THE POPE'S DAUGHTER

CAROLINE P. MURPHY

The Pope's Daughter

faber and faber

First published in 2004
by Faber and Faber Limited
3 Queen Square London WC1N 3AU

Typeset by Faber and Faber Limited
Printed in England by Mackays of Chatham plc, Chatham, Kent

A CIP record for this book
is available from the British Library

ISBN 0-571-22107-6

2 4 6 8 10 9 7 5 3 1

In Memory of John Shearman

Contents

CONTENTS

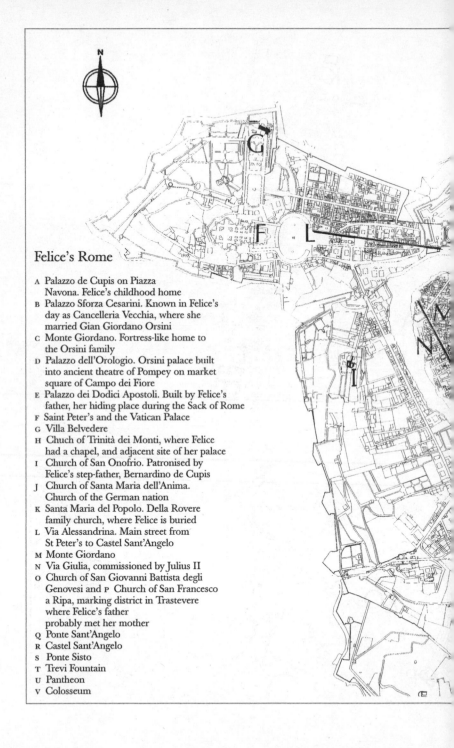

Felice's Rome

A Palazzo de Cupis on Piazza
   Navona. Felice's childhood home
B Palazzo Sforza Cesarini. Known in Felice's
   day as Cancelleria Vecchia, where she
   married Gian Giordano Orsini
C Monte Giordano. Fortress-like home to
   the Orsini family
D Palazzo dell'Orologio. Orsini palace built
   into ancient theatre of Pompey on market
   square of Campo dei Fiore
E Palazzo dei Dodici Apostoli. Built by Felice's
   father, her hiding place during the Sack of Rome
F Saint Peter's and the Vatican Palace
G Villa Belvedere
H Chuch of Trinità dei Monti, where Felice
   had a chapel, and adjacent site of her palace
I Church of San Onofrio. Patronised by
   Felice's step-father, Bernardino de Cupis
J Church of Santa Maria dell'Anima.
   Church of the German nation
K Santa Maria del Popolo. Della Rovere
   family church, where Felice is buried
L Via Alessandrina. Main street from
   St Peter's to Castel Sant'Angelo
M Monte Giordano
N Via Giulia, commissioned by Julius II
O Church of San Giovanni Battista degli
   Genovesi and P Church of San Francesco
   a Ripa, marking district in Trastevere
   where Felice's father
   probably met her mother
Q Ponte Sant'Angelo
R Castel Sant'Angelo
S Ponte Sisto
T Trevi Fountain
U Pantheon
V Colosseum

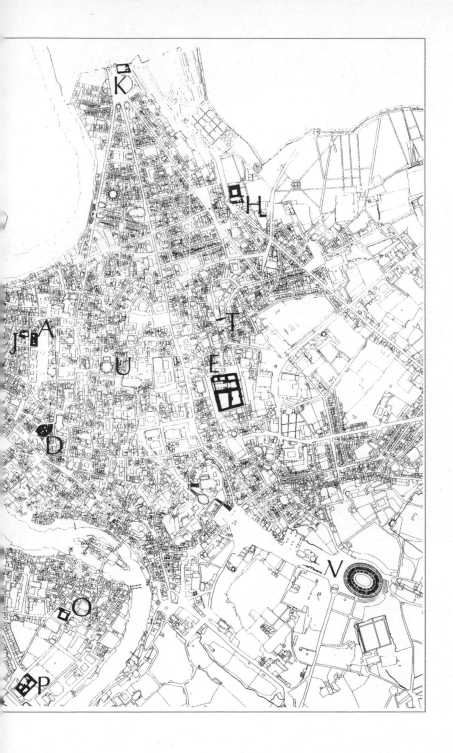

Acknowledgements

The name of this book's protagonist, Felice means lucky or fortunate. The word applies as much to the author, as it does to the heroine. I am immensely fortunate in all the help I have received from so many people.

It was my husband, Henry Dietrich Fernández who found Felice for me and encouraged me to write this book. Any number of ideas within are his, for which he is both credited and un-credited, and he has spent countless hours, at any time of the day or night talking about Felice, her friends and associates, making them into living people.

At the University of California, Riverside, I owe a great deal to my research assistant, Catherine de Luca, who not only retrieved, but also discovered documents in the Orsini Archive at UCLA, and who has provided equally valued service in Florence. My departmental colleague Steven F. Ostrow is the one who first saw Felice in the Mass of Bolsena and Conrad Rudolph first alerted me to Felice's ancestor, Jacopa Normanni. UCR's Academic Senate research fund provided financial support for the project

In 2001–2, I went for a year to Italy, where I was supported by a John Paul Getty Postdoctoral Fellowship and the Harvard University Center for Italian Renaissance Studies at Villa I Tatti in Florence. I would like to thank everyone at I Tatti who made a contribution in some way to this book, including Andrew and Jacalyn Blume, Kurt Barstow, Christopher Hughes, Suzanne Cusick, Katherine Gill, Marilena Falzerano Cirillo, Deanna Schemek, Geraldine Albers, Allen Grieco, Paul Hills, Lawrence Jenkens and Michael Rocke, Bruce Edelstein and Jonathan Nelson. I Tatti's director, Joseph Connors, will recognize that I have appropriated his idea about Guidobaldo Della Rovere, Clarice Orsini and Titian's Venus of Urbino.

Others who have also helped in different ways include Bruce Boucher, Evelyn Welch, Olwen Hufton, Sara Matthews Grieco, Carolyn Valone, Sheryl Reiss, Gillian Malpass, Silvia Evangelisti, Sabine Eiche, Kathleen Wren Christiansen, Sinead O'Flynn, Piers Baker Bates, Robin Bledsoe and Jacqueline Marie Musacchio. I am also grateful to the staff of the many libraries and archives I consulted, including those of the Library of

Congress, Harvard University, UCLA Special Collections, Villa I Tatti, The Biblioteca Vallicelliana, the Archivio Storico Capitolino of Rome and the Archivio di Stato of Rome, Florence and Mantua

Ruth Harris introduced me to my agent, Gill Coleridge, who has helped so much to bring this book into being; practically, emotionally and intellectually. Thanks also go to my US agent Melanie Jackson and to Lucy Luck.

At Faber, I have been extremely felicitous to have had Julian Loose as an editor, because he taught me so much about the art of biography and story-telling, and this would be a very different book without his input. Thanks also go to everybody at Faber who have helped in its production, including Henry Volans and Nick Lowndes, and to my copy-editor, Jill Burrows.

It grieves me, however, that the person who gave in an overwhelming way to this book is not here to see its publication. Professor John Shearman died suddenly in August last year, but in 2000 he bequeathed me the detailed notes he had compiled over the years on Felice, on my promise that 'I would take them seriously', and I have consulted them until the very last moment of this book's completion. He helped me obtain the fellowships I needed to finish my research, and it made me very proud when he asked me to be included among his students at his retirement party in Florence. I always intended that the book would be his, but I never expected to have to dedicate it to his memory. But it is to his memory, with affection and gratitude, that I dedicate *The Pope's Daughter*.

Casa all'Arco Cenci Tavani, Rome, July, 2004

Author's Note

For the sake of readability in English, quoted translations are not always literal ones from Latin and Italian, but have been adapted to facilitate greater reader comprehension.

Prologue: Finding Felice

In the left-hand corner of *The Mass of Bolsena*, part of the fresco cycle Raphael painted in 1512 in the Vatican Palace apartments of Pope Julius II, an attractive young woman stands out from those surrounding her. Her companions' hands frame her face and direct the viewer's eye towards her. She is the only individual in her group to be dressed in black – unusual for a young woman of the time. Equally striking is the alertness and intelligence of her gaze, as she looks across the painting to the figure of Pope Julius II, who is depicted receiving Holy Communion. A sharp-eyed viewer might notice that the Pope and the engaging young woman share a physiognomy: sloping forehead, nose and chin. But what few could possibly know is that this figure is an image of Pope Julius II's only daughter, Felice della Rovere, who became the most powerful woman in Rome of her day.

The story of Felice della Rovere lies at the heart of Rome, embedded deep within the fabric of the city, and she is still to be found there. Felice is present at the Piazza Navona, where the palace in which she spent her earliest years still stands. She exists in the narrow medieval streets of Governo Vecchio and the Via de' Banchi, down which she rode her mule. There are the fifteenth-century palaces of Sforza Cesarini, the old Palazzo della Cancelleria, where she got married, and Monte Giordano,

View of Rome, sixteenth century

where she spent much of her adult life. The eighteenth-century Spanish Steps lead to the Pincian Hill, the site of a villa and a church she loved. We can cross, as she did, the Ponte Sant'Angelo, and enter into the region of the Vatican, the fortress of Castel Sant'Angelo, where she attended parties, and the Vatican Palace itself, where Felice visited her father, and where her image still remains. Other buildings that contain her belong to the seventeenth century, and include the Oratory designed by the architect Borromini, home today to the Archivio Capitolino, which houses her official papers and the thousands of letters she wrote and received.

A woman whose presence can resonate in such a way through the modern city, who has her tale to tell, was clearly a 'somebody' in her own day. That is a rare feat when one remembers that Felice lived half a millennium ago, at a time when a woman who achieved any kind of distinction was the exception, not the rule. Her status as a pope's daughter immediately imbues her with the frisson of scandal and an attendant sense of intrigue. However, the source of this fascination goes beyond the fact she was the daughter of a catholic priest. Felice della Rovere is a complicated and complex woman, both bound and buttressed by the circumstances of her birth. Her tale is a story of personal achievement, one in which she strived to scale the ladders of ambition, who crept along and then sailed down the corridors of power. How far she was able to go, those who facilitated her climb, those she knocked out of her way and those to whom she extended a helping hand are all a part of her tale. Hers is also a story of sacrifice; ambition is rarely achieved without cost.

Felice's father was a cardinal at the time of her birth. There was no expectation that Giuliano della Rovere, as he was born, would become Pope Julius II in 1503. He was only one of a number of cardinals, and by no means the most important person in Rome. Any children he might have had were of little significance to the wider world. Consequently, his daughter has a ghost-like existence until Giuliano becomes pope, when Felice was about twenty years old. From the available material, I have re-created those early years out of a combination of speculation and inference, set within the social and political history of the time. The Felice you see unfold in these pages is fashioned from chronicles, correspondence and diaries, account books and inventories – her own and those of others. Whenever possible, her letters are used to allow her to speak clearly for herself. When they do not survive, I have reconstructed her life, thoughts and ideas from other documents, such as the letters of those who corresponded with her, or who commented and reported on her actions and activities. Bringing Felice to life is like bringing together the components of the *paragone*, the Renaissance debate on which art form – sculpture or painting – is superior. Like a piece of sculpture, she must be seen in the round in order to become a fully three-dimensional character. Like a painting, she needs colour, light and shadow to appear as a vibrant part of this world. But instead of being formed of modelling clay or pigment minerals, she emerges here from a few printed pages, and a collection of almost forgotten and faded sixteenth-century documents.

PART I

The Cardinal's Daughter

CHAPTER 1

Felice's Father

In the year 1480, Pope Sixtus IV commissioned the artist Melozzo da Forlì to create a fresco image of himself, his librarian and his nephews in the library he had instituted at the Vatican Palace. The most compelling presence in the picture is the tall cardinal standing in front of his uncle. He possesses great dark eyes, a hawked nose and angular cheekbones. This man is Cardinal Giuliano della Rovere. With his red cardinal's robes and tonsured head, this is very much how he would have looked when he first met Felice's mother. Before that moment, Cardinal Giuliano had had more than his share of triumphs and disappointments.

Although Giuliano holds a dominant position in this picture, his status in the arena of contemporary Vatican court politics is one of greater complexity. Giuliano della Rovere was born on 15 December, probably in 1445, in a tiny village called Albissola.[1] His family home, however, was nearby Savona, a coastal town in the western province of Liguria, some thirty kilometres to the north-west of its more prosperous neighbour, Genoa. Being a Ligurian, a man of the sea, was very much a part of Giuliano's identity, and he shared his sense of adventure and vision with a fellow Ligurian, Christopher Columbus of Genoa, less than a decade his junior.

But if Columbus's fortune was made through sea-faring, the della Rovere family fortune was built on the Church. For much of the fifteenth

St Peter's and the Vatican under construction

century, the della Roveres were obscure, endowed with neither noble blood nor a history of achievement. Julius's father, Raffaello, might have been a sailor and his mother, Theodora, possibly Greek. This in itself is unusual. It was rare, and still not the norm in Italy, to marry outside one's own town, let alone country, and it was certainly an unusual son who was born from this union.

The della Rovere family might have continued to languish in anonymity were it not for Giuliano's uncle Francesco, who forged a distinguished clerical career for himself.[2] A Franciscan friar, Francesco was a highly effective preacher, and rapidly became a prominent member of the order. By 1462, he was its General. Five years later, Pope Paul II made him a cardinal. Customarily, every cardinal was given a church and its holdings from which he derived his title, and as Francesco's titular church the Pope gave him San Pietro in Vincoli in Rome. He became the first of several della Rovere cardinals to take possession of this church, whose most precious relic was the chains (*vincoli*) believed to have bound Saint Peter when he was imprisoned in Rome.

The position of cardinal gave Francesco admittance to the College of Cardinals and, with it, the power to help shape the future of the Church. He now had a vote in papal elections and indeed the possibility of becoming pope. In 1471, following Pope Paul II's sudden death, Cardinal Francesco della Rovere, only four years after his appointment, emerged as the unexpected favourite at the conclave, the papal election. On 25 August, Francesco della Rovere of Savona was crowned Pope Sixtus IV.

Despite his membership of a mendicant order, with its vows of poverty, Sixtus instituted a nepotistic papacy, placing the advancement of his family above the needs of the Church. He had numerous nephews, many of whom received positions of secular or ecclesiastical importance. Sixtus' favourite nephews were the sons of his sister Bianca. Pietro was made a cardinal only a few weeks after Sixtus' election. To keep him company, Sixtus made his cousin, Giuliano, a cardinal as well.

Pietro and Giuliano were already members of the Franciscan order, ordained in their youth, possibly under pressure from their uncle The cousins, both nearing thirty, were scarcely able to believe their good fortune at making such a rapid advancement from being lowly friars to joining the ranks of the Church's most powerful men. They were so excited by their new appointments that they disregarded Church decorum and scandalously began wearing their scarlet hats before they were officially elected to the College of Cardinals. 'It is an unheard of thing to appear in public with the hat before the announcement is yet published,' the ambassador from Mantua wrote home disapprovingly, stressing what was widely perceived as the *arriviste* nature of the new papal family from a Ligurian backwater.[3]

The cousins might have shared a common excitement at their promotion and its attendant benefits, but they were rivals for their uncle's attention, and his preference became very clear. Pietro Riario spent heavily and was a lavish entertainer. He could be relied on by his uncle to host just the right kind of splendid occasion to impress both visiting dignitaries and Roman citizens. To celebrate St Peter's feast day in 1473, Pietro staged 'a most noble representation of the Tribute that came to the Romans when they ruled the world, and there were sixty mules all harnessed and covered with cloths bearing his coat of arms, and they processed from the Popolo Gate to the Palace of Santi Apostoli [the home Pietro had built for himself]'.[4]

Pietro was a natural showman in a way that his cousin Giuliano was not, and was seen to be of greater value to Sixtus. Giuliano, as cardinal, had received his uncle's own former titular church of San Pietro in Vincoli, but he was conscious of being the underdog at the Vatican court, his uncle's less favoured nephew. But sometimes such treatment hardens and sharpens determination and ambition. Rather than become a jealous, passive martyr as others in his position might have done, or spend time scheming to bring about his cousin's downfall, Giuliano concentrated instead on honing and improving his own skills and abilities. He had an innate sense of survival, an instinct for management, and a fondness of the military that in later years was to earn him the title of 'Warrior Pope'. Rather than simply existing on the periphery of the Vatican court, conscious of his second-class status, Giuliano became Sixtus' troubleshooter. He went out across the Italian papal states, arbitrating in disturbances and insurrections. In June 1474 Giuliano was sent to Todi, a hill town north of Rome whose lord, a *guelph*, and therefore a supporter of the papacy, had been murdered. The province had descended into anarchy. At the head of a troop of soldiers, Giuliano entered the city and succeeded in quelling the disturbances. He had similar success at the Umbrian cities of Spoleto and Città di Castello and began to enjoy his warrior-like image. On Giuliano's return to Rome from Città di Castello on 9 September 1474, one observer wrote, 'All the cardinals had been instructed to go and meet him, but the hardy Ligurian was too early for them. Before the sun had risen he was at the church of Santa Maria del Popolo [sponsored by the della Rovere family].'[5]

Giuliano's successes prompted Sixtus to send him even further afield. In February of 1476 Sixtus made him Archbishop of Avignon in France. Because of tensions between France and Rome, Giuliano travelled there a month later to provide a strong ecclesiastical presence in the country. He stayed over a year. During that time he forged good relations with the French crown and with important French prelates.

Pietro Riario died in 1477, and Giuliano was left as the only della Rovere cardinal. Giuliano was confident he would grow in favour with his uncle. But his return to Rome at the end of 1477 revealed to Giuliano that, despite his hard work, Sixtus was still not going to make him his right-hand man. Giuliano's power was further diluted when, in December 1477, Sixtus created seven more della Rovere nephews and cousins cardinals, including his great nephew, the sixteen-year-old Raffaello Riario, who soon became his uncle's obvious favourite.

In June 1479 Giuliano chose to go back to Avignon, where he was welcomed warmly, and where he felt his position and influence were more clearly appreciated. This time, his absence from Rome was to last three years.[6] It was an important period in the life of the man who would come to refashion Rome. The Palais des Papes at Avignon, the residence of the popes during their exile from Rome in the fourteenth century, was at this time a much more splendid establishment than the Vatican Palace. The Italian cardinal was impressed by the Avignon palace's splendid stairways, dining rooms and audience halls, exquisite decoration and wall hangings. For the first time in his life, Giuliano, the former mendicant friar, became a patron of architecture, renovating the bishop's palace at Avignon with fashionable new windows. The underdog cardinal could feel the thrill of putting his own stamp on a building.

For the rest of his life, Giuliano della Rovere, like no other cleric before or after him, set about establishing his identity through highly decorated architectural works of art. He understood completely the rationale of the fifteenth-century Florentine nobleman Giovanni Rucellai, who noted in his diary that when it came to leaving a legacy, constructing buildings was at least as important as fathering children.

Fathering children, or rather the act required to achieve it, probably interested Giuliano less than it did many of his ecclesiastical counterparts. In 1517, four years after Giuliano's death, the northern humanist Erasmus of Rotterdam, a long-standing critic of the cardinal who became Pope Julius II, published the *Julius Exclusus*, in which he imagines Julius barred from entering paradise. The satirical dialogue is a conversation between Julius and St Peter at the gates of heaven, in which Peter grows increasingly appalled at the worldly nature of what Julius considers his life's achievements. When Julius mentions his daughter, Peter, incredulous, asks, 'Do you mean to tell me that popes have wives and daughters?' Julius replies, 'Well, they don't have wives of their own of course. But what's so strange about their having children, since they're men, not eunuchs?'[7]

Despite Erasmus's view of him, Julius's behaviour was no worse, and in fact much better, than that of many of his colleagues. This was the period in which the Catholic Church was at its most magnificent, and also at its most corrupt. Sexual activity was only one abuse among several committed by the clerical elite, and few in Italy commented adversely on such conduct. Only occasionally did men such as the anti-clerical Roman lawyer Stefano Infessura write in his diary in 1490 that the life of a Roman cleric 'has been debased to such an extent that there is almost not one who does not keep a mistress, or at least a common prostitute'.[8]

It is impossible to count the number of children who called cardinals their fathers in fifteenth-century Rome. Those that are recorded – such as the children of Pope Alexander VI, the infamous Borgia pope, or his immediate predecessor, Innocent VIII – are known because their fathers became popes.[9] Both these popes, who had fathered their children when they were cardinals, openly acknowledged them. As cardinals they had led lavish, decadent lives. They were as much playboys as ecclesiastics.

Such a way of life interested Giuliano della Rovere less than it did his colleagues. In Avignon he worked hard, with variable success, as a papal diplomat. Then in February 1482 he returned to Rome, and his life changed. If Giuliano was still playing second fiddle in Sixtus' affections to his young cousin Raffaello, his standing at the Vatican court did, none the less, improve. He received additional bishoprics, including those of Pisa and the Roman port of Ostia, and he began to acquire a greater number of friends and allies in the College of Cardinals.

Giuliano's new status in Rome led him to relax to some extent, even to imitate the lifestyles of his cardinal friends. At any rate, some time after he returned to Rome, he met a young woman named Lucrezia. If he did not actually fall in love with her, he was sufficiently attracted to her to break his vows of celibacy. Unwittingly or not, Julius was to add fathering a child to his earthly legacy.

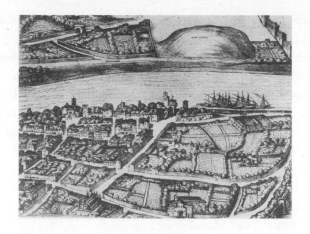

CHAPTER 2

Felice's Mother

It is rare for much to be known about the life of cardinals' concubines, and it is only through a certain amount of teasing out of the available evidence that Giuliano's mistress, Felice's mother, comes to life. In later histories of the popes, Lucrezia's surname is given as Normanni, which makes Felice's matrilineal line particularly interesting, and in fact more venerable than that of her father.[1] The Normanni formed one of the oldest Roman families; their name indicates they could trace their roots back to the eleventh-century Norman invasion of Italy and the sacking of Rome. They lived in fortified palaces on the opposite side of the Tiber from the main part of the city of Rome, in the area known as Trastevere, and were allies of that district's most bellicose clan, the Pierleoni. That Lucrezia came from Trastevere is itself significant.[2] This was the same district in which the Ligurians – the Genoese and the Savonese – resided. Although Cardinal Giuliano's own palace was on the other side of the river, he visited compatriots in this part of Rome, which would have given him the opportunity to meet Lucrezia. Giuliano could have encountered her on the street, perhaps on the Via degli Genovesi, which runs through the heart of Trastevere. In the village-like atmosphere that still permeates old Trastevere, it would not have been difficult for him to track her down.

View of Trastevere in the sixteenth century

There were in fact several prominent women from the Normanni family, of whom the best known is Jacopa, born at the end of the twelfth century, and known as Jacopa dei Settesoli (seven suns). As a wealthy widow she became an extremely fervent supporter of St Francis of Assisi. She founded the first Roman seat for the Franciscans, the Ospedale di San Biagio, now the church of San Francesco a Ripa, in Trastevere, the centre of Normanni family terrain. The street leading up to the church is now called the Via di Jacopa dei Settesoli. St Francis called her 'Brother' Jacopa in praise of her fortitude, integrity and ability to live with manly austerity, and made her a kind of honorary friar. 'Fra Jacopa' is the name she chose to have inscribed on her burial tomb in Assisi.[3] Coincidentally or not, Felice would also possess similarly 'masculine' qualities to those of her illustrious ancestor.

However, over the centuries, like many of their counterparts who had held sway in Rome in medieval times, the Normanni family found its prestige and power declining as the city fell into chaos. By the end of the fifteenth century the Normanni were apparently of little account in the city. Yet even if the family was no longer wealthy, Lucrezia's parentage means she was not a street girl, and it seems unlikely that she had become a courtesan, as they tended to be women who were not native to Rome. That Lucrezia came from a good family does not make her unusual as the choice for a cardinal's sexual liaison: Vannozza Cattanei, who in the 1470s and 1480s was the mistress of Cardinal Rodrigo Borgia – the future Pope Alexander – and mother of Cesare, Joffre and Lucrezia, came from a similar background.

One does not know if Giuliano and Lucrezia had a lasting relationship or a brief encounter. Lucrezia might have been impressed by the compelling cardinal, the nephew of the Pope, and willingly acquiesced to his advances. It is also possible her impoverished family might have encouraged her to yield to him in the hope they would all benefit. Whatever the duration of the liaison, Felice was certainly the only fruit of this union to grow to adulthood.

CHAPTER 3

The Birth of Felice

The date of Felice's birth is not known, so logic and common sense must play a part in its determination. Felice cannot have been born earlier than 1483, because Giuliano did not return to Rome until late 1482. And it seems unlikely that she was born any later because, by 1504, she will be exhibiting a maturity and sense of self beyond that of a teenage girl.

From the perspective of Giuliano's and Lucrezia's child, it was vital that Giuliano should acknowledge paternity. Lucrezia was of sufficient standing that honourable arrangements were made for her following her pregnancy. The baby would not go to any of Rome's convents or hospitals which took in foundlings, such as the Santi Quattro Coronati, or the Ospedale di Santo Spirito, the destination of many a cleric's bastard child. Nor was her mother to live, shamed, as a fallen woman. Instead, she was married, probably either just before or soon after Felice's birth, to a man named Bernardino de Cupis. While the indications are that the relationship between Giuliano and Lucrezia ended with the birth of Felice, the marriage kept both Lucrezia and her baby within the orbit of the della Rovere family. Bernardino was *maestro di casa*, the major-domo who ran both the household and the life of Giuliano's cardinal cousin Girolamo Basso della Rovere. In contrast to his relationship with his Riario cousins, Giuliano was close to Girolamo. In 1507, he paid for Girolamo's magnificent tomb, sculpted by

'Infant Girl', from Christofano Bertelli, *The Ages of Woman*, 1580s

the Venetian artist Andrea Sansovino, in the della Rovere family church of Santa Maria del Popolo.

Of the little that is known about Lucrezia, it can be accepted that she was a loving mother. Felice, her half-sister Francesca and half-brother Gian Domenico were very fond of her. The four formed a tight-knit unit much later in life, valuing their family connection above other ties. That Lucrezia was allowed the opportunity to be a good mother to Felice is interesting in itself. It was not usual in Renaissance Italy for the mothers of the illegitimate children of the elite to be allowed to form a bond with their children, who were usually immediately absorbed into their father's families. The mothers of the Medici bastards are completely unknown, including the mother of Giulio, the future Pope Clement VII. Duke Alessandro de' Medici's mother, a North African slave girl known as Simonetta, was later married to a mule-herder and vanishes from sight. Even though Vannozza Catanei, Lucrezia Borgia's mother, established an identity in her own right as a substantial property-holder in Rome, she had little contact with her daughter. Rodrigo Borgia removed Lucrezia at a young age from her mother and placed her in the care of his new mistress.

If Felice, unlike many of her counterparts, had not spent her earliest years at her mother's side, it is unlikely that she and Lucrezia would have been as close as they were when Felice was an adult. Felice had similarly strong relationships with her half-brother and half-sister, suggesting that the house Lucrezia ran was a happy one. As a wife, Lucrezia met with Bernardino's satisfaction. He made her one of the outright heirs to his estate in his will of 1508, an unusual act given that he had sons, suggesting that he thought well of her. She is referred to as 'Magnifica Matrona' ('magnificent matron'), a title that attests to the position she had obtained in Rome, a long way from being a cardinal's unwed teenage lover.[1]

It is also probable that it was Lucrezia rather than Giuliano who gave their daughter her name. Felice, pronounced '*feh-leee-chay*' in Italian, is a girl's name sometimes used in the English-speaking world today, pronounced with a soft *c*. But in Italy, then as now, it is a boy's name. A girl should more correctly have been called Felicia or Felicità. The word '*felice*' means lucky, fortunate, happy. As a name indicative of a situation, it might be chosen by a mother in Lucrezia's position rather than by a cardinal

father. In this instance, the name Felice could well refer to the circumstances of the baby girl's birth. She might, for example, have survived a
difficult delivery. Or perhaps her name refers to the fortunes of mother
and child. A pregnant young mother, banished from her family home,
could easily have been obliged to place her child in an orphanage. Instead,
Lucrezia's daughter had a lucky start in life, and Lucrezia herself had what
she saw as a fortunate new beginning.

CHAPTER 4

Felice's Stepfather

It was common practice for male members of the elite to make honest women of their mistresses by marrying them off to high-ranking servants or those loyal to the family. Cecilia Gallerani, the mistress of Ludovico Sforza, Duke of Milan, immortalized by Leonardo da Vinci as *The Lady with an Ermine* in 1491, was married a year later to a Sforza associate, Count Ludovico Carminati de Brambilla. Rodrigo Borgia arranged for Vanozza Cattanei first to marry Domenico d'Arignano, and then, on the death of this first husband, Giorgio della Croce. Both of these men were apostolic secretaries at the Vatican Palace. To accept such a bride meant that these men were assured the gratitude of their wives' powerful former (and sometimes continuing) lovers, and could expect attendant benefits. Nor did they necessarily have to have anything to do with the children that were not their own, if these children were not actually raised by their mothers.

Bernardino de Cupis clearly shared a background with the husbands chosen for Vannozza Catanei. He differed from them in that he was involved in several aspects of his stepdaughter's life, even though it was fully recognized that Cardinal Giuliano was her father. There can be no doubt that Bernardino's life and activities did in some way shape Felice's own outlook and ways of doing things. He was unflinchingly loyal to the Rovere. For Bernardino, taking on a discarded Rovere mistress and her

'Platea Agonalis', now Piazza Navona; No. 7 is Palazzo de Cupis

illegitimate child further sealed the bond with the family he served. At the turn of the sixteenth century he commissioned the Sienese artist Baldassare Peruzzi to paint a fresco in the apse of the church of San Onofrio up on the Janiculum Hill.[1] San Onofrio was some distance from the de Cupis home in the heart of Rome. Its attraction for Bernardino was perhaps that it belonged to the Hieronymite monastic order, which derived its name from St Jerome, as did his employer, Girolamo della Rovere.

For San Onofrio, Bernardino chose images of the Madonna and Child, distinctly similar to those the more established painter Pinturicchio had depicted in 1483 at Girolamo's burial chapel at the Rovere church of Santa Maria del Popolo. Bernardino chose as decorative device the acorn, the Rovere emblem, a reference to the meaning of the family name, 'oak', in the borders of his chapel's painting. Bernardino himself is depicted as kneeling donor, every inch the prosperous bureaucrat, whose modern equivalent would be the company man.

The extent of Bernardino's duties as a *maestro di casa* can be gleaned from a handbook, first published in 1598, by Cesare Evitascandalo, entitled in English *The Maestro di Casa; which contains exactly how much and in which the Maestro di Casa must be instructed.* The manual contains over 380 'notable points', covering the nature of the *maestro di casa*'s authority over the rest of a cardinal's servants, and how to deal with each one individually, including, among other issues, how to handle any fraud committed by servants, and what to do 'when the cook is drunk'. He needed to know the rituals of the religious calendar and which vestments his master should wear on what days. The *maestro di casa* was responsible for the acquisition of every type of provision, barley for the horses, wax candles, sugar and wines. He needed to cultivate 'someone at court who could advise him of the occurrence of any ill deeds'. In addition, he needed to be both his master's 'shield' and 'cover his own persona with that of his master's'.[2]

Bernardino came originally from the Umbrian hill town of Montefalco, the heart of St Francis country, and he was resident in Rome by 1462. He had clearly received a good education, more than sufficient to succeed as a high-level bureaucrat, arguably one of the best positions in Renaissance Rome. The bureaucrats were the men who ran Rome; they had all the connections they needed to receive tips, advice and bribes that allowed them a more than comfortable existence. On the other hand, they were not so powerful that they had to be constantly on guard for rivals seeking to topple them. Bernardino performed his duties well. Girolamo Basso della Rovere had much in common with his Riario cousins, showing little interest in ecclesiastical politics but having a great love of magnificence and display. While Girolamo enjoyed the sumptuous life of a cardinal in Rome, Bernardino often assumed his master's role. Girolamo received income as Bishop of the towns of Macerata and Rieti in the eastern province of the Marche. Like many Italian bishops of his day, he was not only a pluralist but he was continuously absent, leaving Bernardino to travel to the Marche to act on his behalf. Bernardino clearly did his job there to Rieti's satisfaction. In 1486, the community promised him that on the birth of his first male child they would present him with 'the sum of 25 ducats from which to buy a gift for his wife'.[3] In 1499, it was to Bernardino, not Girolamo, that the community of Macerata wrote to ask about obtaining a loan of 200 ducats.

Bernardino was clearly successful in donning the persona of his cardinal as if it were his own and he was personally well rewarded for his efforts on behalf of the della Rovere family. He could not only afford a chapel, whose frescos number among the jewels of early sixteenth-century Roman painting, but he also built a magnificent family home. If he did not live as lavishly as most cardinals, he certainly exceeded the standard of living of most ecclesiastical servants. It is likely that, in addition to his salary from Girolamo della Rovere, he received remuneration from Felice's natural father, who would also have provided Lucrezia with a dowry when Bernardino married her.

Lucrezia's dowry contributed to the cost of the house Bernardino built and in which Felice spent her earliest years. The large palace that was once Palazzo de Cupis is to be found on what is now the Piazza Navona, the long rectangular square adorned with Bernini's Fountain of the Four Rivers. The piazza's shape derives from its original function in the ancient world, as the stadium of Domitian, built in AD 92, where foot races were held and whose ruins lie beneath the present-day square. In Bernardino's time, the square was located in relation to the major church in the piazza, Sant' Agnese in Agone, and was known as the 'Platea [square] in Agone' – from which the word 'Navona' derives – or the Campus Agonis. Bernardino chose Piazza Navona for his home partly for its proximity to his employer's palace. Girolamo lived on the Via Recta, which extended out from the piazza, near to the church of San Agostino. But in other ways this piazza was a shrewd choice of location for a bureaucrat who wished to be at the centre of everything. Over the course of the fifteenth century Piazza Navona had gradually changed from an abandoned ancient sports arena into a highly prestigious Roman address.[4]

Given that he was a servant, Bernardino built a palace for himself of remarkable splendour flanked by the Via dell Anima, across from the church of Sant' Agnese in Agone. He took advantage of a bull passed by Sixtus IV, *Et si de cunctarum civitatum* ('for the benefit of the city'), designed to promote regeneration and renewal in the city of Rome. The bull authorized the enforced selling of properties whose owners could not afford restoration and repair. Bernardino bought up a series of small houses and shops along one side of the Piazza Navona. He gutted them and concealed them behind a monolithic façade, in much the same way that the great architect and humanist Leon Battista Alberti did for the Rucellai family at their famous palace in Florence. The eventual magnificence of the residence Bernardino created was such that the writer Francesco Albertini called attention to it in *De Mirabilibus*, his 1510 guide to Rome's architectural marvels, ancient and modern. He described it as the 'house of Bernadino di Montefalco in the square of Agonis, which has a most beautiful well'.[5] In Rome, easy access to fresh water was a great luxury. There was only one major public fountain, the Trevi. Most citizens depended on the Tiber river for their water, for both personal and industrial needs, from which its level of purity may be imagined.

Bernardino's house was the home in which Felice della Rovere spent the first part of her life. Michelangelo, Felice's senior by no more than a few years, and who will play his own part in her story, claimed he was destined to become a sculptor. He believed it because he had ingested dust with the breast milk of his wet nurse, the wife of a stonemason in the little village of Settignano, up in the hills above Florence.[6] In a similar fashion, the young Felice, living at the Palazzo de Cupis, absorbed the smells and sounds of Rome, right at the very heart of the city. Getting to know her city is another way that we can catch a glimpse of the young Felice, and understand the woman she would become.

CHAPTER 5

Felice's Rome

Visitors to Rome today often comment on the city's multi-layered quality, the way the strata of different civilizations and periods exist side by side, quite different from anywhere else in the world. There is still an ancient Rome, visible in structures as vast as the Colosseum or the Pantheon, or as small as the antique columns embedded in doorways of less ancient buildings. The Rome of the era following the legalization of Christianity can be seen in such ninth-century churches as SS Cosmas and Damian or Santa Pudenziana with their vivid mosaics depicting the life of Christ and his saints. Medieval Rome is still apparent in the narrow streets, still called *vicoli*, tall houses and surviving towers, such as the thirteenth-century Torre di Conti, around which Rome's English community lived. Renaissance Rome is present in the palaces and churches built in the re-appropriated classical language of ancient Rome, using travertine stone, once brightly gleaming and now darkened after a century or more of petrol emissions.

This is the Rome that Felice knew over the course of her life. The grandiose churches and palaces of the seventeenth century, the enormously wide city streets blasted through by Mussolini, so punishing in the summer heat, are part of a future that would have surprised, impressed and in some instances appalled her. But what she did experience was a Rome that grew and evolved and in many ways re-evolved in a way that it

Maarten van Heemskerck, Pantheon, 1530s

had not since it had been the capital of the ancient world. The Rome Felice was born into was one vastly different from the city of a century before her birth, and the Rome she died in was different again. Rome in the late fifteenth century changed dramatically in a way that the other great Italian cities, such as Florence and Venice, did not. Neither of those cities had had to transform itself from a war zone.[1]

Over the centuries, Rome has seen its fair share of invaders. The fifth-century Goths and Visigoths had torn apart much of what was left of the great ancient city, whose decline was marked by the Emperor Constantine moving the capital of the Roman Empire to Constantinople in AD 330. Most critically, the Goths had destroyed Rome's hydraulic system, leaving only the underground aqueduct Acqua Vergine untouched. The resultant lack of water in many parts of the city caused a systematic population shift closer to the banks of the river Tiber, known as the *abitato*, 'the inhabited'. The large abandoned areas of the city were called the *disabitato*, 'the depopulated'.

Rome did, however, remain the capital of the Christian world. The pope's residence was the Lateran Palace, adjacent to the church of San Giovanni in Laterano, founded in the fourth century on the edge of the city. It is San Giovanni that is still the cathedral, the bishop's seat of Rome, and not the church of St Peter. Any new pope must still make a journey, a *possesso*, to the Lateran from St Peter's before he can take possession of the papal tiara, his 'tiered' triple crown, the symbol of his power.[2]

But by 1309 even the papacy, represented in some form in Rome since the time of St Peter, was forced to leave the city; it was not to return for more than a century. This time, the cause was not the threat of invasion but the city's internal conflicts. A city so fractured by violence over the course of centuries had created a perpetual siege mentality. The most powerful Roman families did not live in the splendid palaces with ornate façades commonly associated with Renaissance Rome. Instead, they lived in barrack-like buildings, described as *insediamenti*. These palaces were like fortified cities within a city. Individual homes were built on the sloping terrain upon a mount, surrounded by thick walls. Two huge examples still stand in the city: Monte Giordano, property of the Orsini family, and the eponymous Monte dei Cenci. By the twelfth century, different families controlled different parts of the city: the Colonna ruled the Quirinal and

Esquiline hills; the Frangipani family ruled the Palatine and the area around the Colosseum, and the Savelli ruled the Aventine hill and the stretch of the river Tiber at its foot. Over in Trastevere, there was an alliance of sorts between the families of the Pierleone, the Papareschi, the Tebaldi and the Normanni, Felice's mother's family. The Orsini family controlled the area around the Ponte Sant' Angelo, one of the few bridges across the Tiber, as well as the heart of the *abitato*.

The intense rivalry between these families cannot be overstated. They make the relationship between Shakespeare's Montagues and Capulets seem positively cordial. It was turf war, feirce and bloody. The popes and the governing body of Rome, the senate, supported and endorsed different families. Those that did not could meet with serious consequences. The Cenci family kidnapped Pope Gregory VII, a long-standing enemy, on Christmas Eve 1075, and in 1145 Pope Lucius II was killed as a result of his opposition to a Roman government led by Giordano Pierleone.

The Roman families made a lot of money, often legally, from the collection of tolls to cross bridges or to pass in and out of sanctioned areas, such as the Jewish ghetto. But by the turn of the fourteenth century gang warfare had escalated to such an untenable degree that no one was safe in the streets. In 1308 members of the Church, especially the non-Italians, took the opportunity to canvass moving the seat of the papacy from Rome to the more peaceful city of Avignon, in southern France. Their case was reinforced by a great fire that rendered the papal palace at the Lateran uninhabitable. It is certainly possible that it was deliberately set by the French in order to hasten the departure to Avignon.

Exile from Rome lasted almost a century, until the election of Pope Martin V. As the former Oddo Colonna, a member of the important Roman family, Martin wielded sufficient influence to negotiate a return of the papacy to a more peaceful Rome in 1420. He is credited not only with returning the papacy to Rome but with bringing the Renaissance to the city as well. Fifteenth-century Rome still had more in common with postwar, twentieth-century Beirut than it did with prosperous fifteenth-century Florence. There were still vast no-go areas in the city, made dangerous not only by lawlessness but also by the swampy, malaria-ridden terrain that needed to be drained before it could be inhabited. Scores of buildings had been abandoned, their residents having fled the turbulent times or succumbed to outbreaks of the plague. Other structures had been rendered uninhabitable by an earthquake in 1349. Even as late as 1413, only seven years before the return of Martin V, King Ladislas of Naples had taken advantage of Rome's weakened state to invade and plunder the city. The main streets were almost impassable, access to St Peter's near impossible. A city uninviting to pilgrims, who might otherwise have come to venerate the bones of St Peter, was denying itself a valuable economic resource.

But what the troubles of the previous century had done was to undermine the power of many of the Roman families responsible for the initial disruption. The Pierleone, the Normanni and the Frangipane lost a great deal during the fourteenth century, and they never really recovered from the changed financial situation. The Colonna and the Orsini, however, wealthy by virtue of all the land they owned in the Roman countryside, retained and even consolidated their footing as Rome's first families. Although this strengthened the rivalry between them, members of the families who had become clergymen were particularly committed to restoring the city their ancestors had helped to destroy.

Fifteenth-century commentators on Rome provide accounts of the disrepair into which the city had fallen: 'In the absence of the Pope Rome had turned into a cow pasture; sheep and cows were grazed where there had once been merchants' stalls,' wrote Vespasiano da Bisticci.[3] In 1443 a Florentine visitor, Alberto degli Alberti, wrote from Rome to Giovanni de' Medici, to tell him, 'The modern houses, those built of brick, are plentiful, but in disrepair. The beauty of Rome is its [ancient] ruins. The men that are now called Romans are in some way different in their bearing and habits from the ancients; to summarize, they all tend cows. Their women have beautiful faces, but they do not keep the other parts of their body very clean [not surprisingly, given the lack of recourse to water in the city].'[4] To return Rome to its former magnificence would be a challenge, and the labour of a century or more.

Yet under a succession of popes, commencing with Martin V, Rome experienced a radical transformation. The city underwent a rebirth, becoming a 'Renaissance' city in the truest sense of the word. Martin V began by reviving the old office of *maestro di strada*, which had been 'neglected for a very long time'.[5] The tasks of the *maestri* were to supervise the clearing, repaving and restoration of the city's streets and squares. They enforced restrictions such as preventing private dwellings encroaching on public streets or the construction of unauthorized buildings on the banks of the Tiber, and regulated the supply of water.[6]

Eugenius IV, Martin's successor in 1431, had a rather more turbulent and consequently less productive papacy, yet even he succeeded in cleaning up the Piazza della Rotonda in front of the Pantheon. He removed the hermits who lived in the ancient temple as well as the sheds and shops that had sprung up around it. But it was Nicholas V and Sixtus IV, both Ligurians, who took the task of rebuilding Rome most seriously. Nicholas, who succeeded Eugene in 1447, was arguably the first Renaissance pope for whom the encouragement of art and culture was more critical than the promotion of spirituality. As a student in Bologna, he had tutored the sons of wealthy Florentines and beaome aware of the extraordinary developments in their city. Nicholas, benefiting from a more tranquil Rome, was able to concentrate his energies on his vision of an ideal planned city.[7] Even if few of his ideas were carried out during his eight-year papacy, they were sufficiently well conceived to be put into effect by his successors. As the adviser for Nicholas's new Rome, the Pope brought to the city the greatest architect, humanist and conceptual thinker of his day, the Florentine Leon Battista Alberti. In Rome, as the art historian Giorgio Vasari would write a century later, Alberti did 'many useful things that are worthy of praise, the Acqua Vergine, which was broken, he fixed, and he made the fountain in the Piazza de Trevi, with those marble decorations that one still sees'.[8] Apart from the Tiber river, the fountain was Rome's chief public source of water, and certainly the cleanest. Nicholas repaired the city's walls and many of its churches and took advantage of the virtual gutting of the Lateran Palace to argue for the development of the papal palace on the Vatican hill, next to St Peter's.

Nicholas produced a template for Roman reconstruction that his countryman Sixtus followed rigorously when he ascended the papal throne in 1471. Sixtus' propositions for urban planning were equally aggressive. He drew up the previously mentioned bull, the *Et si de cunctarum civitatum*, designed not only as a means of beautifying the city but also as a means of social engineering. The bull compelled 'owners not occupying their houses to sell them to neighbours who do occupy, and who wish to rebuild their ruined houses for the sake of the appearance of the city'.[9] Bernardino de

Cupis benefited from such a mandate as he expanded his property on the Piazza Navona. Sixtus was also responsible for the removal of the medieval porticoes along Rome's streets, the kind that can still be seen in modern-day Bologna. The reason Sixtus gave for his plans was that they rendered the streets 'so narrow that it is not possible to stroll through them conveniently'. However, the porticoes had made it very easy for Roman families to barricade their streets and homes in times of conflict, so for Sixtus it was another way to weaken the power of the native citizenry. Those that were not torn down were bricked up.

Sixtus also reconstructed the bridge across the Tiber, whose origins dated back to 12 BC. The bridge, whose state of disrepair had earned it the name Ponte Rotto (broken bridge) became the Ponte Sisto, and is still in use today. The Ponte Sisto provided Sixtus' Ligurian countrymen, who lived in Trastevere, with better access to the rest of the city, in particular the commercial districts. Sixtus also strengthened his own family identity by having the architect Baccio Pontelli rebuild the church of Santa Maria del Popolo, soon to become filled with della Rovere family tombs and chapels. A substantial social initiative was his reconstruction of the Ospedale di Santo Spirito, a hospital still in use as a medical centre. Patients were treated in wards whose walls are decorated with frescos commissioned by Sixtus in 1475 depicting significant events from his life.[10]

Nor did the Vatican Palace, the new papal home, escape his attention. There he built a great new chapel, decorated with a star-spangled blue ceiling and pictures in the lower storeys by the most fashionable Florentine painters, such as Sandro Botticelli and Domenico Ghirlandaio. Despite the exceptional additions that were to be made by the Pope's nephew Cardinal Giuliano later in his life, the chapel is still known as the Sistine Chapel. It was the first substantial demarcation of della Rovere identity at the Vatican Palace.

CHAPTER 6

Felice's Childhood

Even if by 1483, the time of Felice's birth, Rome was still some way from being the marvel of Renaissance Italy, Cardinal Giuliano's daughter was born into a city filled with a new optimism and a sense of excitement. Moreover, Felice spent her childhood right at the heart of things. The Palazzo de Cupis became a social centre of the new Rome. It was constantly filled with the 'Pope's men', apostolic secretaries, chamberlains, *maestri di strade*, and merchants and lawyers.[1] They spoke a language of their own, exchanged rumours and gossiped about events in the city, made deals, accepted bribes. A small girl did not necessarily understand the meaning of it all, but an intelligent one could recognize the importance of such activity. These were the men who made her city work. What Felice learned from her proximity to them had tremendous bearing on how she would later conduct her own life.

Equally important to Felice della Rovere's development was that in Bernardino de Cupis's circle she had her own worth. Her father, who had kept something of a low profile during the reign of his uncle Sixtus, achieved much greater prominence on Sixtus' death in 1484.[2] The new pope, Innocent VIII, was a fellow Ligurian. Giuliano della Rovere became his chief adviser, to the extent that Lorenzo de' Medici was counselled by his ambassador to Rome to 'send a good letter to the Cardinal of St Peter,

Maarten van Heemskerck, detail showing re-use of ancient Roman columns

for he is Pope and more than Pope'.[3] This meant, of course, that Rome came to regard Cardinal Giuliano in a newly respectful light. The Cardinal now held the key to the kinds of rewards and promotions that Bernardino's associates lived for. By association, reverence was paid to his young daughter. One does not how know much Giuliano saw of Felice, but she knew she was his child, and everyone else knew it too. She was always Felice della Rovere, never Felice de Cupis. Other members of the della Rovere family in Rome treated her as one of their own as well. Her cousin Girolamo della Rovere, Bernardino's employer, was sufficiently fond of her and perhaps generous to her that later Felice would name one of her sons Girolamo; so she clearly had good memories of him.

There is no doubt that Felice did spend her childhood in a loving and stable environment, often so fundamental to a child's, and the subsequent adult's, sense of self-belief. For Lucrezia, the child was her lucky one; the pair had a good life that might not necessarily have been theirs. For her stepfather Bernardino, she was a part of the family he served so devotedly. Nor did Felice lack for company of her own age; her half-sister Francesca was only two years younger. The girls might not have been allowed to play outside, but the Piazza Navona was an exciting place to watch from a window. They could look down on the bustle of its daily market, or at the pomp of the festive tournaments that were held at the beginning of the year. Moreover, Felice was special. For Lucrezia and Bernardino, illegitimacy did not make her inferior to the rest of the family. In fact, the reverse was true. She was a cardinal's daughter, and the blood of a pope ran in her veins. If they behaved towards her any differently than they did towards her siblings, it was probably to be rather more respectful, perhaps more indulgent, because of who she was. In other words, her mother and stepfather treated her more as they might a favoured son than a normal daughter of the time. Consequently, Felice grew into adolescence secure in the love of those around her, confident of her own identity and perhaps somewhat wilful, certain that she would get her way in the end.

And then, in 1492, Pope Innocent VIII died, and everything changed for Cardinal Giuliano and his daughter.

Enter the Borgia

The year 1492 was to be the year of the Spanish. It was Christopher Columbus of Genoa who discovered the New World but he claimed it in the name of Ferdinand of Aragon and Isabella of Castile. And the new pope, who took the name Alexander VI, elected on 11 August 1492, was Rodrigo di Borgia y Borgia, a native of Jativa near Valencia in Spain. Sixtus IV and Innocent VIII had been nepotistic popes, but Rodrigo would redefine nepotism. He ascended the papal throne as the father of at least eight children by at least two women; while he was pope he would father two more, by his mistress Giulia Farnese. Giulia might have replaced Vaonnzza Catanei in Alexander's affections but his children by Vanozza – Juan, Joffre, Lucrezia and Cesare – were never superseded. Alexander immediately began planning splendid marriages for the first three and made Cesare a cardinal. By 1498, however, Cesare had abandoned his ecclesiastical position and the following year married the sister of the King of Navarre, adopting grandiose secular ambitions.[1]

Alexander was an excellent administrator and did much to centralize and secure papal power. But these achievements will always be overshadowed by his ultimately thwarted ambition to forge a dynasty out of the Borgia, a family whose origins were at least as humble as those of the della Rovere. Most important for Felice's story is the way the Spanish pope treated his daughter. Lucrezia Borgia, roughly three years older than Felice, has been the subject of perhaps a hundred biographies, fictional, non-fictional and somewhere in between. Perception of her has been coloured by unfounded tales of her murdering her second husband, who actually died at the hands of her brother Cesare. In truth, it is hard to get a sense of her personality. She begins life as a pleasure-loving young girl and ends it as a pious Duchess of Ferrara, spending long periods of time in seclusion in convents.

Alexander loved his daughter extravagantly and his treatment of Lucrezia scandalized the city of Rome. In June 1493 her marriage to the Count of Pesaro was celebrated in the Sala Regia, the papal throne room at the Vatican Palace, with Lucrezia attended by a hundred and fifty Roman noblewomen. The marriage was dissolved in 1497 to make way for a more politically useful union with the southern Duke of Bisceglie. He in turn was murdered and Lucrezia's third husband was Alfonso d'Este of Ferrara, who ranked among the first families of northern Italy.

In the years following her father's election, Lucrezia was a regular presence at the Vatican court. On at least one occasion her father left her as his deputy during his absence from the palace, although her power was purely nominal. But certainly women were a constant presence at the court of the Borgia. Alexander regularly hosted events at the palace where the entertainment was provided by courtesans. At a ceremony in the basilica of St Peter's Lucrezia and her outrageous Neapolitan sister-in-law, the illegitimate Sancia of Aragon, scandalized the College of Cardinals by sitting in seats strictly reserved for canons of the church, an act sanctioned by Lucrezia's father. An air of sexual anarchy pervaded the Vatican of the 1490s and it infected Lucrezia. In August 1498, a Bolognese correspondent wrote, 'Perotto, the first *cameriere* [chamberlain] of Our Lord [Alexander], who was no longer to be found, I now understand to be in prison for having made His Holiness's daughter pregnant.'[2] Perotto was subsequently found dead in the Tiber, bound hand and foot, and Lucrezia gave birth to a child who then disappears from history.

The 1490s were a time of Vatican court state ceremonies, lavish entertainments and romantic trysts. As Lucrezia Borgia, the daughter of one former cardinal, played at the Vatican court, her father was forcing another cardinal's daughter out of the only home she had ever known.

CHAPTER 8

Felice's Departure

For Giuliano della Rovere, of all the cardinals to be elected successor to Innocent VIII, there could have been no worse a choice than Rodrigo Borgia. For some time there had been friction between Giuliano and Rodrigo, himself the nephew of a former pope, Calixtus III. Rodrigo had endorsed Innocent VIII in conclave and raised support for him but felt the Pope had given him little reward for his efforts. He and Giuliano had quarrelled at Innocent's deathbed, when Giuliano had defended the Pope's right to distribute papal money to members of his own family, an act Rodrigo had protested against. Given that, as pope, Rodrigo would take benefiting his own family to an entirely new level, there is certain irony to be derived from such objection. Before the conclave began, Rodrigo embarked on a breathtakingly comprehensive plan of bribery to purchase the cardinals' votes. He promised Cardinal Sforza the office of vice chancellor, to the Roman cardinals Orsini, Colonna and Savelli, he offered fortified towns or abbeys with large holdings in the Roman *campagna*. Rodrigo even included della Rovere relatives in his scheme, promising benefices to Raffaele Riario and a Benedictine abbey in Turin to a cousin from Savoy, Domenico della Rovere. But he knew he could not buy Giuliano della Rovere's vote, nor that of Girolamo Basso della Rovere, who were united against Rodrigo by their own particular sense of family. However, their alliance was insufficient to

The Aventine Port in Rome, sixteenth century

withstand the overwhelming wave of Rodrigo's supporters, all eager to collect their rewards to supplement their already lavish lifestyles. Infessura
noted sarcastically, 'As soon as [Alexander] became pope, he dispersed his
property to the paupers.'[1]

Giuliano was not alone in his reservations about Alexander. The Borgia
Pope planned to play on a much larger political stage than his predecessors had done. Like Sixtus, he made his family's advancement a primary
goal but Alexander had much greater ambitions, aiming to secure not
just cardinals' hats but dukedoms for his sons. And as a Spaniard, it was
Spanish interests he promoted. Consequently, he made other European
rulers, such as the Duke of Milan and the King of France, very uneasy.
Seeking a cardinal who might stand with them against Alexander, a
Milanese envoy wrote to his lord, 'If Cardinal Giuliano can be got to ally
himself with France, a tremendous weapon will have been forged against
the Pope.'[2]

Giuliano was willing to turn himself into such a weapon. The position
he had held when Innocent was pope had given him the opportunity to
wield political influence and indulge in statesmanship in a way he had
never experienced during his uncle's reign. He had no desire to return to
a life where he existed only on the periphery of power. But such a decision
was not without consequence. To take a public stance in Rome, with the
intent of overthrowing the incumbent pope, posed a threat to his very life.
Alexander's ambition outstripped that of his predecessors, and so did his
ferocity; he would not hesitate to have Giuliano assassinated. On 24 April
1494, Cardinal Giuliano della Rovere set sail, under cover of darkness,
from the port of Rome at Ostia, a bishopric he had once held. He stopped
briefly in his home territory of Genoa and Savona, and from there he
made his way to France. He would not see Rome again for almost a
decade. His principal mission now was to advise Charles VIII, King of
France, on the best ways to attack Alexander in Italy.[3]

However, it was not simply a matter of Rome now being too dangerous
for Giuliano. Felice, too, was at risk. Many parents valued their children
for what they might bring to the family in later life, in the form of a spouse
or a position of influence. But for those in a politically volatile state, children
could be a weak point, a means by which a parent could be controlled.
Giuliano understood very well the potential of this kind of threat. Some

years later he had the young Ferrante Gonzaga held as hostage at the Vatican court in return for his father's, the Marquis of Mantua's, loyalty to the papacy. This kind of hostage-taking had a long history, dating back to the ancient world. Giuliano might have been a somewhat distant father to Felice, but he knew that Alexander would not hesitate to seize her if he felt that he could then force her father's hand. It would not be safe for Felice della Rovere to stay in Rome any longer.

The assertion that this is what happened to Felice is based on a combination of speculation and available historical material. It is evident that Felice did spend her earliest years with her mother and the de Cupis family because of her closeness to them later on, not to mention her almost instinctive understanding of how Rome worked. Yet, in 1504, contemporary accounts describe her as 'Madonna Felice da Savona' implying that the della Rovere home town was now her place of residence.

Felice was taken from the de Cupis palace, from the home of her mother and stepfather, brothers and sisters. She knew that, like other girls, at the age of fifteen or sixteen she would have left home to be married. But she was little more than eleven, young to be leaving the only home she had ever known. Moreover, even on her marriage, she might not have expected that she would have to leave her city, because it was very likely that her husband would have been a Roman. She could never have imagined that she would have to leave, by boat, for her father's native city of Savona, to be placed in the care of her della Rovere relatives.

As a young girl living in the centre of Rome, Felice had had little opportunity or need to travel very far. It is probable that the longest journey she had ever taken was to cross the Tiber river to visit St Peter's or her mother's family in Trastevere. Now she boarded a boat, a mode of transportation that was completely alien to her, to undertake the five-hundred-kilometre journey north along the Tyrrhenian coastline. Nor were sixteenth-century ships remotely comfortable; their decks sloped, making moving around challenging for the uninitiated.[4] The voyage can have served only to heighten Felice's fear and growing indignation.

That Felice was well aware that it was the Borgia who were driving her out of her native city is indicated by a story she would tell a little later in life. While at sea, she believed a Borgia ship was chasing her boat and she vowed that she would throw herself into the water rather than be taken by its sailors. Her father's enemy became her own. In fact she had her own personal grievance against them: they had taken her from her family. Awaiting her in Savona might be her blood kin, but Felice della Rovere, despite her name, was a daughter of Rome not of Savona.

CHAPTER 9

The Adolescent Felice

Savona was very different from Rome, not simply in terms of its size and history, but also in its social structure. Unlike Rome, Savona was not a city that fed off the Church, populated by bureaucrats, and where a cardinal's daughter, living in their midst, was revered as something special. Instead Savona was a small harbour town, whose important men were its merchants.[1] In Rome, the della Rovere cousins Felice knew, such as her cousin Girolamo Basso, were churchmen. Now she was to encounter secular relations such as her aunt Luchina, Giuliano's sister, and her cousin Lucrezia, who was almost the same age as her. If Giuliano had given any thought to the matter at all, he might perhaps have expected Luchina to become a second mother to Felice and Lucrezia a new sister.

But the absence of any contact between Felice and Luchina and Lucrezia once Felice was an adult suggests that their relationship did not develop along these lines. It is not hard to imagine the young Felice, on the cusp of adolescence, arriving in Savona unhappy at having been taken from the only family she knew and with preconceived ideas about herself. Felice felt no stigma from her illegitimacy. She was proud of her parentage because those around her were proud of it on her behalf. Her Savona cousins, however, who might have profited from the Church but whose lives did not revolve around it, probably did not see Felice in the way she saw herself.

Savona in the 1500s

For them, she was simply a family bastard, an insignificant girl at that, who did not merit any special treatment from them. This cool attitude in itself might have surprised her. It is also possible that Felice arrived, not only full of self-confidence, but with a marked sense of superiority too. She was Roman, from the *caput mundi*, a city that was second to none, while Savona lived in the shadow of its more prosperous neighbour, Genoa. Felice came from a city filled with ancient temples, churches and palaces. During the papacy of Sixtus IV, Savona's cathedral had been enlarged when he built a sumptuous chapel for his parents. In 1490, Giuliano della Rovere gave a magnificent altarpiece by Vincenzo Foppa to Savona's Oratory of Our Lady, featuring the Madonna and Child, and Giuliano himself kneeling as a donor, and the merchants' houses became adorned with stylish *all'antica* decoration.[2] The Roman Felice could see it was hardly comparable to the city she had left behind. Undoubtedly she arrived with all the preconceptions city-dwellers have towards places they deem less sophisticated.

There were plenty of ingredients for conflict between a headstrong and lonely girl and her Savonese relations. They did not even share a first language. The Italian used for written correspondence or spoken between Italians of different towns or provinces was *toscana*, the language of Tuscany. But even today each province still has its own dialect, spoken exclusively by its natives. At home, Felice would have spoken *romanescha*, the language of the Romans. Her relatives in Savona spoke a Savonese variant on the Ligurian dialect. This linguistic difference would have served only to widen the gap between them.

What is important about this turn of events in Felice's life is how it moulded her attitude towards her family. Her instinct was to trust and turn to those family members who were churchmen. She always had good relations with them, perhaps because she had had good experiences with the clergy in Rome as a child. But secular family members were a different matter. She tended to regard them with suspicion and isolated herself from them. Whatever might be said about there being little difference between legitimate and illegitimate children, the legitimate ones were always prepared to use their status as a trump card. It seems likely that Felice's provincial relatives, taken aback by the self-possession and self-confidence of a child they viewed as a marginal member of their family, chose to remind her that she was not really one of them. Felice was not one to forget such slights.

Whether she liked it or not, Savona was to become her home. With Rome out of Giuliano della Rovere's reach, he turned his attention to shaping Savona into a kingdom for himself. Part of his grand scheme was to encourage the French, his current allies, to invade Italy and take Genoa and Savona, then establishing him as prince in his native land. He spent a good deal of time in France trying to bring this about, but that did not mean he left Savona unattended. In a foreshadowing of his behaviour in the following decade, Giuliano set about creating a residence in Savona fit for its potential new lord. He hired the Florentine architect Giuliano da Sangallo to build him a splendid palace in the style of those occupied by the Medici and their associates in Florence. The Palazzo della Rovere was the largest the city had ever seen, located at the highest point in Savona overlooking the harbour, on a parcel of land bought originally by Sixtus IV. The palace, which was more magnificent than surrounding buildings, dominated the harbour front. It could easily be seen from the water, a symbol of Giuliano's control of his city. The building was so impressive that in 1500 the town of Savona conferred citizenship on Giuliano da Sangallo, 'master of stone and design'.[3]

Re-creating Felice's part in her father's Savona plans is something of a challenge. Some time after 1497, when she was fourteen, the acceptable age for girls to be married, Giuliano found a husband for her. Supposition, based on the available evidence, provides the following picture of the young Felice's attitude to married life. Marriage was not at all to her liking.

CHAPTER 10

Felice's First Marriage

In 1505, it would be said of Felice that she liked being widowed, and had turned down several husbands her father had put before her when he was a cardinal. Assuming that an inexperienced fourteen- or fifteen-year-old girl, even without Felice's apparent degree of pride and arrogance, would not have been so defiant or independent that she could refuse to marry the man her father proposed, we can deduce that she had accepted a husband at that age. This would have been around 1497–98. We do not know the identity of her husband but logic dictates he would not have been a politically or socially powerful figure beyond the immediate community. He was most likely someone of local political influence, either from Savona or Genoa, who could assist Giuliano in his dealings in the area. Her spouse, who was undoubtedly dead by the beginning of 1504, probably died some time before that date, as there had to be an opportunity for Felice to refuse further husbands her cardinal father proposed for her. So this was a brief marriage and, judging by her reluctance to repeat the experience, she did not enjoy it very much.

Of all the lacunae in Felice's early life, this one is the most frustrating. It is impossible to determine exactly what went wrong to make her so resistant to the idea of remarrying. Did she enter marriage with the expectation of receiving from a husband the affection she had not been granted by her

Wedding ceremony from *La Novella di Gualtieri*, 1553

Savona relatives, and then found it lacking? Was she simply angry at being forced to marry a man from Liguria, which would mean that she would never be able to return to Rome? Whatever it was that happened in Felice's first marriage, it certainly left a deep and apparently negative imprint on her psyche.

How, then, did widowhood affect the young Felice? Herein lies the key to understanding how Felice, widowed perhaps as young as sixteen, recognized her potential power. As a widow, she had some degree of financial independence. On her husband's death, according to law, she would have received the dowry she had been given on her marriage. It was not necessarily large, but it would have provided an adequate means of support and was at her disposal for as long as she remained unmarried. Her recognition of this probably contributed to her reluctance to accept another husband. Why should she relinquish this degree of financial independence in exchange for another disagreeable marriage? Her father's regular absence from Savona also meant that there was nobody who had direct control over her, who could try to force another husband on her. Felice never answered to another della Rovere relative.

Along with this financial independence came a certain status. In Savona, a della Rovere widow was far removed from a della Rovere bastard, and Felice saw the usefulness of the respect accorded her. It provided her with her first opportunity to negotiate with the business community of Savona.

As a widow, Felice would have lived in the new palace that Giuliano had built in Savona. In her father's frequent absences, she became its chatelaine, and the position gave her a taste of power. The palazzo was more than simply a palatial home. It was the symbolic seat of his own power, and those anxious to ingratiate themselves with the cardinal came to its doors. Visitors included captains of the ships that docked in Savona's harbour; they left gifts that might entice the cardinal and his family into future transactions. As did Savona's merchants. There was a sense of intrigue about the palace. on those occasions when Felice's father was in residence, emissaries would arrive for discussions on ways to overthrow Alexander. For Felice, this new life in the Palazzo della Rovere could in some ways replicate life in the Palazzo de Cupis. If she was not directly involved in the acts of international diplomacy, she certainly enjoyed the frisson of being so close to policy and intrigue. She wanted her own part in it.

On his return visits to Savona, Giuliano could see for himself that his daughter had a talent for negotiation. Felice knew almost instinctively how to set a deal in motion, how to get the most out of it, how to command the respect and trust of those with whom she bargained. At this level, and at her age, the negotiations might not have been very substantial, the acquisition of small amounts of foodstuffs or clothing materials, but it was very good training for what was to come later in life for this cardinal's daughter.

There were also those who came to the palace door seeking help, those in Savona who had fallen on hard times, or who needed the influence of the town's leading family. The last few years of her life had shown Felice a world in which she was perceived as an outsider. That sense of being on the outside looking in had made her unusually sympathetic to those on the margins. She was always willing to champion an underdog, to extend help and influence where she could.

These distractions aside, Felice was still anxious about her immediate future. A point would come when her father would lose patience and insist that she take a husband, perhaps again from the local community. Her position of relative independence could not last for ever. But then, another death occurred, one that once more changed the destinies of the exiled cardinal and his daughter. What has up to now been Felice's phantom-like presence in history's chronicles rapidly acquires deeper shadow and substance and colour.

PART II

The Pope's Daughter

CHAPTER I

The New Pope

By August 1503, Alexander VI had grown obese as a result of all the gluttonous and sybaritic events he had staged at the Vatican Palace. 'This month is a bad one for fat people,' lamented the Pope. By 12 August he had succumbed to the malaria carried by the mosquitoes that riddled the many as yet undrained swampy areas of Rome. A week later, the Spanish pope was dead. He was buried in the ancient rotunda once attached to St Peter's called, ironically, Santa Maria della Febbre ('Our Lady of the Fever'), designed to protect the faithful from the plague.[1]

Cardinal Giuliano della Rovere wasted little time in returning from exile and he arrived back in Rome on 3 September to participate in conclave. 'I have come here on my own account,' he said, 'and not on other people's.'[2] Anxious to secure the tiara for himself, that September he was to be unlucky. Too many opposing interests, including a strong French desire to see the election of one of their own, meant the crown fell into the hands of an outside candidate on 22 September. This was the aged Sienese cardinal, Francesco Piccolomini, who took the name Pope Pius III in memory of his own uncle, Pius II.

It seemed as if Giuliano's run of bad luck, which had begun over a decade earlier with the election of Alexander, was not yet over. But his fortunes were to change faster than he might have imagined. Just two weeks

Bringing Dinner to Cardinals at Conclave

after becoming pope, the frail Pius fell ill. He was dead by 19 October. This time Giuliano did not intend to fail. He adopted the same recourse to bribery that had earned Alexander the tiara. He made promises he had no intention of keeping, in particular to the contingent of Spanish cardinals, whom he particularly loathed because of their affiliation with Alexander. None the less, as the Ferrarese ambassador remarked, 'The Spanish cardinals do not intend to be poor when they come out of conclave.'[3] On 31 October, the cardinals entered conclave. They cast their votes in the Sistine Chapel and slept on trestle beds put up in the Vatican Palace's audience halls, the Sala Regia and the Sala Ducale. This temporary accommodation was, this time, required for only one night. The cardinals returned with the quickest decision in the history of the process thus far and emerged the very next day, announcing the della Rovere cardinal as their new pope. Coincidentally, the *conclavisto*, the official responsible for locking and unlocking the cardinals in their sequestered quarters, was Bernardino de Cupis.[4] So it was her stepfather who presented to the world Felice's biological father as *Il Papa*, the father of every Christian soul.

When Cardinal Giuliano della Rovere ascended the papal throne in November 1503, he performed the same ritual every pontiff before him had done; he took a new name. No pope's name was a neutral choice, but Giuliano's selection of Giulio, or Julius, was ripe with symbolism. Officially, he chose the name in honour of a predecessor, the fourth-century Pope Julius I. Julius II, a Franciscan as his uncle Sixtus had been, was devoted to the cult of Mary: Julius I had erected the church of Santa Maria in Trastevere, close to the district the Ligurians in Rome called home. The name Julius was also unusually close to his baptismal one, as if the former cardinal was reluctant to relinquish entirely his previous identity, and wanted his old self to enjoy this most exalted of ecclesiastical positions. Moreover, the name of Julius also had an association with Julius Caesar, whose endeavours had first made Rome great. The city of Genoa even greeted Julius's election with a eulogy praising him as being endowed with 'the soul of a Caesar', a seemingly strange analogy for a churchman.[5]

Like his namesake, Julius II wanted to be a great statesman, a great builder and a great soldier. He was determined to carry on the work launched by his fifteenth-century predecessors of beautifying both the Vatican Palace complex and the city of Rome. Florence, steered by the

Medici family, obsessed equally by art and power, was acknowledged as the great Renaissance city of the fifteenth century. Julius's mission was to ensure that in the sixteenth that title belonged to Rome and that he would be fêted for eternity as the engineer of the new magnificence of the *caput mundi*. Beyond the city walls, Julius wanted to consolidate the papal states, to see cities such as Bologna returned to their rightful owner, the papacy, and he was prepared to go to war in person to claim his prizes. Everything he did throughout his entire reign was tempered by this Caesarian spirit of bellicose aggression. He was not called the Warrior Pope for nothing. Julius's years in exile had given greater focus to his dreams and ambitions. They made the taste of his papal victory all the sweeter and made him all the more determined to create a personal identity and legacy that would surpass that of any previous pontiff – including that of the very first. In his satire, *Julius Exclusus*, Erasmus writes of Julius arriving at the gates of heaven and informing Peter, bewildered and scandalized by his successor's attachment to worldly goods, 'You are still dreaming of that old Church, in which you and a few starveling bishops ran a really frigid pontificate, subject to poverty, sweat, dangers and a thousand nuisances. Time has changed everything for the better. The Roman pope is now quite a different thing; you were pope in name and title only. If you could see today so many sacred buildings erected by kingly wealth, so many thousands of priests everywhere (many of them rich), so many bishops equal to the greatest kings in military power . . . so many cardinals dressed in purple with regiments of servants crowding round them . . . what would you say?' Peter's response is, 'That I was looking at a tyrant worse than worldly, an enemy of the Christ, the bane of the Church.'[6]

Very soon after his election, Julius, this 'bane of the church' became known as 'Il papa terribile'. His monstrous temper was quick to flare if his demands and desires were not met. Approaching sixty, Julius knew he had no time to waste if he was to achieve everything he wanted in the time left to him. He personified *terribilità*, the ability to inspire awe-struck terror in those who served him. Giorgio Vasari later praised the portrait that Raphael painted of the Pope towards the end of his life as 'so wonderfully life-like and true that it inspired fear as if it were alive'.[7] Raphael captured the Pope's brooding gaze, averted from the self-avowedly unworthy and timorous viewer, and his be-ringed, white, claw-like hand as it gripped his

43

chair. It is an image very different from the fresco of the della Rovere men Melozzo da Forlì had painted more than thirty years earlier. Then Pope Julius was still Cardinal Giuliano, Sixtus IV's less favoured *nipote*, obliged to bend to listen attentively to his uncle's instructions.

Julius was not the only della Rovere family member whose personality was shaped by enforced absence from Rome. Up in Savona, twenty-year-old Felice della Rovere greeted the news of her father's election with a mixture of relief and elation tempered by caution. Relief, because it meant that her own years of exile were over; she could now go home to the city of her birth and see her family again. She knew, moreover, that her father's new-found glory would also have its impact on her own life. There were plenty of cardinals' daughters, but Felice was now unique; she was the living pope's only daughter. Such status confirmed her sense of her worth and rarity, and she knew that the possibility of being something exceptional was within her grasp. Yet she also recognized that such ambitions might not necessarily be reached without a struggle. She had resisted, successfully, her father's attempts to marry her off while he was still a cardinal. But such resistance in those turbulent times, with her father constantly distracted and often far away in France, was relatively easy for a headstrong girl fixed on self-governance. Felice knew the stakes were much higher now. For her father, Felice was a valuable asset. He could use her to seal any number of political deals through a marriage alliance, and he might not consider his daughter's personal wishes unless she voiced them forcibly. In such papal strategies Felice della Rovere did not want to be a pawn; she wanted to be a queen. She was more than prepared to enter into a battle of wills with her father in order to achieve her ends.

CHAPTER 2

The Reluctant Bride

Cardinal Giuliano's coronation as Pope Julius II took place on 28 November 1503. The new pope spent between fifty and sixty thousand ducats on this lavish affair, which was marred by rain.[1] There is no indication that he invited his daughter to travel from Savona for this momentous day in his life. This was typical of his attitude towards her throughout the course of his papal career. Felice was to appear at the Vatican Palace only when Julius needed her, although he was to come to need her more often than he might initially have thought. It was not necessarily that Julius was mean-spirited. The relationship between father and daughter defies easy categorization, but Julius certainly valued her. He was, however, guided by certain rules and, as pontiff, he did not want to flaunt his illegitimate daughter. Julius was partly influenced by his own sense of what was decorous and appropriate behaviour in his position. In comparison with his predecessors, his uncle Sixtus included, Julius was markedly restrained in distributing largesse to members of his family. But his treatment of Felice was also predicated on his desire for his reign to be seen as the polar opposite of Alexander VI's. Julius's loathing of Alexander was so great that he even hated living in the same Vatican apartments as his predecessor had done. Alexander had certainly taken nepotism to levels even the indulgent Sixtus IV could not have imagined. Yet Julius could appreciate the reasoning behind

Maarten van Heemskerck, Detail of View of St Peter's and the Vatican under Construction

Alexander's bestowal of cardinals' hats on his sons, and his making his favourite, Cesare, lord of the provinces of the Romagna. Even the multiple marriages Alexander organized for his daughter Lucrezia were a comprehensible component of the family advancement that had become the norm for papal policy. Where Alexander had gone too far was in his overtly public love for his daughter. As his popularity with the city of Rome waned, there was speculation that yet another Borgia bastard was in fact the product of an incestuous relationship between Alexander and Lucrezia.[2] Julius could not remove from his mind the idea that should Felice, his unmarried daughter, be present at his crowning, the same rumours and whispers would begin about their relationship.

Despite her absence from the coronation, Felice was clearly on Julius's mind during its aftermath. The first surviving written reference to Felice della Rovere dates from January 1504 and is embedded in the dense multi-volumed chronicles of the political life of Italy compiled by the Venetian Marino Sanuto. It reads, somewhat tersely, 'The Pope is arranging a wedding for his only daughter Felice who is in Savona and is awaited in Rome, to the Signor of Piombino, Lord Appiano.'[3]

Felice still had more than a month to prepare herself for her return to Rome. At the end of February, there was further news of her travel plans: 'Madama Felice, the daughter of the Pope, is coming from Savona, and the Pope has sent some of the galleons that are at Ostia to honour her. Also this week the prefects and the Cardinal of San Pietro in Vincoli will come, and he will do them great honour.'[4]

This brief description of Julius's different modes of honouring his visiting relatives is telling. In Renaissance Rome, how, when and where the pope's visitors – friends, family or political emissaries – were greeted was an indication of the esteem in which they were held.[5] The implications of such social manoeuvring were thus telegraphed to the visitors themselves and to the wider diplomatic world. The prefects of Rome were Julius's brother Giovanni della Rovere, Lord of Senigallia, and his wife, the sister of the Duke of Urbino, Giovanna da Montefeltro; the title was purely honorary. The cardinal was Julius's favourite nephew, Galeotto Franciotto della Rovere, who had inherited his uncle's old titular Roman church of San Pietro in Vincoli. These distinguished family members were to be welcomed with an event in the city of Rome itself, something, the missive implied, of a spectacular nature. On the other hand, Julius sent his daughter a welcoming committee to meet her at sea, before she even landed on *terra firma*. Such a reception met several of her father's requirements for Felice's entrance into Rome. It acknowledged his daughter's arrival in an impressive and not inexpensive fashion. The launching of galleons at full sail was a costly enterprise. In fact, the further out a papal retinue travelled from Rome to meet an incoming guest, the greater the perceived prestige bestowed by the pope on the visitor. Felice could not feel that her father had not made some effort to honour her arrival. Perhaps more to the point, from Julius's perspective, those with an interest in her presence in Rome, such as the Lord of Piombino, would note her father's acknowledgement of her. Felice's stock on the marriage market would depreciate if it was perceived that she was of apparently little worth to her father. At the same time, however, this meeting at sea was, by dint of its location, discreet. It meant that Julius did not have to arrange a public ceremony in Rome to honour his daughter. At sea, apart from his sailors and an unnamed Vatican emissary, there would be no onlookers, no audience to witness her arrival, as there would have been in the city itself. Such an ostentatious event, Julius felt, could have compromised his own position as supreme pontiff, given that he was determined to be seen as very different from his predecessor, at least in the eyes of the plebeian faithful.

Felice's return to Rome meant a return to her childhood home. Decorum did not permit the young widow to stay at the Vatican Palace, but the Palazzo de Cupis was waiting for her. Her family was there – Lucrezia, Bernardino, Francesca and Gian Domenico – all delighted to see their cherished girl transformed into a young woman. Life in the Piazza Navona had undergone few changes in her absence, but the de Cupis, like Felice, were well aware of the impact Julius's election could have on their future. They could not have imagined that the cardinal's daughter would return as the daughter of a pope and that in due course they would profit from the family connection. In 1506 Julius made Bernardino Treasurer of Perugia and Umbria. On the death of Girolamo Basso della Rovere in 1507, Bernardino's brother Teseo received the bishoprics of Recanati and Macerata which had been held by Girolamo.[6]

For Felice, there could be no better base than the Palazzo de Cupis. Her stepfather was *conclavisto*, the keeper of the key in more than name: any information passing through the Vatican would be diverted sooner or later into the de Cupis home. If she were to agree to marry him, Felice wanted a lot of information about the Lord of Piombino.

The Lord of Piombino, Jacopo Appiano, had been a victim of Borgia aggression and had only recently had his lands returned to him by Julius. Piombino was relatively small, but its geographical location was not without its usefulness to a Ligurian pope and his family. The city was a port some seventy kilometres to the south of Livorno and was important in terms of both trade and defence along that stretch of the Tyrrhenian coast. Julius's own coastal upbringing made him unusually conscious for a pope of the strategic value of port towns from both a financial and a defensive point of view. At the port situated at the mouth of the river Tiber, which connected Rome to the sea, he maintained a large fleet of ships, including those sent out to greet Felice. Later, in 1508, he would add a large fortress, designed by Donato Bramante, to the port of Civitavecchia, about a hundred kilometres to the south of Piombino. Bringing Piombino into the family fold would make a significant nautical contribution to della Rovere control of the coastline between Rome and Savona.

Furthermore, Jacopo Appiano brought a number of advantageous political alliances to the marriage table. He was on good terms with Florence, Pisa and Siena and his family also had a long-standing alliance with the Kingdom of Naples. Via the Lord of Piombino, Julius could add the Appiano allies – the most important Tuscan towns and Naples – to his own.[7] With his strategically positioned city and the right sort of friends, Jacopo Appiano had attractive qualities as a bridegroom, at least from Julius's perspective.

There was also inducement for Felice to accept the match. The Medici secretary, Bernardo Dovizi da Bibbiena, reported from Rome, 'The daughter of the Pope, Madonna Felice, is to be married to the Lord of Piombino with those conditions that Pope Alexander wished to place upon the [marriage] of Madonna Lucrezia. That is to say that the said Lord will make a priest of the son that he already has and if Madonna Felice should bear a male child he will inherit the state, and if the Lord dies without children the estate shall go to the said lady who can dispose of it as she pleases.'[8]

Effectively to disinherit a son from a first marriage so that a son from a second could inherit was not necessarily abnormal in contemporary marital politics. The second part, that should there be no children Felice would receive Piombino, was much more unusual. Furthermore, Bibbiena remarked that she could dispose of the estate as 'she' pleased. He gives Felice an autonomy rare for a woman of this time, indicating her instinct to protect herself and her interests.

Less than a month after Bibbiena's report, however, the Piombino match was off. A Venetian in Rome wrote home in March noting that Julius had sent an emissary to France 'to arrange a marriage between the Pope's daughter with the son of the Duke of Lorraine'.[9] Perhaps Julius decided he would benefit more from a French liaison, with its international implications, than from the provincial Piombino match. The Duke of Lorraine, René d'Anjou, was an old political ally of Julius, and a marriage between their children would further cement this relationship.

However, Felice herself might have voiced the opinion that the Piombino marriage was not to her liking. If it was in Julius's interests to hold out for something better, then certainly the same was true for Felice. After meeting Jacopo Appiano, she perhaps felt that the potential prize of Piombino would not compensate her fully for however many years of matrimony she might have to endure. The Vatican officials and bureaucrats who were constant visitors to her stepfather's house chattered and gossiped and probably told her, directly or indirectly, all she needed to know about Jacopo Appiano. Of great interest to her was that he had been passed over as a husband for Lucrezia Borgia. Felice might not have paid a great deal of attention to Lucrezia Borgia while she was herself only a cardinal's daughter. However, what Lucrezia had been given was now a benchmark for what Felice wanted for herself. The notion of settling for a Borgia reject was not something she would have been able to tolerate.

Nor did anything come of Felice's potential Lorraine marriage, although whether interest waned on the bride's or groom's side is not known. Shortly after the French union was broached, Felice sailed back to Savona for a brief period. Her return is the first indication that Julius did see his daughter as more than material for the marriage market, for when she went back, he had her act as an agent of good will between himself and the Savonese mercantile community. They were evidently anxious to hear that they would receive favourable treatment in Rome now that there was a pope who was one of their own. Julius's uncle Sixtus had seen himself as specifically Savonese; inscriptions emblazoned across the Vatican Palace from his reign read 'Sixtus IV Saonensis'. Julius was not quite so parochial in his outlook. He preferred to identify himself by way of his province, Liguria, which meant he could exploit a connection with the more powerful and wealthy city of Genoa. None the less, he had no desire to alienate his native city's business people and was ready to take advantage of the good relations his daughter had established in Savona. Before she departed again for Rome, Felice, awaiting a boat from Genoa, wrote once more to the Savonese *commune*, assuring them that the 'Pope holds you dearly in his heart and loves the city more than any man has ever loved his *patria*'.[10]

This stay in Savona provided Felice with a period of respite from the ongoing campaign to find her a husband. It also allowed her to perform in a role that was instinctively hers. Ironically, she was a natural cardinal *nipote*, she loved mediation and diplomacy, and particularly enjoyed helping those weaker than herself. Julius was described as 'always on the alert to shield the humblest of his subjects from oppression', and in this respect, as in others, Felice was her father's daughter, taking time to deal with small grievances in the midst of major crises.[11] Like her father, Felice did not shy away from conflict with her peers, but it gave her pleasure to feel that she had the power to smooth any ruffled feathers in the town to which she had arrived, as an outsider, a decade earlier.

Felice's period of respite from the matrimonial carousel was, however, brief. At the end of May, Julius summoned his daughter back to Rome, this time in the company of her aunt Luchina.

CHAPTER 3

The della Rovere Women in Rome

On 31 May 1504, the Venetian ambassador at the Vatican court, Antonio Giustiniani, reported on the arrival of Julius's sister Luchina in Rome. She was expected there soon, 'in the company of Madonna Felice, daughter of the Pope, for whom galleys set sail several days ago to fetch from Savona'.[1] He reported their arrival at the port of Ostia on 8 June and noted that the following day they would make their formal entrance into Rome. Their entrance was still discreet, however, with few onlookers for 'the plague is making great progress, and there are few places in the city that are not infected . . . the Pope is inclined to leave Rome, although it has not been determined where he shall go'.[2]

Despite the threat of disease, Julius did not move from Rome, and a few days later he hosted a celebratory event for the arrival of his female relatives. 'These ladies,' the Venetian ambassador wrote, 'the daughter and sister of the Pope, in the company of the Prefectress have gone *publicly* [his emphasis] to the Pope's Castle attended by many courtiers from the family of the Pope and other Cardinals, and they enjoyed themselves until late in the evening with His Holiness.'[3]

The Venetian ambassador took pains to imply there was a hint of scandal attached to Julius carousing with the women. Julius would not have hosted such an event for his daughter alone; even in the company of her

Maarten van Heemskerck, View of Villa Belvedere, 1530s

aunt her 'public' entrance warranted underscoring in Giustiniani's missive. None the less, that Luchina was there did dilute the impact of Felice's presence. Moreover, the festivities took place at 'the Pope's Castle', Castel Sant' Angelo, the Castle of the Holy Angel. This vast circular structure, originally the mausoleum of the Emperor Hadrian, was converted into a fortified, moated castle in the Middle Ages, its name changed to remove its association with the pagan past. It stood at the foot of the Ponte Sant' Angelo, the bridge over the Tiber leading to the Vatican Hill. It was close to the Vatican Palace, to which it was connected by a secret passageway, yet was recognized as a separate building. Julius could thus entertain his female relations in splendid fashion, but outside the ecclesiastical complex itself, thus maintaining Church decorum.

To maintain decorum while catering to family needs became Julius's first priority as the patron engineer of Vatican Palace additions. His recent predecessors, from Nicholas V onwards, had all made renovations and amendments to the palace structure, but the palace was still a disharmonious collection of medieval buildings, assembled one on top of the other on the Vatican Hill. Julius would have the man best described as his 'partner in design', the architect Donato Bramante, make numerous improvements to his papal residence.[4] Bramante was originally from Urbino, but had worked for many years at the Sforza court in Milan. He and Julius shared a similar vision of Rome. Both were enamoured of the idea of returning the golden age of ancient Rome to the Julian city. The first task Julius gave Bramante, in the spring of 1504, was to make the Villa Belvedere more easily accessible. The villa was built in the 1480s by Innocent VIII, the Ligurian pope Julius had so closely assisted, and was described by those that visited it as 'a most exquisite and delightful place'.[5] Located north of the Vatican Palace on the Mons San Egidio, it became Julius's favourite site for family entertainments. Like Castel Sant' Angelo, the villa was close to the Vatican Palace proper, yet was not actually part of it. Julius could host dinners and dances that his female relations could attend, and not fear comparison with Alexander VI, who had no compunction about staging parties in the palace itself with Lucrezia or mistresses and courtesans present. Julius had Bramante design the Cortile del Belvedere, defined by two corridors extending from the palace across a deep valley to the villa. The villa was three hundred metres away from the palace, across difficult terrain, a challenge the ageing Pope and his architect would overcome. This was only one phase of Julius's plans for the Cortile del Belvedere. Bramante also added a courtyard and garden for the Pope's growing collection of antique sculpture, which included the famous *Laocoön*, the *Belvedere Torso*, and *Apollo Belvedere*.[6]

It was at an event at the Villa Belvedere that indications of Felice's discomfort among her female della Rovere relatives became apparent. While Felice had established herself as a figure of sufficient substance to mollify the people of Savona, her relationship with these women was more complex. Throughout her life, she contrived to have little to do with them. Her lack of ease when with them was described in a letter written on 11 July 1504 by Emilia Pia. Emilia Pia was lady-in-waiting to Elizabetta Gonzaga, Duchess of Urbino, and she was writing to Elizabetta's niece by marriage, Isabella d'Este, the Marchesa of Mantua. Emilia is reporting a meal given by Julius in honour of his female relatives at the Villa Belvedere:

> And then Madame the Prefectress [Felice's aunt Giovanna da Montefeltro della Rovere] entered with Madonna Costanza her daughter and the two married nieces of His Holiness. The first, Madonna Sista, married to the nephew of the Cardinal of San Giorgio, Signor Galeazzo Riario . . . she wore a dress of gold brocade covered with slashed crimson silk and a mantle of gold taffeta. The second niece, called Madonna Lucretia, married to a nephew of the Cardinal of Naples, who is the son of the Duke of Ariano, wore a dress of black and gold silk with pearls at her neck and jewels on her head of not much worth; and these two are the nieces of the Pope, the daughters of a sister of His Holiness, called Madonna Luchina. And Madonna Costanza preceded all, with a yellow dress covered in slashed white pendant trimmings and a headdress of diamonds of some worth, believed to have been given her by the Pope. Madonna Felice did not appear at all, as she was feeling ill.[7]

At such significant events as this dinner at the Villa Belvedere, one that the Pope was giving in honour of his female relatives, one of those relatives would have to be on the brink of death to fail to attend. The obviousness of Felice's absence was noticed, and remarked on by the sharp-eyed and sharp-tongued Emilia Pia. The inference is that she deliberately chose to stay away. Although Felice was the Pope's daughter, and Rome was her city, precedence on this occasion went to his niece Costanza, causing Felice irritation, if not downright humiliation. Felice was already a known quantity at Italy's courts. Emilia Pia did not have to describe who she was to Isabella. She did, however, have to explain the identity of Felice's Savonese aunt and cousins, suggesting that they had lived in obscurity until the time of Julius's election as pope. Felice could not countenance the possibility of being thought of only as their equal, or even their inferior, when she was quite certain that she ranked above them.

Another reason Felice preferred not to attend this event is quite understandable for a young woman. She would have been made to feel underdressed. It is clear from Emilia Pia's description that the women were arrayed in their finest gowns of lavishly slashed and decorated silks of golds, scarlets and yellows, adorned with jewels. Felice was a widow, so she would wear black widow's weeds. Such garments gave the widow who was the regent of a family a sense of personal control; they declared her power and sexual unavailability. Felice, however, was not a powerful matriarch. On this occasion all that her widow's habit would have done would be to make her appear drab amidst the adornment of the other young women.

But Julius had not brought Felice back to Rome simply so that she could avoid social interaction with her cousins. Three days after the party at the Villa Belvedere there was a report that he was seeking to consolidate relations with the powerful Roman baronial family the Colonna. This he thought to effect 'through a marriage with Madonna Felice, daughter of the Pope, with Signor Marcantonio Colonna'.[8] This occasion was the first on which Julius considered a Roman marriage for Felice. Two further possibilities, in the autumn of 1504, were with sons of Ercole d'Este, the Duke of Ferrara. The first was with his youngest son Ferrante, whom Julius proposed should be given the cities of Modena and Reggio Emilia. However, Ferrante was just a boy. While it was common for women to go as brides to older husbands while they were still children themselves, a boy taking an adult woman as his bride was almost unknown. The plan to unite the eleven-year-old Ferrante and the twenty-one-year-old Felice went no further. An alternative proposal was that Ercole's second son, Ippolito, be divested of his cardinalship, betrothed to Felice, and made heir to the d'Este dukedom. This would have deprived

Ercole's oldest son, Alfonso, from his inheritance – a situation Julius would have preferred, as Alfonso was a friend to Venice, a city currently hostile to the papacy.[9]

Had such a marriage to Ippolito d'Este taken place, Felice would have deposed Lucrezia Borgia, Alfonso d'Este's wife, as duchess-in-waiting, and become Duchess of Ferrara herself. It is difficult to imagine that such a future would not have appealed to Felice. It was all too evident how different Lucrezia's relationship with her father Alexander was from her own, and hard for Felice not to feel envious of her. Lucrezia had lived close to the Vatican Palace in the Palace of Santa Maria in Portico. Alexander adored his daughter so much he had stipulated in the contracts of her first two marriages that she was not to move from Rome during the first year of her married life, as he could not bear her departure. Ceremonies and entertainments were held in the Vatican Palace exclusively in Lucrezia's honour. In other words, unlike Felice, Lucrezia was not sent back to the Borgia home town when her presence was not required in Rome. She was not met discreetly at sea, or welcomed publicly into Rome only if in the company of other female relatives. Admittedly no one accused Felice of an incestuous relationship with her father and brother, as they did Lucrezia with Alexander and Cesare Borgia. Nor were there any rumours of Felice bearing an illegitimate child, as Lucrezia was believed to have done. None the less, it would have taken a hugely suppressed ego not to feel the sting of being treated so differently from one's predecessor by one's father, and such self-abasement was not in Felice's nature.

Yet Julius's brusque treatment of his daughter served only to define further Felice's personality at this critical juncture in her life. Lucrezia Borgia, indulged and adored from childhood, was marked by a passivity that rendered her incapable of making any protest when her brother Cesare killed her beloved second husband, Alfonso of Naples. Nor did it help Lucrezia at the d'Este court, where many were hostile to her and her father-in-law withheld her dowry funds from her. By contrast, Felice della Rovere's alienation from her della Rovere relations contributed to her fearlessness, which was quite astonishing in a woman of her time. This character trait revealed itself most distinctly in the incidents surrounding her proposed marriage to Roberto di Sanseverino, the prince of the southern city of Salerno.

CHAPTER 4

The Prince of Salerno

The tales of Felice's five previous potential suitors – Piombino, Lorraine, the Colonna and d'Este sons – are somewhat fragmented. Their names appear in correspondence emanating from the Vatican Palace, but then references to these potential matches disappear, leaving only speculation as to why the matches were abandoned. However the affair of the Sanseverino Prince is very well documented. The negotiations to marry him to Felice lasted over the course of several months, from December 1504 to February 1505.

Roberto was the son of Antonello di Sanseverino, who at one point had numbered among the most powerful of the Neapolitan barons. Roberto also had a della Rovere connection through his mother, Costanza da Montefeltro. Costanza, daughter and sister to the Dukes of Urbino, Federico and Guidobaldo, was also sister to Julius's younger brother Giovanni's wife, Giovanna. There was a long-standing accord between Julius and Antonello, who had spent many years in political alliance when Julius was still a cardinal. Rumours spread that were Roberto to become Julius's son-in-law, he might become the most favoured of his relations, his secular *nipote*, rather as his own cousin Girolamo Riario had been to Sixtus IV. That Julius did indeed have some personal investment in Roberto is suggested by the fact that the Sanseverino Prince came to the marriage

Maarten van Heemskerck, View of New Saint Peter's under construction, 1530s

bargaining table with some serious personal problems. In a failed rebellion, which Julius as Cardinal Giuliano had encouraged, against the King of Naples, Roberto's father Antonello had been forced into exile and stripped of his estates.[1] As the discussions of a marriage with Felice progressed, Roberto was a prince in name only.

One of the preconditions of the match was that Julius would negotiate the return of Roberto's estates with King Frederic of Naples. In addition, recounted the Venetian ambassador, on good authority from the Cardinal of Naples, 'His Holiness has promised to provide, as a dowry, 40,000 ducats from the bank of San Giorgio in Genoa and a house in that same city valued at 10,000 ducats. Five thousand ducats will come in the form of silver, jewels and clothing for the lady and, for a yearly living expense, 6000 a year, four to the prince, and two to the lady. However, His Most Reverend Cardinal has informed me that the Pope has no capital at the Bank of San Giorgio right now, and the house is not worth that much because it is old, abandoned and miserable.'[2]

The match was not regarded enthusiastically by the extended Montefeltro clan. Guidobaldo, the Duke of Urbino, paralysed by gout and rendered impotent by syphilis, felt that Roberto was attempting to usurp his own position with the Pope. He claimed that Roberto held private audiences with Julius in order to tell him that Guidobaldo was 'weak and crippled and what the Pope needs is a man of action, and other words about his own virility'.[3] Another not in favour of the union was Ferrante Colonna. Married to yet another Montefeltro sister, Agnese, he had hopes that his line might inherit the Duchy of Urbino when the childless Guidobaldo died. Such a possibility would become less than likely if Roberto di Sanseverino became the candidate sponsored by the Pope to become the Urbino heir.

But no one was more vocally opposed to the marriage than Felice herself. The first indication of her resistance comes in a letter of 28 January 1505, from the Venetian ambassador. He remarked that although the Prince of Salerno might claim the negotiations were concluded, the Cardinal of Naples had told him that there were 'difficulties in bringing it about as the lady [Felice] has contested it, which she has simply done by saying no, and that she has not shown respect towards her father, who has wished for the union'. Less than two weeks later, on 10 February, the Venetian had much more specific information about Felice's objections:

Finding myself today with the Duke of Urbino, His Excellency apprised me of the fact that the marriage of Madonna Felice with the Prince is in difficulty and the cause is the lady, who does not want it to take place, citing his poverty and also because it is said that he has another woman. The Duke believes the whole affair is in disarray as the difficulties are great, because, he says, this woman has let her words be heard and now they have reached the ears of the Prince. Even if the objections of the state [of Naples] were to cease, the lady would not wish to enter into his hands due to her fear of having an unhappy life with him. The Duke then accused the lady of instability, stating that many times the Pope, even when he was a cardinal, had wished her to marry. But she has remained a widow, and has always found reasons to be opposed to the men proposed, saying that she prefers to be left to depend upon her own resources. However, now the Pope is disposed to give her away to anyone, and to send her away from Rome, so as not to have to behold this shameful creature in front of his own eyes.[4]

In a world of diplomatic correspondence where information is usually conveyed in oblique and subtle forms, the words spoken by Felice and the Duke of Urbino are quite startling in their directness. Felice, who had clearly done her own research into the Prince's suitability to become her husband, stated categorically why she was refusing Roberto di Sanseverino: he had no money and he had a mistress. She was not enthusiastic about a life of penury, the prospect of living in a rundown palace in Genoa and her husband's attention directed towards another woman. She was evidently sceptical of her father's promises to persuade the King of Naples to return Roberto's lands to him. She perhaps also feared that Julius would be unsuccessful in his negotiations with these Aragonese princes or that, once the marriage contract was signed, he would become occupied with other matters. Even if they had not spent a great deal of time together over the course of her life, Felice had taken pains to know her father's methods of doing business, some of which she emulated. She had seen for herself or heard tales of where and when he might be inconsistent or go back on his word, not least at the moment when he was elected pope. So Felice did not entirely trust her father, and felt he did not have her personal interests at heart when it came to choosing a husband for her.

She was not afraid to stand up to Julius. Julius might have personified *terribilità*, and encouraged those facing him to feel fearful in his presence. But Felice stood apart from her contemporaries when dealing with her father. She shared his stubbornness and tenacity, and she refused to be cowed by his demands and wishes.

Guidobaldo da Montefeltro's comments about Felice are equally enlightening. His claim that she was 'unstable' reflects perhaps more on him than on her. Women of Renaissance Italy did not, as a rule, defy their fathers. They tended to defy their fathers even less when they were illegitimate, marginalized by society and thus grateful for any provision their fathers might make for them. Felice's outspokenness and her fearlessness shocked Guidobaldo. Even if he did not want this particular marriage to take place, he had seen his three sisters accept their chosen husbands without protest, and saw such behaviour as a woman's duty. To his mind, Felice's consistent refusals could be explained only by a degree of instability. Why else would a woman act in such a way?

Equally fascinating is the independent state of mind Felice had evidently maintained since the time her father was a cardinal. She was not only highly selective about whom she was prepared to take for a husband; she had no qualms whatsoever about remaining on her own. Her widowed status helped her. It was the only state in which an unmarried woman could live honourably in the outside world; otherwise the convent was her destination. If Felice had been born a boy, she would have been by now, over a year into her father's reign, a fêted and powerful cardinal. But the only ecclesiastical life made possible for a woman, the cloistered existence of a nun, had no appeal for her.

Her first marriage, unsuccessful as it might have been, had provided her with some kind of financial independence. Julius had given her a dowry. It was the law that as long as a woman remained a widow following her husband's death, her dowry could be used to provide her income. The funds could be reappropriated by her family only at the time of remarriage. Generally speaking, such reappropriation happened quickly and without complaint, especially with a woman of Felice's young age. But Felice's status was made more complex because of her illegitimacy. Exactly who controlled her, especially as Julius did not wish to assume an active paternal role, was a much more complicated issue than it was normally

and allowed her greater room to manoeuvre. Felice had no plans to relinquish her financial and personal freedom for an unsatisfactory marriage. She still had certain things she needed to do before she was ready to become a bride again.

Holding out for a husband who met her specific standards was only one part of Felice della Rovere's strategy for personal advancement. As self-confident and self-assured as she might have been on many levels, she did not delude herself. Her transition from cardinal's daughter to pope's daughter had brought her a considerable increase in status. However, while the daughter of a duke was groomed from infancy to take her place within the circles of the elite, the illegitimate daughter of a cleric was not. Felice's upbringing had been in the house of a Roman bureaucrat, and the earliest years of her life as an adult had been spent among the provincial elite and the merchants of a small port town. This background had certainly provided her with several beneficial experiences: life with the de Cupis family had shown her that it was the *haute bourgeoisie* of Roman society who got things done in the city and that they could be the most valuable allies. In Savona, as her father's sometime representative, she had become a voice of reassuring authority with the *commune*. At the same time, however, Felice was conscious that she had not grown up as the equal of the great ladies of Italy. She might have felt compensated for this sense of inequality had her father favoured her in an open and lavish fashion and welcomed her to Rome with open arms. But Felice was only too aware that such paternal treatment would not be hers. Instead, she desired equivalence with the Italian elite, which would stem from a recognition and admiration of her personal qualities and abilities. Such recognition for herself as herself, and not purely as daughter or wife, could outlast a father's reign or a husband's life. To achieve it, she needed to establish a reputation for herself in her own right.

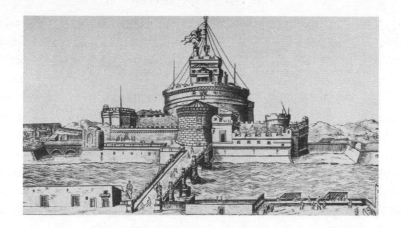

CHAPTER 5

Self-Promotion

In Raphael's fresco *The Mass of Bolsena* Felice della Rovere, dark like her father, is portrayed as an attractive young woman. Throughout her life she took good care of herself, soliciting, among other things, recipes for tooth-paste. However, her dark looks did not necessarily meet the traditional standards of beauty at the turn of the sixteenth century in Rome. Blondes were still favoured, although interestingly this was to change during the reign of Julius, when the Madonnas painted by Raphael evolve from blonde to brunette. There is a great deal of commentary on Lucrezia Borgia's long golden hair, delicate features and graceful dance steps. No such specific descriptions exist of Felice, which suggests she lacked, or did not develop, these more traditional charms. But that was not where Felice's interests lay. Instead, as she came to prominence in Rome's social and cultural orbits, there were few who did not comment on her *prudentia* – wisdom or intelli-gence. Such a reputation endured throughout her life. The scholar Angelo Firenzuola, writing in defence of the female intellect, cites among the female luminaries of his time: 'the *prudentissima* Felice della Rovere . . . of whom with no small amount of praise do many men speak, with a resounding voice'.[1]

Prudentia was in fact a much greater asset to Felice than mere prettiness. It was a far more enduring quality than physical beauty, which would

View of Ponte Sant' Angelo and Castel Sant' Angelo, sixteenth century

quickly fade. Moreover, *prudentia* could lead to the acquisition of personal attributes that could manifest themselves physically and which Renaissance Italy valued as highly as *bellezza*. *Magnificentia* (magnificence) and *grazia* (grace) contributed to the formation of a compelling persona, and allowed one to cultivate a quality still highly prized in modern Italy: *la bella figura*. *Fare la bella figura*, literally to 'cut a fine figure' means every movement, gesture, manner, activity is flawless. In Renaissance Italy, *bella figura* was understood as *sprezzatura*, which is best translated as the achievement of brilliance with apparent ease and lack of effort. To possess *sprezzatura* was the supreme goal of every ambitious Renaissance courtier. *Sprezzatura*'s chief proponent, who also provided advice and lessons on how to acquire it, was Baldessar Castiglione. Castiglione's friendship and approbation was something Felice sought out following her father's election as pope.

Castiglione was Mantuan by birth and had grown up in the orbit of the Gonzaga court. In 1499, at the age of twenty-one, he entered the service of Francesco Gonzaga, the Duke of Mantua. His humanist education and knowledge of Latin and Greek made him a prime candidate for the Mantuan diplomatic corps and over the next few years he journeyed to Milan, Pavia and Naples as the representative for Mantua. In late 1504, Francesco Gonzaga, whose aunt Elizabetta was married to Guidobaldo da Montefeltro, agreed to let him transfer his service to the court of Urbino. He became invaluable to the artist Raphael, a native of Urbino, and gave him personal advice on how to conduct himself at court, contributing greatly to the success of his artistic career. In return, Raphael painted a portrait of his friend which is the visual embodiment of *sprezzatura*. The palette of the portrait is muted, greys and browns, which renders his piercing blue eyes all the more striking. Castiglione appears soberly dressed, in a hat and fur doublet. But the hat covers his baldness and fur was usually worn on the inside not the outside of a coat, for greater warmth. But how then would the viewer of his image know that Castiglione was the proud owner of such a luxurious garment? Renaissance Italy produced many career diplomats but none whose ear was so finely attuned to the subtleties and nuances of the position of the courtier than Castiglione. No one better understood the importance of self-presentation. For Castiglione, the manner in which one did something – speaking, singing, playing an instrument, telling a story or a joke – was as important as the actual substance of the activity. The critical element in courtly exchange was perception. How one was perceived by colleagues and superiors at court was at least as important as what one actually was. Such notions were deeply embedded in the Italian way of thinking. The ancient Latin word *honestas* meant honest and worthy but it was also the word for reputation and the respect given you by others.

Castiglione's experiences and advice for the aspiring courtier would eventually be collected in his manual of etiquette and behaviour, *Il Cortegiano*, or *The Book of the Courtier*. *Il Cortegiano* endured as an international bestseller for well over a hundred years and was translated into seven languages. Its use as a conduct book is best summarized by the addenda to the title of the 1561 English edition: 'Verie Necessarie and Profitable for Young Gentlemen and Gentlewomen, Abiding in Court, Palace or Place'.[2]

Although his book was not published until 1528, the year before his death, Castiglione began writing his text in 1514. Most of its characters, stories and examples were drawn from the early 1500s, when Castiglione first went to work for the court of Urbino. *Il Cortegiano* is conceived as a series of evenings of imaginary conversation between the real-life nobles and scholars whose presence frequently graced the court of Urbino. Castiglione's gathering included Elizabetta Gonzaga da Montefeltro, the Duchess of Urbino; her lady-in-waiting, Emilia Pia; her nephew, Cesare Gonzaga; Medici family representative Cardinal Bernardo Bibbiena and the humanist poet L'Unico Aretino. The group began by considering what made the perfect male courtier. Although the protagonists disagreed over whether being well born was a necessity, they determined he should speak and write well and be an able fighter and an accomplished musician.[3] Over and over again they stressed the importance of grace to the courtier, judging that 'he should accompany all his motion with a certain good judgement and grace', or that 'some are born indeed with such grace, that they seem not to have been born, but rather fashioned with the very hand of some God'.[4]

The participants in Castiglione's dialogue next turned their attention to defining the quintessential female courtier. Much of the discussion focused on her intrinsic qualities rather than any acquired skills. Grace and good manners were paramount, as were modesty and elegance in both her person and dress. For some, she should be little different from her male counterpart.

'I will', declared Cesare Gonazaga, 'that this woman have accomplishment in letters, music, drawing, painting, skilful in dancing and in divising sports and pastimes and the other principles that have been taught the courtier.'[5]

Cesare Gonzaga also emphasizes that the ideal courtly lady should possess 'nobleness, courage, temperance, strength of mind, and wisdom', and directs the conversation towards the importance of a woman's sense of personal honour and chastity. He asks, 'How many do the vilest things from fear of death? And yet a tender and delicate girl often resists all these fierce and strong assaults, for many have been known who chose to die rather than to lose their chastity.'[6] Another participant, Gaspare Pallavacino, expresses scepticism that such women exist 'in the world today', which provides Cesare with the opportunity to provide multiple examples of such heroic women. His first examples are actually anonymous: a young Capuan woman, captured by the French soldiers, who chose to drown herself rather than be ravished by them; a Mantuan peasant girl who had been raped and who too preferred a watery grave to a life dishonoured; a Roman girl lured to the dark recesses of the church of San Sebastiano by a man inflamed by lust for her, who killed her after she refused his advances. And then Cesare says:

> But to speak of persons known to you, do you not recall having heard how Signora Felice della Rovere was journeying to Savona and fearing that some sails that were sighted might be ships of Pope Alexander in pursuit of her, made ready with some steadfast resolution to throw herself into the sea in case they should approach and there was no means of escape. And you must not think she did this out of any passing whim, for you know as well as anyone else what intelligence and wisdom accompany this lady's singular beauty.[7]

Felice della Rovere is *Il Cortegiano*'s only example of a modern noblewoman prepared to die to defend her honour. Cesare Gonzaga then had to move into somewhat tamer territory, praising the chastity of his aunt, Elizabetta Gonzaga, in the light of her husband Guidobaldo's well-documented impotence. This story about Felice is certainly the most dramatic reference to a real-life woman to be found anywhere in the book. Female rulers such as the Empress Matilda and Isabella of Castile are revered for their governing abilities and the women of the d'Este family – Isabella, Beatrice and their mother Eleonora di Aragona – are extolled for their multiple virtues. Yet again, the story of Felice's journey and her brave resolution confirms how unusual she was in Renaissance Italy.

Undoubtedly Castiglione had heard this story about Felice's adventures from Felice herself. In January 1505 he arrived on secondment in Rome to discuss the matter of who would inherit the Urbino dukedom with Pope Julius II. There he met Felice, currently in the throes of arguing with her father about Roberto di Sanseverino. For Felice, winning Castiglione's confidence was a strategic move. The diplomat held sway and influence at two important Italian courts, Urbino and Mantua. His good opinion of her could prove invaluable political cachet.

There is no doubt that Castiglione was intrigued by Felice della Rovere. While the Duke he served found her 'unstable', for Castiglione she was lively and intelligent. Their friendship lasted several decades. Castiglione exhibited some contradictions between his prescriptions for ideal female behaviour and the actual women whose company he enjoyed. The female courtier of his book is supposed to be endowed with modesty and a good degree of subservience; in real life Castiglione admired intelligent, lively and outspoken women who could 'entertain all kinds of men with talk worth the hearing'.[8] The most engaging participant in Il Cortegiano is the feisty Emilia Pia, who is always ready to mock her male companions. Described by Castiglione as 'endowed with so lively a wit and judgement that she seemed the mistress and kingleader of all the company', she was likely to have been the model for Shakespeare's own most lively heroine, Beatrice in Much Ado About Nothing.[9] Felice's reputation as headstrong and self-assertive and her own 'ready liveliness of wit', undoubtedly appealed to Castiglione before he had even met her.

The tale recounted in Il Cortegiano of Felice at sea, fleeing from the Borgia ships, reveals a great deal not only about her personality but about how she wished to be perceived. Certainly her declaration that she would rather throw herself in the sea than be taken alive by Borgia sailors is in keeping with that same strength of character that flouted her father's wish for her to marry the Sanseverino Prince. At the same time, there was also a level of calculation to Felice's retelling this event to a man with a good classical education. It casts her in the guise of an ancient Roman heroine, Lucrezia, Sofonisba or Artemisia, who all chose death rather than relinquish their virtue. Julius's Vatican court was one obsessed by the recovery of ancient Rome. It was appropriate that the spirit of such women should be found in the daughter of the Pope who had named himself for a hero of the ancient world. At the same time, the story also allows Felice to make reference to her della Rovere roots. Not only was she travelling to Savona, her ancestral home, but she was at sea, which played an important part in della Rovere mythology. *The Miracle of Savona*, one element of the autobiographical fresco cycle commissioned by Sixtus IV at the Roman church of Santo Spirito in Sassia in 1476, depicts a legendary event from the Pope's life. As a young boy, he fell into the sea but was rescued from drowning by St Francis and St Anthony of Padua. Felice, recognizing that her place in the della Rovere family had been marginalized, was anxious to affirm her standing within the family in the public sphere by identifying herself with the sea, a distinct della Rovere emblem. Metaphorically, to throw herself into the sea rather than be taken by her father's enemies was to return to the bosom of the family.

Felice's tale also suggests that the relationship between herself and Julius was closer than it might have appeared to those at the Vatican witnessing the sometimes awkward father–daughter dynamic. The event at sea took place when Julius was still a cardinal and Alexander VI occupied the papal throne. The enmity between Alexander and Julius, who spent much time scheming to disrupt the Borgia papacy when he was a cardinal, was well known. One of the points to Felice's story is to suggest that the Borgia were prepared to attack Julius by boldly kidnapping his daughter at sea, an act hardly worthwhile if Julius did not value her. Moreover, Felice's own decision to die rather than be taken by the Borgia indicates that the enemy of the father had become the enemy of the daughter. Without even mentioning her father in this story, the bond between the Pope and his daughter is made explicit.

This meeting between Castiglione and Felice at the Vatican court cemented a lifelong friendship between the two. It was also a conduit to another relationship that Felice greatly desired, friendship with Isabella d'Este. Seven years Felice's senior, Isabella was the eldest daughter of Ercole d'Este, the Duke of Ferrara.[10] In 1490 she had married Francesco Gonzaga, the Marquis of Mantua. Isabella and Felice were not unlike in character: both were strong-willed, and each had a tremendous sense of herself, a fixed determination to get what she wanted, and a dislike of compromise. But whereas Felice had had to fight for her place in the world, Isabella had grown up only too secure of hers. She was wife, daughter and sister to Italy's wealthiest dukes; her own sister Beatrice was the wife of the Duke of Milan. Isabella was undoubtedly the best socially connected woman in Renaissance Italy. Although undeniably self-indulgent and never a ruler in her own right, Isabella nonetheless actively participated in the brokering of marriages between royal households. She fashioned herself as a patron in the tradition of the great male *maeceni* of the Renaissance, such as Cosimo and Lorenzo de' Medici. She commissioned and secured works by many of the great Renaissance artists, Mantegna, Leonardo, Michelangelo, Titian. An enthusiastic singer, she developed a choral group at Mantua, and also encouraged humanist scholarship. She amassed a large personal library, and promoted poets and writers at the Mantuan court. Her 'personal' poet, Niccolò da Correggio, coined for her the name with which she is still associated, 'la prima donna del mondo', first lady of the world.[11]

Isabella took her title of *prima donna* very seriously. She was antagonistic towards her sister-in-law Lucrezia Borgia, who, having married Isabella's brother Alfonso, eventually became Duchess of Ferrara. Isabella was rather disdainful about Lucrezia's origins and made concerted efforts to slight her sister-in-law on visits to Ferrara.

Felice della Rovere wanted Isabella's approbation. The Mantuan Marchesa's good opinion of her could be transmitted across Italy's most important cities: to Ferrara, where Isabella was more highly regarded than Lucrezia, who was reigning duchess there, and to Milan, where Isabella's sister was duchess, not to mention Venice, Florence and Naples, the home of Isabella's mother. Isabella could also reinforce Felice's relations with Urbino, where her husband's aunt was Elizabetta Gonzaga. There could be no more useful female friend to Felice. Eliciting the support of Castiglione was an important step in making overtures to the Marchesa.

Of further assistance in her endeavour was securing the approval of Gian Cristoforo Romano. A goldsmith and sculptor, Gian Cristoforo worked primarily at the Vatican court, striking papal medals. In January 1506 he participated with Michelangelo and Giuliano da Sangallo in assessing the newly recovered Hellenistic statue of *Laocoön*, recently excavated from farmland near the Baths of Titus on the Esquiline Hill. Gian Cristoforo also had long-standing ties with Mantua, having produced the medallions gracing Isabella's famous *studiolo* at the Palazzo Ducale. He continued to serve Isabella from Rome, acting as an agent in securing the precious artefacts she craved, and he corresponded regularly with her.

On 1 December 1505, Gian Cristoforo wrote to Isabella, enticing her to come to Rome:

> If your ladyship comes to Rome this Carnival, I guarantee you that you will be given beautiful things, and that you are awaited with great desire. I have already assured many cardinals that you are coming to Rome, and much affection would be bestowed upon you, and you will be so pleased by the place and the many different things that you will be sorry to leave and want to come back often. This will be so many in many respects because you would be so comfortable staying here amid sweet female companions, and especially that of Madonna Felice the daughter of the Pope, who is the most noble lady, of a noble intelligence and goodness, and dedicated to letters, antiquities, and all virtuous works, and a slave to your ladyship as she has repeated to me many times in speaking with her.[12]

Gian Cristoforo's words are designed as a letter of formal introduction for Felice to Isabella, calculated to win Isabella over. The artist and agent attests to Felice's good character; he refers to her as both noble and good and it is clear that he wanted to present Felice as a woman with whom Isabella had a great deal in common. Felice was highly intelligent and shared Isabella's humanistic interests. But Gian Cristoforo was also careful to ensure that Isabella should in no way feel threatened by Felice. He made no mention of Felice's physical appearance; even if Felice had been exceptionally pretty, Isabella would not have been pleased to hear it. Although her poets claimed the contrary, Isabella was by no means a beauty herself. She did not like beautiful women, and was always reassured when Lucrezia Borgia's attractiveness was contested. Nor did she care for painters to represent her as she truly was. Later called 'dishonestly ugly' by the salacious writer Pietro Aretino, in her fifties she made Tititan paint her twice.[13] She rejected the first painting the Venetian produced of her. This is no longer in existence, although in the seventeenth century Rubens was able to make a copy showing a rather broad woman in a bright red dress, heavily made up. Only the second painting, portraying her as a comely fifteen year old, met with her satisfaction.

Gian Cristoforo also took pains to make it clear that Felice did not think of herself as Isabella's equal. He informed the Marchesa that Felice had told him 'many times' that she considered herself Isabella's 'slave'. Undoubtedly Felice knew of Isabella's self-regard and temperament, and tailored her own presentation to ingratiate herself with the *prima donna*. Gian Cristoforo's description of Felice as an intelligent, genteel and cultivated woman was an accurate one. It was his job to provide Isabella with honest assessments, whether of members of the Vatican court or of 'a bronze panel with finely inlaid ancient figures', such as he mentions in this very letter. Guaranteeing – a word Isabella liked to hear – that Felice was, as he said she was, a fitting companion for the Marchesa of Mantua was no less important than certifying the beauty and rarity of the works of art he secured for his patron.

Isabella perhaps felt sufficient malice towards Lucrezia Borgia to reciprocate Felice's overtures of friendship simply in order to spite her sister-in-law. It could show Lucrezia that while she disdained one pope's daughter she was happy to spend time with another. But Isabella did in fact find Felice to be 'the sweet companion' Gian Cristoforo Romano had promised her. They formed a relationship that bordered on genuine friendship, but that certainly had a marked element of courtly expediency, each aware of the other's usefulness.

CHAPTER 6

The Education of Felice della Rovere

When Felice approached Isabella d'Este, it was as a woman who shared her scholarly interests. Felice's dedication to 'letters and antiquities' was an important aspect of her strategy for acceptance into courtly circles; the Medici, d'Este and Gonzaga families all prided themselves on their learning and cultivation. A new age of humanism had arrived in Rome and Felice wanted very much to be a part of it. It allowed her to charm and impress such men as Baldessar Castiglione and Gian Cristoforo Romano, as well as the cardinals at the Vatican Palace. Felice was also aware that Lucrezia Borgia had set a precedent as an educated woman. Alexander VI's daughter had even cultivated a kind of literary salon at her palace at Santa Maria in Portico, attended by such scholars and poets as Raffaello Brandolino, Serafino Aquilino and L'Unico Aretino. While Felice's father would not approve of his daughter forming such a circle, with all its consequent publicity, he did not prevent her from forging friendships with scholars and poets who came to the Vatican.

The Bolognese poet Giovanni Filiteo Achillini cites Felice in the *Viridario*, a poem he composed in honour of various luminaries at the papal court at Christmas 1504, in which he describes her as, 'the lofty Felice, whose elegant manners deserve so much merit, praise and honour'.[1] The Spoletan poet Pier Giustolo had worked for the Borgia and entertained hopes that

Tiber Island in the sixteenth century

Felice might become his new patron.[2] In 1506, he wrote a poem about the time he had met Felice, two years earlier, on a summer visit to the fortress at Senigallia belonging to her uncle, Giovanni della Rovere.

Giustolo described how, on his own arrival at Sengallia, he had admired the fortress and Senigallia's market but had been most taken with Felice herself. He praised her physical, moral and intellectual qualities. He also made much of her widowhood, and her appearance in a widow's veil, which is seen to endow her with a certain mysterious unattainability. In anticipation of procuring future commissions, the poet wrote that he desired nothing more than to be able to sing her praise on the occasion of a future marriage.[3]

Felice also actively solicited the help of those who could assist her with acquiring some kind of a humanist education. She became acquainted with Scipione Carteromacho, a humanist scholar working as the secretary for her cousin Cardinal Galeotto Franciotto della Rovere. Carteromacho was a close friend of the Venetian Aldo Manutius, the most prolific publisher in early sixteenth-century Italy. On 11 December 1504, he wrote to his colleague in Venice, 'You remember how I wrote to you about having visited Madonna Felice and she commissioned me to write to you to find out what you have published in either Latin or the volgare [Italian], and if you would be willing to send her some work or another. I haven't returned to see her, however, because I wanted to be able to tell her what she could have from you.'[4] A month later, on 13 January, he wrote again to Manutius, 'I read some details of your letters to Madonna Felice, who took great pleasure from them, and asked me to thank you greatly and to recommend her to you. In fact she told me she is in constant desire for books, and so I am writing you to send what you could let her have. I ask you to address the books to me, so that I can continue to be the intermediary as I have been in word.'[5] Such a transaction assured Carteromacho would continue to work as Felice's agent, and she be in his debt.

There is something poignant about Carteromacho's account of Felice's fervent desire for books. Over and beyond how books helped her appear to her best advantage in fashionable scholarly circles, they also served as her companions during those times when her father deliberately excluded her from courtly events. Books were a means to shut out the trials of ongoing bargaining, and negotiations for a husband she did not want. Reading was one of the great pleasures of Felice's life. She came to possess magnificent volumes of such ancient authors as Pliny and Suetonius. These were manuscript editions, illustrated, bound in plush leathers and sealed with silver clasps. But such books were in large part for show, artefacts to be placed on display. The real testimony to the fact that she was a serious reader is her possession of numerous unnamed books. Bound in cheap vellum, they were of little monetary worth, cited in inventories of her property only by bulk, the equivalent of a stack of well-thumbed paperbacks today.

Felice was determined to focus on aspects of her personal identity and social connections that reached beyond a role as wife to an Italian lord. None the less, the issue of a new husband still loomed. Felice's refusal of Roberto da Sanseverino had made her father really angry. The Duke of Urbino had declared that Julius wished to banish his daughter from Rome, Julius did not actually carry out this threat, although relations between himself and Felice did cool. He called a temporary halt to the line of bridegrooms that had been paraded before Felice since January 1504. Following the Sanseverino incident, there is no mention of Felice in any Vatican-related documents until late in 1505. Felice might have been made to return to Savona for much of 1505, or perhaps she continued to stay at the de Cupis palace in Rome. Julius, in the meantime, had other matters demanding his attention.

CHAPTER 7

Enter the Orsini

In 1505 Julius was also preoccupied with matters other than finding his increasingly irritating daughter a husband. This was the period in which he began his career as papal *maecenas* in earnest. Bramante's work on the Vatican Palace complex continued. Giuliano da Sangallo, architect of the della Rovere palace in Savona, built the Pope a loggia on the south side of Castel Sant' Angelo, complete with inscription on its frieze reading, 'Iulius Pont Max Anno II' ('The second year of Julius's pontificate'). It is still visible today.

February 1505 brought thirty-year-old Michelangelo Buonarotti to Julius. Michelangelo was by then unquestionably Italy's most brilliant sculptor. He had been accommodated in Rome, at the Palazzo Riario (now Cancelleria), during 1496–97 while working for Julius's cousin Raffaelle. For Riario he had produced the *Bacchus* sculpture now in the Bargello in Florence and, for a French cardinal, the exquisite *Pietà*, now in St Peter's.[1] Julius, exiled from Rome in the 1490s, had yet to have the opportunity of employing the Florentine artist. Now he brought Michelangelo, fresh from working on the colossal *David*, back to Rome to plan what Julius wanted to be the greatest, the most magnificent, papal tomb imaginable. Michelangelo, thrilled at the prospect of creating something so extraordinary, spent several months in discussion with the Pope, and then went

Caradosso, Portrait Medal of Pope Julius II, obverse, Bramante's design for New St Peter's, 1506 to Carrara to oversee the quarrying of marble that had to be perfect for such an enterprise.

Julius, meanwhile, turned to a project even dearer to him than his own tomb. Ever since he had been a cardinal, he had dreamed of re-creating St Peter's church. He believed it was his destiny, that his uncle Sixtus had heard a divine voice telling him one of his nephews would become pope and rebuild the old, fourth-century basilica.[2] Julius turned to Bramante, his partner in design, to produce a church that would 'embody the greatness of the present and the future'.[3] The crumbling Early Christian church was to be demolished and rebuilt as a grandiose domed interpretation of an ancient temple, a successor to the temple of Solomon. On 18 April 1506, the ceremonial stone of New St Peter's was laid. Only once this stone was in place did marriage plans for Felice begin again in earnest.

Felice turned twenty-three in 1506. By the standards of the time, when girls of the elite married at fifteen and sixteen, she was old to be a bride. Although she was admired by members of the intelligentsia, forward-thinking men of their age, the same could not be said of the nobility, who had a more old-fashioned outlook. Felice was fast becoming a less than attractive marital prospect: illegitimate and to outward appearances, not especially beloved by her father; stubborn, blunt and past her first fresh-ness. She herself undoubtedly knew she was rapidly reaching a point of no return. Young widows who did not remarry were not allowed to main-tain the public, independent existence Felice had enjoyed in the previous few years. Eventually, they would be obliged to take holy orders and enter a convent. Felice della Rovere had not cultivated a character fashioned on ancient Roman heroines, or sought friends of the standing of Isabella d'Este, to spend the rest of her days cloistered.

The bridegroom her father now proposed, Gian Giordano Orsini, might not have been a Mantuan or a Ferrarese duke, but he offered attractions of his own. He was the leader of one of Rome's two most powerful families. Marriage to Gian Giordano would assure Felice's place in Rome. As wife of the Orsini Lord, Felice could stay in Rome; there was no threat of relegation to a small Tuscan port town, or to France, or to southern Italy, or to a ramshackle palace in Genoa. Instead, she would acquire increased status in the city of her birth, elevated to a position not contingent on the vagaries of her father's recognition.

'I have decided to write', wrote Francesco Sansovino in 1565, 'of the illustrious deeds of the Orsini family, who are the most noble among all others, not only in Rome, but throughout Italy, filled with honourable merit, as much for their military deeds as their civil ones, and who, for a long time now, have done many things worthy of eternal memory.'[4] Sansovino's story of the Orsini family is a long one. As he promises, it is filled with daring military exploits, which firmly fix the family's presence on the international political stage over the course of several centuries. The Orsini were old Roman aristocracy. Many of Rome's new elite were obliged to invent their roots, often claiming a lineage older than Rome itself to inflate themselves. The Sienese banker Agostino Chigi, who by the early sixteenth century was the wealthiest man in Italy, fashioned a lineage for himself dating back to the Etruscans. Pope Alexander VI claimed he was descended from the Egyptian Pharaohs. The Orsini had no need of such devices. Everyone in Rome knew that their solid baronial roots could be traced back as far as the twelfth century, which endowed them with a five-hundred-year history on a par with that of the Neapolitan kings and longer than that of the d'Este, Gonzaga or Sforza families. The Normanni, Felice's mother's family, were equally venerable, but they no longer had the wealth and power of the Orsini.

The family name Orsini was derived from Cardinal Orso Boveschi, nephew to Pope Celestine III, who was elected in 1191. Orso established a powerful curial dynasty, with attendant financial benefits.[5] The family bought vast tracts of land in the Roman *campagna*, giving them a substantial stake in Rome's food supply, as well as control of the roads approaching Rome. In the city itself, they possessed numerous houses and palaces, but had two particularly important residences. One, a palace that came to be known as Palazzo dell'Orologio because of its clock tower, was embedded into the fabric of the ancient Theatre of Pompey, located next to Rome's most important market, Campo dei Fiori. The other, which came to be known as Monte Giordano, was less than a quarter of a mile away, just by the bend in the Tiber river. It was built upon a *monte*, a small hill now believed to been built up of discarded amphora from ancient Rome, unloaded from docks on the water over time. The character of the palace was that of *insediamento*, a fortified stronghold, rather like a walled village, containing various palaces and residences belonging to a number of family members.[6] Here Lucrezia Borgia spent some of her childhood, as at the time her father was having an affair with Giulia Farnese, the wife of Orso Orsini, and he placed his daughter in the care of his mistress. Monte Giordano's main entrance was on Via Papalis, the papal processional street. Felice herself regularly passed Monte Giordano at its rear, on the Via dei Coronari, as she made her way from Piazza Navona to the Vatican. The Orsini dominated that district of Rome, and Felice had seen at first hand their importance to the city.

In 1277, the Orsini acquired a pope of their own when Gian Gaetano Orsini became Nicholas III. Nicholas concentrated on developing the Vatican Palace as a papal seat of residence. The traditional papal palace was attached to Rome's cathedral, St John the Lateran, several miles away on the other side of the Tiber river. However Nicholas sought to inflate the importance of the Vatican as it was located no more than half a mile from the Orsini terrain of Monte Giordano. In so doing, he expanded and consolidated the power of his family until it essentially ruled that part of Rome between the Tiber river and the Campus Martius. Being close to Rome's major source of water, the area was the most highly populated in the city.

For the next two hundred years the Orsini family continued to grow, until it comprised twenty-nine distinct branches. The most important line was that of the Bracciano Orsini – to which Felice's future bridegroom belonged – named for the huge estate they controlled to the north of Rome. They occupied castles in the Roman *campagna* and individual *palazzi* protected by the walls of Monte Giordano, or in the fabric of the Theatre of Pompey.[7] The sheer number of the Orsini, backed by financial power, made the family troublesome, if not downright dangerous, for the papacy. The Orsini's bitter enemy was the other hugely powerful Roman family, the Colonna, and the fighting between them had been one of the justifications for the papal capital being moved from Rome to Avignon.

When the papacy did return to Rome, under the helm of the Colonna pope, Martin V, Cardinal Giordano Orsini immediately took advantage of these newly peaceful times to attempt to create a different atmosphere in his titular home. Cardinal Giordano wanted to bring Florence's new humanist culture to Rome. He collected an impressive library of ancient writings, which he wished housed in a fitting setting. He augmented, embellished and modernized his palace, commissioning architects to use

the latest *all'antica* architectural language in its building. This style had orig-
inated in Rome, but had not been used in the city for many centuries,
although it was visible in the column capitals in Monte Giordano's courtyard. He also hired the Florentine painter Masolino, the associate of
Masaccio, to paint a vast fresco cycle picturing the lives of famous men.[8]
Biblical and classical heroes adorned the walls of the palace's *sala grande*.
The room impressed Giovanni Rucellai, the Florentine banker who
believed so firmly in architectural magnificence that he hired Alberti to
design his family palace and adjacent chapel and believed building to be as
important as fathering children. On his visit to Rome for the Jubilee of
1450, he made note of 'Monte Giordano where the Cardinal Orsini lives,
where there is a most beautiful room decorated with well-executed figures,
and with certain windows which have alabaster in place of glass'.[9] This use
of alabaster allowed a golden, glowing light to filter into the room. Cardinal Giordano's *sala* became a theatrical *salon*; Rome's humanists would
meet there, dressed up in ancient costume to conduct discussions appropriate to the intellectual ambience of this palatial environment.

The peace between the Orsini and Colonna was an uneasy one and
fighting broke out again towards the end of the century. In 1482 the
Colonna ransacked Monte Giordano, and they returned again in 1485 to
attempt to burn the Orsini stronghold to the ground. Although most of the
structural fabric of the palace was saved, Cardinal Giordano's spectacular
fresco cycle, among the most significant paintings in fifteenth-century
Rome, was destroyed.

For Pope Julius II, the threat of ongoing conflict between these families
was disturbing. How could he continue the quest for a magnificent new
Rome if the Orsini and Colonna still insisted on acting out their feudal
disputes in the city's streets? How could he build his glorious new creations
when there was the constant risk of fire? What would happen to the ecclesiastical economy if pilgrims shunned a city made dangerous and violent
by the barons who were supposed to be leading it? Julius needed a truce
between the two sides, and he needed a means of controlling them. His
sympathies inclined towards the Orsini, who had traditionally been *guelphs*
– supporters of the papacy – while the Colonna were *ghibellines* and supporters of the Holy Roman Emperor. Furthermore, he shared a common
enemy with the Orsini: the Borgia. Pope Alexander VI and his son Cesare,

having forged an alliance with the Colonna, had systematically waged war on the Orsini, whom they saw as a threat to their supremacy in Rome. They had attacked and confiscated much Orsini property, which had been returned to the family by Julius when he became pope. None the less, Julius did not want to appear to favour the Orsini too openly, as this would only further antagonize the Colonna and provoke disturbances.

Julius's solution was to bind both families to him with matrimonial ties. He had once considered having Felice marry the young head of the Colonna family, Marcantonio. Now, he offered him his twenty-one-year-old niece Lucrezia, the daughter of his sister Luchina, dissolving her now less politically useful marriage to Alberto Carafa of Naples. The newly proposed husband for Felice, Gian Giordano, was head of the Orsini of Bracciano.

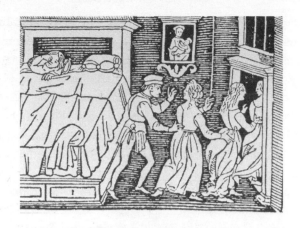

CHAPTER 8

Gian Giordano

Francesco Sansovino provides the following summary of Gian Giordano Orsini: 'His Imperial Majesty (the Holy Roman Emperor) always honoured Gian Giordano. This hero who for his incomparable fortune and valour, and for the stable reputation of his paternal state was a prince of the house of Orsini, not only revered by the Emperor and by Ferdinand, King of Naples, who gave him for his wife the lady Maria d'Aragona his daughter, but by all of Rome.'[1]

Born in the 1560s, so about twenty years older than Felice, Gian Giordano was recently widowed. He had married his first wife, Maria d'Aragona of Naples, the illegitimate daughter of Ferdinand of Aragon, in 1487, when Felice was four years old. Maria died in 1504, but not before she had borne him three children: two girls, Francesca and Carlotta, and a boy, Napoleone, born in 1501. Gian Giordano's profession, like that of his father, Gentile Virginio, and numerous Orsini ancestors, was that of *condottiere*. The *condottiere* was a contracted soldier of fortune, who hired himself and troops, often recruited in the medieval feudal manner from the villains on his estate, to the highest bidder.[2]

In Gian Giordano's case, that highest bidder was France. The Orsini *condottiere* became a loyal Francophile, organizing public displays in Rome to celebrate French military victories – sometimes of an incendiary nature.

The Wedding Bed, Venice, 1540

To commemorate the outcome of the battle of Marignano in 1515, Gian Giordano set alight an entire block of houses he owned near Monte Giordano. Small wonder then, that some, such as Felice's younger cousin Francesco Maria della Rovere, would later describe him as 'pubblico pazzo' ('plainly mad').[3] France, with its emphasis on the chivalric past, was perhaps a place more in keeping with the sympathies of this soldier for hire than his own native country. Francesco Sansovino describes how 'in France, he was singled out at court. King Louis XII marvelled at the greatness of this illustrious baron. When the King lost 20,000 ducats to him at cards, Gian Giordano performed a most royal act, for he spent the money on a superb and noble palace at Blois, where the court assembled. This building is still called the palace of Gian Giordano, and all say that the Orsini chose not to spend French money anywhere but France.'[4]

Gian Giordano had been favoured by the French, but he also had good reason to be grateful to Julius II. He had suffered especially under Borgia rule. Alexander VI had poisoned his father Gentile Virginio in 1496 and confiscated his lands. Not only did Julius return them; he engineered the downfall of Alexander's son Cesare, which could only give Gian Giordano considerable satisfaction. For Gian Giordano, taking Felice in marriage assured him continued papal support, and that was his prime motivation in making her his wife. The Italian nobility freely acknowledged that Gian Giordano was 'moved to take a bastard of the house (of della Rovere), the daughter of a pope, to comply with his needs at the time'.[5] Maria d'Aragona had borne him three children, so he was not in need of an heir. Felice, with her difficult reputation preceding her, was hardly the most enticing marriage prospect. Nor was Julius prepared to provide a lavish dowry, so Gian Giordano had no great financial incentive. He was to project a carefully studied casual attitude to his bride on the occasion of their wedding.

Julius did exact some revenge on Felice for her attitude towards the potential husbands he had put before her. Her dowry was 15,000 ducats, less than half the 40,000 Julius had declared he would offer Roberto Sanseverino although Gian Giordano agreed to settle a further 5,000 on Felice. On 26 May 1506 a meeting took place, notarized by the Orsini lawyer, Prospero d'Aquasparta, described as 'an act of procurement by Gian Giordano Orsini to allow Bernardino de Cupis di Montefalco, and Paolo and Giacomo Oricellai to extract the dowry of the lady Felice della

Rovere from the Reverend Lord Cardinal of San Pietro in Vincola [Gale-otto Franciotto della Rovere], Vice Chancellor and the Illustrious Lord Prefect of the city [Julius's brother, Giovanni]. This act has taken place in Rome in Monte Giordano.'[6] This agreement was immediately followed by a second transaction, a 'declaration by Giacomo Rucellai, the procurator of Gian Giordano Oricellai, that he has received from the Cardinal of San Pietro in Vincola and from the Lord Prefect 15,000 ducats as a part of the 20,000 for their sister, and wife of Gian Giordano, Madonna Felice della Rovere, which will serve for the recovery of Marcellino in Monteverdi, [next to the Janiculum Hill in Rome] and Monte della Spagna at Tivoli.[7] These were estates Gian Giordano had lost during the Borgia pontificate.

Gian Giordano might have been able to buy back some property with money from Julius, but the sum seemed somewhat paltry in comparison to the dowry Julius gave Felice's cousin Lucrezia. Marcantonio Colonna received 10,000 ducats and his palace at the church of Dodici Apostoli (adjacent to the Colonna family palace) as well as the town of Frascati. Nor was it just a matter of money. Julius evidently sought also to embarrass Felice by the manner in which he ordered her to be married. In November of 1505 he had arranged for the marriage of his nephew Niccolò to Laura Orsini, daughter of Orso Orsini and Giulia Farnese, Alexander VI's mistress. That marriage was celebrated in the Pope's Vatican apartments and the union blessed by Julius himself. Felice was present to witness it, and to see the gold necklace set with a diamond, two emeralds and a ruby worn by the bride, a gift from the Pope. A book of poems was commissioned to commemorate the wedding. A similar celebration was conducted for the marriage of Lucrezia della Rovere and Marcantonio Colonna, after which there was a public procession from the Vatican to the Colonna palace. The wedding ceremony offered to the Pope's daughter could not have been more different.

CHAPTER 9

The Orsini Wedding

Felice della Rovere's wedding was staged over 24 and 25 May 1506. Julius issued a public ordinance, banning any public celebration of the event: 'The Pope does not wish there to be any demonstrations, as Pope Alexander would have done, because she is his daughter,' wrote Sanuto.[1] The nuptial ceremony did not take place within the Vatican Palace, but instead in the palace belonging to her cousin Galeotto Franciotto della Rovere, Cardinal of San Pietro in Vincoli, who had taken part in the negotiations to transfer Felice's dowry to Gian Giordano. This palace, then known as the Cancelleria, the Chancellery, and now as the Palazzo Sforza Cesarini, was originally built in 1458, when its patron, the della Rovere nemesis, Alexander VI, was still Cardinal Rodrigo Borgia. It was appropriated by the della Rovere family to serve as a demarcation of della Rovere territory on the other side of the river from the Vatican palace. Julius would soon begin the construction of a street alongside it, the Via Giulia. Cut, according to ancient prescriptions, as straight as an arrow, the Via Giulia stands to this day in sharp contrast to the winding streets of the medieval city.

So Felice was married in a setting connected with her family, but the Cancelleria was well removed from the Vatican Palace, the site of her cousins' weddings. Moreover, Julius, whose name appeared nowhere on the dowry settlement, was conspicuous by his absence from his daughter's

View containing Palazzo Sforza Cesarini (Old Cancelleria) and Monte Giordano wedding. Paris de Grassis, the pernickety master of ceremonies at the Vatican Palace, was in charge of its organization and he wrote a lengthy description of what took place.

Paris de Grassis found several aspects of the event decidedly off-putting. He described the union as 'doubly bigamous', a reference to the fact that both Felice and Gian Giordano had been married previously, and he expressed doubts as to whether the union should receive official ecclesiastical blessing.[2] The wedding was staged in two parts. The first, on the Sunday, was an announcement of the terms of the marriage. No women attended this ceremonial business meeting and Felice herself was represented by her cousin, Galeotto Franciotto della Rovere. Among those present were twelve cardinals, eleven of whom, Paris de Grassis noted, were wearing red hats, but one, Giovanni de' Medici, the future Pope Leo X, had chosen to wear a purple one. Giovanni de' Medici was an Orsini on his mother's, Clarice's, side, so perhaps he felt entitled to vary his appearance. Paris de Grassis, however, felt this was excessive and commented, 'It would have been better if he had worn one that was the colour red.' Felice's uncle, Giovanni della Rovere, the Prefect of Rome, was present, as were the French, Spanish and Imperial ambassadors, and numerous members of the Orsini family.

This first part of the ceremony took place in the Cancelleria's grand hall. Paris de Grassis had readied the room with carpets, twelve armchairs for the prelates and a stool with a velvet cushion for the Prefect. The other guests were seated on long benches covered in leather, arranged on all four sides of the room. Two notaries arrived, Signor Tancredi from the Camera Apostolica to act on behalf of the bride, and, on the groom's side, Prospero d'Aquasparta, who announced the amount of Felice's dowry and the terms of its disbursement. While these proceedings were taking place, Gian Giordano did not sit still but got up to greet his new relatives, Galeotto and Giovanni della Rovere.

The following day saw the actual celebration of the union. Paris de Grassis comments that Gian Giordano Orsini wished to adhere not to Roman nuptial customs but to those of the French and Spanish. For superstitious reasons, the groom preferred the wedding rings not be exhibited, but instead placed on the finger of the wedding celebrant, his cousin Rinaldo Orsini, the Archbishop of Florence. The rings themselves, Paris de Grassis noted, were poor things, worth no more than a couple of ducats. Although the ceremony was due to start at four o'clock, last-minute astrological consultation meant Gian Giordano insisted on a delay until seven. Felice was obliged to sit and wait for these three hours in the chapel. In the meantime, her bridegroom arrived at the Cancelleria 'not in wedding dress, but in hunting garb, with leather leggings and rough boots, a cheap felt hat, an untrimmed beard, uncombed hair and dismal clothes'. He used the time to call a barber and dress himself in more appropriate attire, a velvet tunic and hat, and a gold chain. De Grassis includes no description of Felice's wedding gown, or whether she wore any jewels, which suggests that she was plainly dressed for a bride on her wedding day.

Gian Giordano injected several elements into the ceremony that were entirely alien both to his bride and to the onlookers. At one point he removed a handkerchief from his jerkin, which he gave to the celebrant, instructing him to give it to the bride, who evidently had no idea what she was supposed to do with it. And that was not the end to poor Felice's discomfort. After the rings and the vows had been exchanged, and the pair declared husband and wife, Gian Giordano turned to Felice and bestowed on her what Paris de Grassis calls in Latin an *osculo galico* – a French kiss. 'That is to say,' he wrote, 'one between her lips and teeth, which caused the bride to redden, and the onlookers to both admire and laugh.'

Following the *osculo galico*, Gian Giordano and Felice immediately consummated their marriage in Cardinal Galeotto della Rovere's undoubtedly lavishly appointed bedchamber. Such a practice ensured that neither side could attempt to annul the marriage later on grounds of non-consummation. They were at least spared onlookers, as Paris de Grassis stresses that no guest was present. That did not prevent those outside the door speculating on what was going on behind it. Emilia Pia, in an account of the occasion which she sent to Isabella d'Este, states that 'they lay together fifteen minutes. Many believed that they were performing other "secret" acts' – a reference to the unexpected and exotic French kiss.[3]

Following this brief act of sexual union, the entire wedding party then proceeded to the palace of Monte Giordano. Here, Paris de Grassis, who, befitting his position as master of ceremonies, disliked untidiness and lack of protocol, remarked on the Orsini palace's state of disarray. There were piles of wood everywhere, partially dismantled walls and blocked-up doors. Gian Giordano still did not have the resources, or perhaps the inclination, given his constant absence from Rome, to repair the damage the Colonna had wrought on his home almost twenty years earlier. Paris also noted that only now was new furniture, presumably for the bride, including a bed, being carried into the palace.

Perhaps the politeness customary to his position precluded Paris de Grassis from saying any more than that. Emilia Pia, however, provided a much more forthright account of what occurred after they left the Cancelleria. An appropriate and decorous journey from the Cancelleria to Monte Giordano would have been for the party to have ridden up the Via Papalis, the central artery linking the two palaces. Instead, they went on foot, down a seedy street, the Via del Pozzo Bianco ('White Well'), named for a white marble sarcophagus that served as a drinking fountain. The journey was short but highly inappropriate none the less. Emilia Pia wrote:

> [Gian Giordano] wished to take a certain street called Pozzo Bianco where stand women of ill repute, even though it was said that he should take another way . . . The women who were with Madonna Felice were Madonna Giulia [Farnese, mother to Laura Orsini, Felice's cousin Niccolò's new wife] and the daughter and the sisters of the Cardinal of San Pietro in Vincoli. Madonna Giulia turned and said with certainty that if the bridegroom was a gentleman then he would have taken another route. As they approached Monte Giordano, a great many sweets [*confecti*] were thrown from the windows and the groom took his hat from his head and put it on the bride's, but she refused it, and thus they entered the palace. The rooms were badly decorated and the meal was worse, especially as nothing had been served at the Cancelleria. There were two shoulders of mutton, half a lamb and half a kid, a capon and three bowls of white veal . . . These things were served on one plate in the French style, there was not a single knife on the table, and so many did not stay, as they could not tear the meat apart with their fingernails. When the groom came to the table he performed certain ceremonies in the Spanish fashion, such as placing his hat on the head of a page while he dined; and at dinner he demonstrated his expertise in the French and Spanish languages, which appeared to be his only virtues.[4]

The day following this peculiar and, for many concerned, wholly un-Italian event the couple departed Monte Giordano. 'At dawn,' wrote Paris de Grassis, 'Gian Giordano left for his home at Bracciano, where he will leave his wife.[5] Felice's new life as an Orsini family member had begun.

The end to Felice's old life saw her father banning public celebration of her wedding, and staying away from the ceremony. She had a bridegroom who had behaved in a decidedly eccentric fashion, and offered her a wedding breakfast of frugal victuals in a palace in sore need of repair. These are hardly the tokens of a romantic event – one supposed to mark every woman's life – even by the very businesslike standards of the Italian Renaissance. Nor would they seem to signify an auspicious future. But neither was the new *Signora* of Bracciano a standard romantic heroine. Felice might have been disconcerted by such an unlikely start to her second marriage. However, her refusal to wear her new husband's hat shows she had no intention of relinquishing her sense of self and strength of will simply because she was newly married. Despite the slights inflicted on her by her father, and her new husband's eccentricities, the twenty-three-year-old Orsini bride was already plotting how to utilize her new position to its best advantage. She could now campaign for the rewards, the power, control and validation she craved, that she believed were rightfully hers, and thus far largely missing from her young life.

PART III

Felix of the Oak and the Bear

CHAPTER 1

A Bracciano

At dawn on 26 May 1506, Felice della Rovere Orsini, as she would now be addressed, weary from the endless events of the previous day, mounted a horse and set out with her new husband to his titular castle of Bracciano thirty kilometres to the north of Rome. Felice's journey was different from the one she normally took when she left Rome. Her trips to and from Savona were always by sea, sailing on galleons from the port of Ostia; as a result, she had seen very little of the Italian countryside. Now she was riding along the Via Clodia, an ancient road constructed in the first century AD. She journeyed through hilly, densely wooded land, admired since antiquity for its beauty, home to Italy's oldest settlements, where thousands of Etruscans still lie in tombs cut in the soft tufa, the volcanic rock. Almost all of what Felice could see around her was Orsini country; one branch or another of the family possessed nearly everything north of Rome all the way to Viterbo.

In the early hours of her first day as *La Signora* of the Orsini family, Felice quickly became conscious of just how great a departure she had made from her old life. Much of the journey was strange for her, and not only the sights of the Roman countryside. She had never travelled on horseback over such a distance. For a young woman who had grown up in a city, mules were the usual mode of transport. These sure-footed animals

Map of Bracciano Orsini holdings to the north of Rome, seventeenth century were more popular in an urban environment than horses and *mulatieri*, mule drivers, were the taxi-drivers of their day. In fifteenth-century Florence, Cosimo, the driving force of the Medici family, rode a brown mule; in sixteenth-century Rome, Michelangelo riding his white mule about town and around his neighbourhood near Trajan's Column was a familiar sight. If she was travelling alone, Felice still often chose a mule over a horse. However, when travelling with her *condottiere* husband, she switched to riding horses. Soldiers did not ride mules, and decorum and practicality dictated that a woman should have the same kind of mount as her husband. Recent decades of horse-breeding, instituted by men such as Gian Giordano, who had spent time in France, had resulted in a mount that was easier for women to ride: short, stocky Italian warhorses had been bred with sleeker French equines to create a more slender animal.[1] Men rode stallions; women rode mares or geldings. And women rode side-saddle. The Italians, Europe's most sophisticated riders, were responsible for developing a pommel on the side-saddle to secure the female rider's seat. Felice was fortunate; women of the Middle Ages had been obliged simply to sit sideways and hold on.[2] And the pace at which Felice now rode to Bracciano was different too. A mule going from the Piazza Navona to the Vatican Palace rarely exceeded a trot on the city streets. Now she was obliged to canter and gallop to cover large stretches of terrain, moving from city palace to country castle. Not so far into the future, Felice the city girl would become an experienced judge of horseflesh, knowledgeable about hunting and saddlery.

As any traveller approaching today, Felice saw the castle of Bracciano on the horizon long before she reached it. It is an imposing fortress, with thick perimeter walls and massive towers built of the local grey volcanic stone.[3] Perched high on a cliff, it overlooks the Lago di Bracciano, Italy's eighth-largest lake, which conceals a Bronze Age settlement in its depths. The castle is sometimes described as great and gloomy and perhaps Felice was to be pitied as she approached her new home. Yet, looking up at Bracciano, she might not have been so sorry for herself. On a summer day with the water of the vast lake sparkling in the sunlight, the snow-capped Sibillini mountains visible in the distance, she might have felt happy to have escaped the heat and smells of Rome. As Felice and the Orsini party approached the castle, they reached a thick stone wall with a moat and drawbridge. As Felice crossed the bridge, the castle rose directly above her and an outcrop of small houses surrounded her. These were home to the hundreds of people who worked for the Orsini, either as house servants at the castle or as labourers on Bracciano's land. Felice had arrived at the hub, the nerve centre, of her husband's family's economy. She quickly came to understand the resonance of her new home – practical, historical and symbolic.

Below the castle, there were fields of grain and barley, staples of the Roman diet, and vineyards producing local wine. The oldest agricultural activity was the raising of pigs, and Bracciano's original name is believed to have been Porcianum. Water from the lake was a precious commodity, and had been since the second century AD, when the Emperor Nerva routed the Aquedotto Traiano by the lake. Later, in the sixteenth century, this water fed the Acqua Paola, the aqueduct installed by Pope Paul V to bring water to Rome. Securing the water rights from the vast lake in 1427 gave a significant boost to the Orsini family finances.

Further contributions to the family economy were provided by the multiple fiefs under the jurisdiction of Bracciano: Santo Polo, San Gregorio, Scrofano, Isola, Campana, Cantalupo, Canemorto, Montorio and Vicarello, to name but a few.[4] A complex network of indentured peasants worked the land. They existed in a feudal system long since extinct and, even in the sixteenth century, increasingly old-fashioned in the growing urbanism of Renaissance Italy. In Felice's time an array of *massari* and *subditi* – the words were used to describe different kinds of labourers and tenants and are no longer current in modern Italian – populated these *feudi*. Their ruler was the *Signor* of Bracciano. They provided their Orsini Lord with a substantial portion of his yearly revenue and looked to him for assistance and protection, frequently from each other. Rivalry was utterly entrenched in these settlements. Like much small-town life, bitter disputes arose over seemingly the most trivial of matters. It was the responsibility of the Orsini Lord, or his representatives, to resolve them.

The Orsini had long-standing interests in Bracciano and its surrounding lands but it had not always been theirs in its entirety. They had once fiercely contested its possession with another old Roman family, the Di Vico. The Di Vico had built the original castle of Bracciano in the late twelfth century when they served as prefects of the nearby city of Viterbo.

Like Felice's maternal family, the Normanni, the Di Vico had since waned in power and prestige but back in the fourteenth century they were as considerable an enemy of the Orsini as the Colonna were in the fifteenth. In 1407 the French anti-pope at Avignon, Clement VI, an Orsini supporter, passed an edict to force the Di Vico family to surrender the castle to the Orsini. Ironically, given his status as a member of the Colonna family, the Orsini's bitter enemy, it was Pope Martin V who ratified Orsini possession in 1419. The castle had thus come to stand as a symbol of an Orsini victory over their local rivals, the Di Vico.

The castle of Bracciano did not undergo any further additions and enlargements until 1470, when Gian Giordano's grandfather, Napoleone, renowned as a 'man skilled in the military arts', invested his earnings as a *condottiere* in its renovation. The castle now acquired its irregular quadrilateral shape, punctuated by six turrets, which together surrounded a courtyard. Significantly, despite rebuilding at the height of the new fashion for *all'antica* architecture, Napoleone did not attempt to modernize his castle or to alter it aesthetically in any way from its late-medieval appearance. He simply made it larger and more imposing. It was important for Orsini family prestige that the castle should adhere to its medieval roots in order to remind all that surveyed it that, unlike the families of the wealthy cardinals now flocking to Rome, this family could trace its roots into antiquity. The new castle certainly impressed those in nearby Rome. Felice's great-uncle, Pope Sixtus IV, spent several months in residence there in the summer of 1481, following a severe outbreak of plague in the city. Sixtus wrote letters in which he indicated he was at 'the house of Napeoleone Orsini, the exceedingly well-fortified palace called Bracciano'.[5] The room in which he stayed was still called the *capella papalina* at the end of the sixteenth century. Other visitors to Bracciano included Medici family members, and Charles VIII of France.

After the death of Napoleone, his son Gentile Virginio continued embellishing the family home. In 1491 he hired a Roman artist known as Antoniazzo Romano to paint frescos recording major events in Gentile Virginio's life. The original location of these images, since transferred inside, was unusual: they were painted on the walls of the covered entry leading up to the castle's principal *cortile*. Anyone arriving at Bracciano was greeted by images of Gentile Virginio. On one wall he was featured at his

1487 meeting with his nephew Piero de' Medici who was *en route* to Rome to arrange the marriage of his sister Maddalena to a nephew of the Genoese pope, Innocent VIII. On the other, Ferdinand of Aragon could be seen bestowing a military command on Gentile, as he did in 1489. Another fresco cycle Gentile Virginio commissioned from the Antoniazzo workshop was intended to emphasize Orsini ties with France. One room was adorned with scenes from *Les Fontaines de Jouvence*, a chivalric French legend about the fountain of youth. Gallic homage such as this would have pleased any French visitor to the castle.

Like Monte Giordano back in Rome, Bracciano had seen more than its fair share of violence. In the late 1490s it was the target of sieges by the Borgia family, but had been defended bravely by Gian Giordano's aunt, Pantasilea, and her *condottiere* husband, Bartolomeo d'Alviano. Small wonder then that much of the Bracciano family identity and sense of pride was invested in the castle.

The castle of Bracciano might have given Felice some reassurance that she had not made a dreadful mistake in marrying Gian Giordano, especially after having eaten cold meat with her bare hands in the fire-damaged great hall of Monte Giordano. True, the castle's interiors might not have been as luxurious as those Felice had seen her cardinal cousins create at their palaces in Rome; nor was its architecture as up to date as that of the palace her father had commissioned at Savona. But the sheer scale of the castle and its elegant frescos commemorating her late father-in-law's deeds, not to mention its historical aura, would have impressed her. And Bracciano was near to Rome; Felice need not feel as trapped or isolated as she might have done with a move to Piombino or Salerno. Here her de Cupis family would never be too far away.

About a month after Felice and Gian Giordano arrived at Bracciano, Marino Sanuto recorded that 'festivities have taken place at Brazano [*sic*] to celebrate the wedding of Madonna Felice with Signor Gian Giordano Orsini'.[6] It is to be hoped that these events were an improvement in style and substance from those in Rome. At least Gian Giordano did mark the occasion, and his acknowledgement of his new bride was important for Felice's standing at Bracciano. She needed to command the respect of the family's high-ranking servants, who included Martino da Bracciano, Philippo da Bracciano and Giovanni della Colle. Highly able men, they ran the estate and were sufficiently well educated to serve as Orsini diplomatic representatives abroad if needed. They in turn commanded the loyalty and co-operation of the lower-ranking servants.

Felice understood very well the need to befriend these men. In terms of their activities, education and background, they were like her stepfather, Bernardino de Cupis. Bernardino came from a small hill town, Montefalco, similar to Bracciano, and he ran Girolamo della Rovere's household in Rome in a similar fashion to the way these men ran the Orsini estate. The smooth functioning of the estate depended on their skills and co-operation. In keeping with her natural inclinations, Felice was probably more interested in securing the good will of the Bracciano staff than she was in making friends with her new Orsini relatives. In Savona, she had chilly relations with her aunt Luchina and cousin Lucrezia but had established a good rapport with the town's merchants. Her relationship with the family into which she married and with their servants was similar. Gian Giordano's younger children, Napoleone and Carlotta, lived at Vicovaro, the Orsini estate to the east of Rome out by Tivoli. However, there was no shortage of Orsini relatives in the neighbourhood of Bracciano when Felice arrived. Carlo Orsini, Gian Giordano's illegitimate half-brother, lived in a castle at nearby Anguillara, on the other side of lake Bracciano, with his wife Portia and son Gentile Virgino. Then there was Renzo da Ceri, who took his name from the costal town of Cerveteri, also not too far away. Renzo, an aspiring *condottiere*, was married to Gian Giordano's eldest daughter, Francesca, and was a regular presence at Bracciano. Renzo's uncle was Giulio, of the Monterotondo branch of the family. If, in the early years of her marriage, there was no open hostility between Felice and most of the Orsini family members, relations seem never to have been more than cordial. As with Luchina and Lucrezia, the Orsini felt that they were inherently superior to the Pope's illegitimate daughter, an attitude Felice did not share.

CHAPTER 2

Felice and the Orsini

While she appreciated the importance of influential friends such as Isabella d'Este, Felice never much liked members of the nobility whose position in life rested solely on blood line or military successes. Neither born into nor brought up as a member of the feudal aristocracy, she had little in common with them. She far preferred those members of society, the curia or scholars, who had advanced through their innate cerebral ability. It was those members of the Orsini family who had entered the clergy with whom she had the most rapport. They in turn gave her greater deference because she was Pope Julius II's daughter than did other members of their family.

Felice had a particularly good relationship with Cardinal Giovanni de' Medici, an Orsini relative through his mother, Clarice, of the Monterotondo Orsini. He was the Cardinal who had distinguished himself at Felice's wedding by wearing a purple hat while his fellow cardinals all wore their regular scarlet ones. Giovanni maintained his family ties with the Orsini and at one point he procured 200 ducats on behalf of his cousin Gian Giordano, 'for repairs to the house of Monte Giordano'.[1] However, his bond with Felice, whose father he served, was stronger. She called on his favour in January 1507, when she wrote to him as 'my most honoured lord', asking him to support Bartolomeo d'Alviano, Gian Giordano's uncle, by marraige, on a diplomatic mission to the King of Spain. Cardinal

Federico Zuccaro, *View of Bracciano*, 1580s, castle of Bracciano

Giovanni's support would in turn sway her father, Julius II, who was still suspicious of any interaction with Spain. The letter shows how schooled Felice was already in the language of charming self-abasement, designed to ensure the writer would get her way: 'I am sure Your Reverence recognizes the superfluity of my intervention here, as much as he knows my love for him . . . However, I beg that your Reverence might wish to help, as to do so would be to do a good deed, as much for the love of the present Lord [Alviano] as for the love of me.'[2] Felice's letter ends with her asking Cardinal Giovanni to 'as always, recommend me to His Holiness, whose feet I humbly kiss'. Protocol dictated Felice not refer to Julius as her father.

Felice's tone was very different with another Orsini cleric, Annibale. He was Gian Giordano's short-lived younger brother, resident at Vicovaro, where he oversaw some of the estate's transactions. On 25 November 1506, an older and less exalted member of the family, Dianora Orsini, had written to him in agitated terms, with the following request: 'I ordered hay from Cola d'Alessandro, and I have learned that Cola refuses to sell to me, which surprises me greatly. I beg of your lordship to order that Cola d'Alessandro should sell the hay at my request, as I have promised it to others.'[3]

A demand for hay might seem like a trivial matter, and the refusal on the part of an Orsini servant to part with it to an Orsini family member surprising. Hay, however, was an essential staple, a valuable commodity, especially in years when there was little yield. Dianora Orsini might well have calculated her own finances based on her acquisition of hay from the family estate. She could exchange it for other goods with merchants from the towns, whose own access to agricultural goods might be limited. However, Cola d'Alessandro, a farm manager at Vicovaro, had evidently decided to sell the hay to someone more influential, or who had something that he himself wanted. Nor did Annibale Orsini apparently pay any attention to Dianora's request to assist her. Feeling that her words appeared to count for very little, Dianora turned to the Orsini family's newest member for help with her appeal. On 17 December, Felice wrote to Annibale, in a firmly authoritative but measured tone, one with which her servants and associates would become very familiar: 'Illustrious Reverend: I have seen Madonna Dianora and I understand that she wrote to you about the farm manager, Cola. And because the matter is of no small importance, I am asking you here to take this money, do what is necessary, and do not do anything less.'[4]

When Felice wrote this letter, she was still only twenty three years old and had been Orsini *Signora* for little more than six months. But its firm tone indicates she had wasted no time in developing her persona as the *chatelaine* of Savona. Behaving as a meek and timid bride was not in her nature. Nor would it help the Orsini family comprehend that she was a force in her own right who demanded respect and obedience. Felice's attitude towards Dianora Orsini is also typical of her personality. Dianora was not a powerful member of the clan and Felice had nothing to gain personally by extending her help to her. Felice, however, seems always to have been compelled to give aid to those who were weaker than herself. She was guided by her innate sense of justice. At the same time, protecting the less fortunate also provided her with a need for personal validation that circumstances had yet to supply.

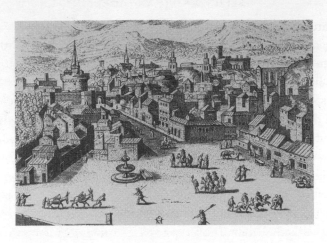

CHAPTER 3

Felice and Gian Giordano

In the months following her wedding, Felice della Rovere Orsini spent more time getting to know her servants and negotiating with family members than she did with her new husband, for Gian Giordano was often absent from the Orsini lands. Not very long after they were married, he set out for Spain, returning to Italy in late November. In fact, the only surviving letter from Gian Giordano to Felice is written after he disembarked at Naples. Barely decipherable, the letter gives Felice a brief account of the highlights of his trip: the King of Spain gave a concert in his honour, and he met up with a relative, Bartolomeo Alviano, an 'exceptionally good man', who had given Gian Giordano several gifts, 'as token of the love he bears me'.[1] Among these were a jerkin and eight *carrone* (yards) of black velvet. The Spanish held a monopoly on this opulent fabric, as the dye came from the log berry tree, which was plentiful in the New World they now controlled, so it was easier to acquire in Naples, which belonged to Spain. Gian Giordano's acquisition of expensive black velvet was something he felt would especially interest Felice. As an adult, Felice wore a great deal of black, interspersed with crimson, as if she were a cardinal. She wore black during her first widowhood and then throughout her second marriage, because her husband, who was an honorary member of the Aragonese family, decreed that they should dress as if they were Spaniards.

View down the Via Alessandrina to Castel Sant'Angelo

This sartorial code struck Italian observers as decidedly unusual. An ambassador to the d'Este court commented on her dress when she made a grand entrance into Rome in 1507. He describes her wearing black, with a white hat, adding, 'in accordance with Spanish custom'.[2]

The sparseness of their surviving correspondence and lack of commentary on their relationship make it difficult to ascertain exactly how Felice felt about Gian Giordano, or he about her. Theirs was an arranged marriage. It was not predicated on modern ideas of affection or sexual attraction, even if its consummation was an immediate imperative in order to ensure its validation. On the day of the wedding, Gian Giordano had taken pains to appear disengaged from the event. His actions, however, were directed more towards the Roman curia than as a deliberate attempt to humiliate his bride. Gian Giordano might well have warmed to Felice when they arrived at Bracciano, a stage on which he was the principal actor. Yet whether Gian Giordano was passionately in love with Felice or not, he certainly came to respect her burgeoning managerial qualities and diplomatic skills. Felice profited from his regard for her in these capacities, and was probably little concerned about anything else. Gian Giordano provided Felice with a status that allowed her to acquire a meaningful position in the Roman world, which she exploited to full advantage. In return, Felice allowed Gian Giordano to gain a papal alliance that protected him from Colonna family aggression. If he kept mistresses, as he undoubtedly did, he was evidently discreet. There was no potential for the type of humiliation Felice was sure she would have suffered had she married the Prince of Salerno, who openly paraded his current mistress. Best of all, perhaps, was that Gian Giordano was apparently content to let Felice concentrate on the things she wanted to achieve, and did not hold her back from her ambitions.

At the very least, Felice and Gian Giordano grew to understand each other. When he was absent, she sent him updates on political events. A servant wrote to him at the end of December of 1506, when he was still in Naples, to expect a letter 'with a postscript written by your lady consort about His Holiness's victory at Bologna'.[3] They performed an intricate act together on the Roman political stage, one in which they could be seen as both independent and united. A description of their meeting with the Duke of Ferrara, on 6 July 1512, outside the Palazzo Ferrari, as they were leaving the Vatican one evening and riding along the Via Alessandrina, best embodies the relationship between them. An emissary reported to the Duke of Mantua: 'The Duke by chance ran into Signor Gian Giordano and Madonna Felice near the palace. They dismounted from their horses, and so did the Duke and they honoured each other with many caresses, and after a great deal of ceremony, at length Madonna Felice remounted, and went on her way, while Gian Giordano chose to accompany the Duke into his home . . . '[4] These brief lines present Felice and Gian Giordano engaged together in a formal display of diplomatic courtesy, and then demonstrate Felice's independence from him, as she continued on her way, riding her horse alone along the papal route.

Together, Gian Giordano and Felice visited Julius at the Vatican, their entrances and exits recorded and described by emissaries. They hosted events outside Rome and Julius visited them at Bracciano and other Orsini castles, such as Formello.

Felice also made sure that Gian Giordano rewarded those servants who had served her well. In January 1508 he ratified the donation of a piece of land known as 'La Pietra del Diavolo', to Oliverio di Bordella, which was to serve as the dowry of Chiara di Parma, described as Felice's chamber-lady.[5] On another occasion, Gian Giordano had arranged for a sizeable pension, 100 ducats a year, for Pasqualino da Piombino, who had faith-fully served him 'in times of peace and war'. However, Pasqualino died soon after the pension was awarded and, at Felice's urging, Gian Giordano agreed to transfer it, 'in consideration of the service and loyalty given to Felice Ruvere de Ursinis, my beloved wife, to Antonietta de Canneto de Proventia'.[6] A yearly 100 ducats was a handsome sum for a woman of this time to receive, and a further indication of Felice's desire to take care of her own.

There was one more thing that Felice required of Gian Giordano: she needed to give birth to a son. As was the case with the aborted Piombino marriage, if Felice could produce a boy, then Gian Giordano's son from his first marriage, Napoleone, would be excluded from inheriting the Orsini lordship. This title would instead pass to Felice's son, ensuring that Felice had a substantial stake in the future of the Orsini family; at the very least, subsequent Orsini heirs would be descended from her. More significantly for Felice, should Gian Giordano die while such a son was still a minor, she could become regent of the family. Even in 1506, such a thought would not have been too far from her ambitious mind. Without such a safeguard, the passing of Gian Giordano, twenty years her senior, from this world to the next, would mean the passing of Felice as a childless widow from the Orsini family. Any potential wealth and power to be derived from the Orsini would fall from her grasp.

Felice's first child, born in 1507, was a girl, Julia, named for her maternal grandfather. A year later, in August, Sanuto reported that, 'a son is born to the daughter of the Pope'.[7] Felice also named the child after Giulio. It is not known how long little Julio lived, but it appears not to have been long.[8] Without a son to safeguard her future with the Orsini, Felice's anxieties returned. What would become of her should she be unable to bear Gian Giordano a son? Many women of Felice's time suffered similar fears, Henry VIII's wives perhaps being the best known. But these women were fearful of the anger of their husbands if no son and heir was forthcoming. Felice's desire for a son was entirely personal. Short of faking a pregnancy and bringing in a baby boy in a warming pan, a deceit certain duchesses and queens are believed to have employed, there was very little that could be done to ensure the arrival of a son. So Felice created a contingency plan to protect her future. And she had her father to thank that she was able to do so.

CHAPTER 4

Father and Daughter Reunion

After Felice married Gian Giordano, she was able to reach an accord with her father. As wife of an influential Roman lord, she had a position in her own right in Rome and her new status appears to have eased the tension and ambiguities between the Pope and his illegitimate daughter. Julius had taken his revenge on his daughter for her stubbornness by removing himself from her wedding ceremony. After the marriage had taken place he felt they could begin anew and that he could give her greater public recognition. On 15 June 1506, Julius II invited the new-lyweds to the Vatican where in his very apartments, as an emissary wrote to Mantua, 'he held a great banquet for them, which they attended, along with several Roman lords, the Prefect of Rome, and four cardinals. There was singing and dancing.' Moreover, 'eight days previously, the Pope had sent the Lady Felice a cross which the Republic of Venice had just sent to him'.[1] This cross, made of diamonds, became a particularly treasured possession in Felice's life, not least because it marked her father's new recognition amidst those at court who mattered most.

In May 1507, the Ferrarese ambassador gave another account of Felice's newly honoured status:

Ruins of Baths of Diocletian, sixteenth century

Yesterday, Madonna Felice, the daughter of His Holiness, entered Rome, accompanied by Gian Giordano, her husband, Lord Antonio de Cordova, Signor Julio Orsini and several other gentlemen. There were around forty horsemen. The lady was dressed in black velvet, and on her head was a white velvet hat, in accordance with Spanish custom. Before her rode the bride of Lord Antonio, who is very young, around twelve years old. She was also dressed in dark damask, and rode a mule which had a saddle fashioned like a chair. They went by way of the Via de Banchi to the Belvedere where they found His Holiness. The party went back to Monte Giordano around midnight. This evening His Holiness went on horseback to the Prati [the fields backing on to the Vatican complex] and took dinner in the gardens of Monsignor Ascanio Sforza, where the lady Felice and these other gentlemen were also to be found. Accompanying His Holiness were the Cardinals of Pavia, Volterra and Urbino.[2]

Felice's status in Rome was due in part to her husband's rank. However, the Vatican's ambassadors found her to be of greater significance than Gian Giordano, who is emphatically a secondary subject in their accounts. In the years when Julius was attempting to arrange Felice's second marriage, she was kept away from the spotlight. Now she made triumphal entrances into Rome and attended parties hosted by cardinals where she was the female guest of honour – if not the only woman present. Such events played a major part in Felice's positioning of herself within Vatican court politics. It became increasingly evident that she was more important to her father than she had initially appeared.

There were other ways in which Julius acknowledged Felice beyond the confines of the Vatican. On 25 March 1508, Julius embarked on one of the year's traditional state processions. The feast day he was celebrating was the Annunciation, when the pope travelled from the Vatican to the church of Santa Maria sopra Minerva in the heart of Rome, not far from the Pantheon. There he enacted a ceremony initiated during Sixtus IV's reign, handing out bags of money as dowries to worthy poor girls of that neighbourhood. The route he chose took him by Monte Giordano as, according to Paris de Grassis, 'he wished to see the repairs to buildings around Monte Jordanus'.[3] For Julius, ceremonial marches were a good opportunity to observe the progress of ongoing urban renewal. The beautification of the Via Papalis, the street on which Monte Giordano was situated, was of particular importance. This 'papal' street was the chief parade route through the city. Restoring it, after all the troubles of the fourteenth century, clearing away rubble and cleaning the façades of damaged buildings, enhanced the prestige of the papacy. However, the crowd of onlookers all recognized that Monte Giordano was his daughter's new home and percieve the symbolism of Julius, on his way to serve as emblematic father to the girls of the parish of Santa Maria sopra Minerva, electing to pass by the Roman home of his real daughter.

Attention, public and private, was not the only way Julius rewarded Felice. He had given his daughter a relatively meagre dowry, but that money was not the last Felice would receive from him. Usually, the dowry was a woman's only share in her family estate. Although law dictated that Felice's dowry would be returned to her on her husband's death, Gian Giordano had spent the money buying back confiscated Orsini land. Extracting it would prove difficult. However, in addition to the dowry handed over to her husband, Julius subsequently gave money directly, if discreetly, to Felice. This cash gift did not pass through Gian Giordano, who could potentially siphon it away from her, to spend as he chose. Late in 1508, Felice received 9000 ducats from her father. Given to her secretly, without legal transaction, the money was more than half of her original 15,000-ducat dowry. It was hers to spend as she wished.

This highly unusual father–daughter transaction is emblematic of the complex relationship between Julius and Felice. On some levels, he treated her poorly, and he would continue to do so until he died. On others, he could almost be described as a progressive parent. As much as he adored her, Alexander VI never gave Lucrezia large sums of money of her own; her dowry passed into her husbands' hands, and she had a good deal of difficulty extracting any for herself. Yet Julius, who distanced himself on so many occasions from his daughter, gave her a financial autonomy rare among women of her time.

What did Felice do with her money? It served as a nest egg for her and alleviated some of her anxiety about what might become of her should her time with the Orsini prove brief. But she did not put it in a bank or purchase an annuity, as was common for women of her day. Instead, she invested it in a way that shows she had paid attention to what Bracciano meant to the Orsini. Like Bracciano, her investment was practical and lucrative as well as spectacular and symbolic. Felice della Rovere, Bracciano's new *Signora*, bought a castle of her very own.

CHAPTER 5

The Castello of Palo

Felice had been an Orsini family member for two and a half years when she became a property-owner in her own right. In that time, the twenty-six-year-old had experienced life amidst a baronial family at first hand. If she was not particularly impressed by individual Orsini family members, she had come to recognize the benefits of life as a landed noble. Through negotiations such as those she had undertaken for Dianora Orsini, she saw the wealth and power that came with access to and control of agricultural produce; these were new and useful lessons for a woman raised within an urban world. Owning a castle, with a surrounding estate stretching out for miles around, was like possessing a small kingdom, of which its owner was the ruler. Money was made in the most direct of ways, through the sale of produce grown on the land. It was not necessarily an easy investment and there was the responsibility of maintenance, of care and protection of the building, its lands and workers, but these were challenges Felice enjoyed. When, in late 1508, the opportunity came for her to buy the seafront castle of Palo, a few miles to the north-west of Rome, from Gian Giordano's cousin Giulio Orsini, she immediately took advantage of it. The purchase was in itself a bold and audacious act for a woman. Few women of Felice's time owned property in their own name and if they did, they had normally received it from a father as part of a dowry, and it would become fully

'Woman Fully Grown', from Christofano Bertelli, *The Ages of Woman*, 1580s

theirs only when they became widows. So, as a married female property-owner, Felice della Rovere was a decided anomaly.

Given how indelibly their property was tied up with the identity of the Roman barons, why would Giulio Orsini wish to part with his castle? Like many of the Orsini men, Giulio Orsini had earned his living as a *condottiere*. His years of service stretched back to the 1480s, when he had worked for the Medici family. The castle Giulio owned at Palo was of particular usefulness and importance. Built in 1367, it was typical of the fortified strongholds of its day and served as a useful depository and point of exchange for all kinds of goods, including weapons shipped down the coast, primarily from Tuscan ports.[1] However, like Gian Giordano, Giulio had suffered under Borgia rule. His estates and their revenues were confiscated by Alexander VI and Cesare Borgia and they had personally occupied the castle for a time. Giulio Orsini was thus considerably impoverished by the time of the reign of Pope Julius. From Giulio's point of view, the idea of selling Palo to Felice might have been somewhat unorthodox, given that she was a woman, but the sale had definite advantages. It provided him with a substantial sum of ready cash – 9000 ducats – and with the purchaser being his nephew's wife, it might seem as if Palo was not actually going out of the family. Giulio perhaps even believed that his son Mario might eventually see its return. Felice, however, viewed Palo in an entirely different light. Once the property was hers, as far as she was concerned, it bore no relation to the Orsini family whatsoever.

In January 1509, a series of notarial acts took place 'in Rome, at Monte Giordano, in the *Camera Magna* of the palace'. This location, the most important room in Monte Giordano, indicates the seriousness of the transactions. Giulio Orsini was present, as was the Orsini lawyer, Prospero di Aquasparta. On 16 January the first meeting held was to confirm the 'sale of the castle situated at Palo with its land holding, done by Prospero di Aquasparta, in the name of Giulio Orsini, in favour of Donna Felice Orsini della Rovere for the price of 9000 golden ducats, of which 8,060 is payable now, and the remaining 940 ducats she promises to pay by the end of sixteen months'.[2] Three days later, a 'receipt and quittance' was made up between Giulio and Felice in which Giulio 'confirms that he has received in hand, and in cash, 8,600 ducats for the sale of Palo made by Prospero di Aquasparta, my procurator, to the Illustrious Madonna Felice Rovere Ursino'.[3]

For Felice, Palo was a practical acquisition, but it was also a property endowed with prestige and replete with symbolic relevance for its new owner. Palo allowed Felice to express her multi-faceted identity, as della Rovere daughter, as Bracciano bride, as the woman who was 'dedicated to letters and antiquities', as well as in her burgeoning role as entrepreneur and businesswoman.

The castle itself dated back to 1367, but its site was among the oldest developments in the history of Italian civilization. Not even the antiquity-obsessed Isabella d'Este could claim she owned anything with such ancient resonance. The Etruscan scholar George Dennis wrote of the site in 1848, 'Palo is well-known to travellers as the halfway house between Rome and Civitavecchia; but few bear in mind that the post-house, the ruined fortress, and the fishers' huts on the beach represent the Alsium of antiquity – one of the most hoary towns of Italy, founded or occupied by the Pelasgi – ages before the arrival of the Etruscans on these shores.'[4]

Its name, the first century AD poet Silius Italicus speculated, derived from Argive Halesus, the son of Agamemnon. In Etruscan times, Alsium had been a major harbour and, in the days of ancient Rome, a popular holiday resort for the wealthy. The Roman general Pompey had a villa there, as did Pliny the Younger's mother-in-law, which she had bought from his guardian, Rufus Verginius, who called it 'the nesting place of his old age'. Several emperors also vacationed here, including Antoninus, whose villa was praised for its location, 'surrounded by hills, and looking out on to the sea'. Destroyed in the gothic invasions, the site was resettled in the early Middle Ages, its new name, Palo, believed to derive from the *palludi*, the marshy terrain, on which it was situated.

While Palo might not have been as resonant a name as Alsium, for Felice it allowed her another link with antiquity. Another first century AD poet, Pollio Felice, had been famous for his seafront villa in the south. Built onto a promontory at Sorrento, this site was one that later attracted the attention of Giovanna, the fifteenth-century Aragonese Queen of Naples. In a Renaissance world delighting in word and name play, Pollio Felice and Palo Felice would provide amusement, reinforcing the idea that it was Felice's destiny to own such a place.

The seafront site itself provided further opportunities for Felice's self-expression and self-assertion. As a della Rovere family member, she would feel that the sea played its part in her identity. As a teenager, she had vowed, as she told Baldessar Castiglione, to throw herself into the sea rather than let herself be taken by the Borgia. She had sailed many times up and down the coast that she could now see from her castle's windows. Looking out over the sea from what was now her own property, Felice could recall herself as a young girl taken from her family in Rome to the safety of Savona, the della Rovere home town. No great future had been planned for the cardinal's daughter. Seeing that castle from the ship she could never have imagined that it would one day be hers. A realization of the heights to which she had now ascended made her new possession all the sweeter.

Palo's location allowed Felice the opportunity to make a further connection with her father. Julius, mockingly called a 'boatman' by Erasmus in *Julius Exclusus*, was a great nautical enthusiast. He maintained a large fleet of galleons at the Roman port of Ostia, the town of which he had once been bishop. At the time of Felice's acquisition of Palo, he was in the process of building a harbour at Civitavecchia, for which in 1510 Bramante designed a large fortress. Palo was exactly halfway between Ostia and Civitavecchia. Julius undoubtedly approved of his daughter's purchase, because it added to della Rovere control of the Roman water.

Although Felice might not have been aware of it, her mother's bloodline could also be traced to this area. The Normanni had once owned property at Castrum di Martignano, located by Lake Martignano, a few miles from Palo. In the twelfth century, the Normanni had owned a castle there, inherited in 1270 by Constanza, the widow of Pandolfo Normanni, who had sold it to family members Giovanni and Stefano.[5] In yet another sense, Felice was returning to her roots. Whether she was aware of this particularly intimate connection or not, Felice understood that possession of Palo allowed her to position herself in her own right within Rome's baronial history. Palo's illustrious past as Alsium allowed her a relationship with the ancient world. The fourteenth-century castle gave her a substantial stake in Rome's medieval past. Felice did not need to invent a venerable Roman ancestry for herself – her mother had already provided her with one – but few could argue that her ownership of the castle cemented her position.

CHAPTER 6

The Entrepreneur

Personal prestige, the augmentation of an identity, a relationship with the ancient world – these were all desirable accoutrements for the Renaissance noblewoman. They were not, however, Felice's primary reason for acquiring Palo. She wanted it to make her money. Private income was her primary safeguard against Gian Giordano dying before she could give birth to an Orsini son and heir. The shoreline of Palo might have been marshy, but the land set back from Palo was exceptionally fertile, the soil almost black. The castle came with substantial acreage, partly dense forest and partly wheatfields.

The importance of wheat to the Roman economy cannot be overstated. Bread was the city's primary staple and many of the city's workers received part of their wages in bread. Insufficient quantities of grain were grown in the Roman *campagna* and, in order to feed its citizens adequately, merchants imported large amounts from elsewhere in Italy. Anyone who played a part in the bringing of grain to Rome had some stake in the city's finances, and with that came a role in the city's politics.

The revenue from the sale of Palo's grain was Felice's own. It made her a wealthy woman in her own right, independent of her husband or her father. She also exploited her newly acquired assets to gain further access to the Vatican Palace, and established a business partnership, which would

Farm labourers, sixteenth century

flourish for more than a decade, with the most powerful secular figure within the Vatican, Giuliano Leno. Giuliano Leno came from a family very much like the de Cupis, whose members were bureaucrats and city officials.[1] The Leno family had long-standing ties with cardinals from the della Rovere family. They also married into another bourgeois Roman family, the del Bufalo; Felice's half-sister Francesca de Cupis was married to Angelo del Bufalo. Leno became the general contractor for the Vatican Palace. No substance, from building material for New St Peter's to firewood or foodstuffs, entered the Vatican without a licence from him. He had worked for Julius when he was still Cardinal Giuliano, overseeing the building of the cardinal's palace at San Pietro in Vincoli. The new purchase made by the Pope's daughter interested him greatly, and he looked to profit from it as well. Felice needed somebody who could help her sell her produce in Rome. She wanted to operate independently of the markets controlled by the major Roman families, including the Orsini. Giuliano Leno could supply Felice with what she needed and he made a contract with her to broker the sale of Palo's harvest in Rome.

Felice, together with Leno, directed much of Palo's yield directly into the Vatican Palace. Thus Felice came to supply a portion of her father's – the Holy Father's – daily bread and his cardinals came to realize that Felice was a financial force in her own right. With this new position came further power and influence for Felice at the papal court, power and influence that could outlast her father's reign.

Giuliano Leno was not the only Vatican official Felice employed in helping her broker the sale of her grain. Nor did all of it go to Rome. A surviving account book from 1511 shows how she exploited Palo's seafront location, her old ties with Savona, and a good relationship with high-ranking Orsini servants. The agents in charge of selling this part of her harvest were Giovanni Paolo, the castellan of Bracciano, and 'Maestro Biasso, captain of the galley of His Holiness'. Felice della Rovere, who recognized the importance of befriending servants, may have become acquainted with Captain Biasso on her journeys from Rome to Savona. Now, some years later, she persuaded him, doubtless with suitable financial reward, to ship grain to locations that were easily accessible from Palo. He would have used a ship from the papal fleet, something he could have done only with the Pope's blessing, which suggests that Julius endorsed his daughter's business activities. Thanks to his assistance, Felice's customers came to include residents of the island of Elba, about sixty kilometres north-west of Palo.

One of the entries in this account book reads: '20 March, 1511: We notify Felix Ruveris d'Ursini, our patron, that we have sold on her behalf to Gian Rinaldo Marcciano of Elba fifty twenty five *rubbios* [13, 608 dry litres] worth of grain from Palo for the price of fourteen *carlini* for every 5 *rubbios*. Signed, Maestro Biasso, Captain of the galley of His Holiness and Maestro Gian Paolo, governor of the Castle of Bracciano.'[2] In this same shipment, Antonio Marcciano of Elba bought 42 *rubbio*; Constantino of Elba, 26; Andrea, 16. On another occasion, Captain Biasso took his ship up to Savona. There he sold 65 *rubbio* to Giovanni di Stefano and 64 to Riccardo Corvello, who possibly numbered among those merchants to whom Felice had written back in 1504, assuring them of a favoured place in Rome now that her father was pope.

Other customers were down in Sperlonga, the coastal town about a hundred kilometres to the south of Rome. One individual entered in this account book, and the only Orsini family member who acquired grain from Felice, is Dianora, on whose behalf Felice had intervened shortly after her marriage, when Dianora wanted hay from the Orsini estate. Felice might have taken it on herself to supply her personally with everything she needed, so she would no longer be reduced to sending fruitless begging letters.

In this account book Felice's full name is latinized as 'Felix Ruveris Ursinis'. This might not be so strange if the rest of the document were not written in Italian, and suggests that the assumption of this expression of her name is a deliberate choice on Felice's part. In Latin it has a very masculine ring: 'The Fortunate One of the Oak and the Bear'. The name denotes strength, durability and ferocity – qualities surpassed only by her father's *terribilità*. It is not the name of someone to cross and an excellent name for use in the context of business and politics. Felice was to exploit its resonance to its fullest.

Purchasing Palo was the shrewdest act Felice had yet undertaken. As a property-owner in her own right, with her identity and authority further enhanced, she was about to take yet another step in her career and become a political negotiator.

CHAPTER 7

Vatican Ambassadress

The January 1509 purchase of Palo marks a point of maturity for Felice. She was now independently wealthy, and that autonomy garnered her greater respect among her peers. Her father saw that he could exploit the influence she now wielded for his own ends. Felice willingly colluded.

In the two years that had passed since Felice married Gian Giordano, Julius had continued to implement his plans and ambitions. He had carried on with his work renovating the Vatican Palace. Bramante had built ceremonial staircases, designed a great window in the main throne room, the Sala Regia, and made progress on the construction of New St Peter's. The stormiest relationship ever between an artist and a patron, that between Michelangelo and Julius, also gave birth to extraordinary works of art. Julius had lost interest in his tomb project but in 1508 he did set Michelangelo to work on new decorations for the ceiling of the Sistine Chapel, the masterpiece of his uncle Sixtus IV's reign whose ceiling was now cracking.

That same year, Julius brought Michelangelo's greatest rival to Rome, the twenty-five-year-old painter Raphael of Urbino, who was, coincidentally, the same age as Felice. The young artist, who grew up at the Montefeltro court, had already taken Florence by storm with his exquisite rendition of the Virgin and Child, redefining the word *sprezzatura*. It gave Julius tremendous satisfaction to steal him from the city whose beauty he was deter-

Medal devised from *Pax Romana* emblem

mined Rome would surpass. But Julius wanted Raphael's skills for his private pleasure: he had no desire to live in the apartments belonging to his predecessor Alexander VI. Their decorations, by the Sienese painter Pinturicchio, consisted of stories from the Old and New Testament with the participants in the guise of members of the Borgia family. Pinturiccho depicted the blonde-haired Lucrezia as St Catherine, her brother Cesare as a Turk, and Alexander as King Solomon. Julius had absolutely no intention of looking up into their faces every day. Instead of simply continuing to live in the same rooms, and have Pinturicchio's work painted over, he decided to move out of them entirely. He had Bramante perform structural work on older papal chambers, known simply as the *Stanze* (rooms). Raphael was to adorn them with frescos symbolically illustrating all the great achievements and dreams of his reign.[1] Among these are *Parnassus*, where Apollo and the Muses sit among scholars and philosophers from Homer to Dante. The multi-figured *School of Athens* includes Bramante depicted as Euclid, Michelangelo as the melancholic Heraclitus, and Leonardo da Vinci as Plato. Raphael himself peers out from the far right-hand corner.

The fruits of Julius's aesthetic vision still endure. His political programme was, however, much more problematic. Outside Rome, Julius's political fortunes waxed and waned. He had had an astonishingly easy victory when he removed the Bentivoglio family from Bologna in 1506. This was in part because the family had made itself unpopular and many citizens of Bologna welcomed his arrival to liberate them from its tyranny. However, the Bolognese proved fickle, and Julius had to fight several times over before he finally subdued the Bentivoglio.

Perhaps Julius's greatest success, primarily a result of his matrimonial strategies, was the 1511 *Pax Romana* – The Roman Peace. The *Pax*, signed on 28 August 1511, was a treaty between the barons and the citizens of Rome. Its most important signatories were, needless to say, members of the Colonna and Orsini families. Giulio Orsini signed for Gian Giordano, who was absent in France. Their names were joined by those of others from the thirteen Roman districts, including such Roman families as the Savelli and the Massimo. All promised to dedicate themselves 'to the honour and exaltation of His Holiness Our Lord Pope Julius II, and to the Holy Mother Church . . . to peace, quiet and good living in the fair city of

Rome, our communal *patria*.[2] While tensions still continued between the barons, Rome gradually ceased to be torn apart from the inside. This relative peace made for an easier existence for Julius and his successors within the city of Rome. A special kind of maiolica, pottery ware, was created to commemorate the peace. This became known as Orsini–Colonna ware and depicted a bear, the Orsini emblem, embracing a column (*colonna*) with the inscription 'we shall be friends'.

Julius had arranged Felice's marriage to Gian Giordano Orsini as a means of making peace in Rome. But Felice had made her own contribution to baronial accord two years before the *Pax Romana*, in 1509, when she had negotiated an *entente* between the Orsini and Savelli families. The Orsini and Savelli were not especially bitter enemies, but Savelli inclinations to ally with the Colonna had caused hostility between the families. Felice, however, had befriended one Savelli family member, Portia, who was married to her brother-in-law Carlo Orsini. It was perhaps through Portia that Felice had engineered a concord on which the Mantuan ambassador reported on 24 April 1509. He described how representatives of the two families had appeared 'in front of the Pope, vowing to quarrel no more. In return, any penalties [for fighting] they had incurred would be dropped. As a guarantee that this peace would be respected, they will deposit 100,000 ducats, supplied by certain cardinals, as well as by lords who are their friends, and the people of Rome.'[3]

Felice's work with the Savelli had coincided with another, much more dangerous, piece of negotiation, when she had contrived to prevent the Orsini forming an alliance with Venice. The Venetian Republic had been a thorn in Julius's side ever since he took the papal tiara. The Venetians consistently challenged papal power and overrode and superseded clerical appointments instituted by Julius. He had been particularly angered by their refusal to appoint one of his nephews, Bartolomeo della Rovere, as Archbishop of Padua in 1508 following the death of his brother, Galeotto Franciotto della Rovere, in whose bed Felice and Gian Giordano had consummated their marriage. By 1510, the Venetians had also begun to assert themselves militarily. They were conscious of the threat of Turkish aggression from the east, and from the north-west the possibility of a French invasion. They wanted to arm and defend themselves. Julius had no desire to see Italy invaded by either side, nor did he want any military action in Italy unless it was under his command, and he disliked the self-assertiveness of the Venetian Republic. He decided to join the international, anti-Venetian League of Cambrai, whose other members were Louis XII of France, the Holy Roman Emperor Maximillian, and the Spanish Ferdinand of Aragon.[4]

In early 1509, the Venetians readied themselves for war against the League. As was common in military practice at this time, they not only had their troops captained by members of the Venetian Republic, they also hired *condottieri* from elsewhere in Italy to augment their capabilities. They entered into negotiations with Giulio Orsini and Gian Giordano's son-in-law, Renzo da Ceri, to serve as military commanders in their war. This situation angered Julius and embarrassed Gian Giordano. The Orsini, through Gian Giordano's marriage to Felice, were supposedly papal allies and from Julius's perspective such an alliance did not allow them to go to war on behalf of the state that Julius had deemed an enemy. Gian Giordano, a long-standing servant of the French crown, was equally uncomfortable with his relatives' choice of new employer. However, there was a reason why *condottieri* were called 'mercenaries' in English. Their services went to the highest bidder and political loyalty, if it was a factor at all, was a secondary consideration for them. There was no denying that Orsini family finances were still in some degree of disarray following the conflicts with the Borgia. Not having shared Gian Giordano's French income, Giulio and Renzo did not share his loyalty to the French. And even though he was head of the Bracciano clan, Gian Giordano was in no position to forbid his relatives to take Venetian pay.

Gian Giordano found himself in a decided quandary. He did not want his family to appear less than united, nor did he want conflict with his father-in-law, or with his French patrons. It was his wife, Felice, who allowed him to save face. She acted as the means by which his Orsini relatives were prevented from serving as mercenaries for Venice.

On 1 April 1509, Julius called a meeting at the Vatican with the two bankers, Agostino da Sandro and Bonvixi, who were responsible for paying out the Venetian salaries of the Orsini *condottieri*. He then absented himself, and the discussion took place with the bankers 'by way of Madonna Felice' to ensure the rest of the money promised them did not reach the Orsini.[5] Felice then 'stayed the night at the palace, with an armed guard'. Clearly, with such delicate and potentially volatile negotiations taking place, it was too dangerous for her to return that night to the palace of Monte Giordano and run the risk of being abducted or even assassinated.

Having stalled Orsini access to the Venetian funds, Felice then approached the Orsini themselves. News of what took place between the two sides came to Venice by way of a courier, Mafio: 'From the mouth of this courier,' Marino Sanuto reported, 'there came news of the Orsini and it is not good. They have reached an agreement with the Pope and the cause of this is Madonna Felice, daughter of the Pope, wife of Gian Giordano Orsini. She went to find these Orsini and had them reconcile with the Pope, and they have returned the 16,000 ducats they had from our orators.'6

What exactly Felice offered to make the Orsini *condottieri* change their minds is still secret. Undoubtedly Giulio Orsini and Renzo da Ceri were bribed in some way to make it worth their while to return this substantial sum of money to the Venetians. Such bribes must have been sanctioned by both Julius and Gian Giordano. Politically, it was wise that neither party appeared to have been involved in such a transaction – Julius, as it would seem as if he was meddling in Orsini family business, and Gian Giordano, as he would appear not to be putting his own family's interests first. Both men were clearly content to have Felice, their daughter and wife respectively, act as the negotiator. It absolved them from any blame, which was particularly critical in the case of Gian Giordano and allowed him to maintain a neutrality with Venice, his relatives and the Pope. The Venetians clearly held Felice responsible for the Orsini cancelling their contract; as Sanuto recorded, she was the 'cause' of the break.

How did Felice profit from her actions? She had no personal interest in whether the Orsini served Venice or not. But the incident allowed her the opportunity to act in the role that she knew would have been hers had she been born a boy, that of cardinal *nipote*. In mediating between the Pope and the Orsini she was performing as her father had once done for his uncle Sixtus, effectively serving as a papal political mediator. The act gave her something she wanted very badly, widespread public recognition. Her reputation spread throughout Italy's courts as ambassadors and emissaries sent out accounts of what had occurred. On 2 April, Lodovico da Fabriano, stressing Felice's involvement in the process, sent word to the Mantuan court: 'Those Orsini have reached an agreement with Our Lord, and came yesterday to kiss the feet of His Holiness, through the mediation of Madonna Felice . . . they have undertaken not to fight without a papal mandate . . . '[7]

The incident also allowed Felice to strengthen the bond with her father. In her negotiations with the Orsini and Venice, Felice did not act primarily as an Orsini wife. In this instance she was all della Rovere daughter. Gian Giordano's relatives recognized where her allegiance lay and it made them uneasy. Although they had acquiesced to the Pope's wishes, this event served to define further the distance between Felice and her husband's relatives. Felice's loyalties were embedded in the Vatican Palace, not at Monte Giordano.

CHAPTER 8

Felice and the Queen of France

By 1510, an accord had been reached between Julius and the Venetians, who were no longer his prime enemy. Instead, he turned his attention to France, whose continued presence in northern Italy he wanted brought to an end. The League of Cambrai dissolved and the Holy League was formed in its place. Its core members were the same as those in the Cambrai League minus France and with the addition of Henry VIII of England, the leaders of the Swiss cantons and, this time, Venice. A letter arrived in Venice from the papal court, with the good news that 'the Pope will lift his censure against us, and he has sent Madonna Felice, the wife of Signor Gian Giordano, to tell Giulio Orsini to prepare himself, as the Pope wishes to be with the Venetians against France'.[1]

But if Gian Giordano's relatives were willing to go into battle against France, the Bracciano Lord himself was not. This new political situation caused Gian Giordano an even greater degree of discomfort than had the Venetian affair. Gian Giordano was not only a long-standing servant of France; he had, in the form of his palace at Blois, a significant financial asset tied up in the country. What was important for Gian Giordano was not necessarily that he succeed in bringing hostilities to an end, but that he at least appeared to be working with that aim in mind. If Julius had called on Felice to assist him with the Venetian arbitration, this time it

Detail of *Fountain of Youth* frescos, Castle of Bracciano, fifteenth century was Gian Giordano who called on her to arbitrate between France and the Pope.

Gian Giordano went on an extended visit to France to put forward negotiations for peace. He returned in July 1511 and went to the Vatican to discuss such a proposal with the Pope. 'Madonna Felice', Sanuto records, 'also came from Bracciano in order to strengthen the agreement.'[2] In other words she supplied moral support for her husband in his dealings with his father-in-law.

To achieve peace with France was an insurmountable task for Gian Giordano, who was a *condottiere* acclaimed more for his loyalty than for his political finesse. Moreover, Julius was only one participant in the Holy League. He had, if not loyalties, certain interests in maintaining good relations with his fellow League members, in particular the powerful Holy Roman Emperor, who was himself not ready for a French accord. None the less, Julius was prepared to utilize his Orsini connections as a conduit for dialogue between himself and France. Such conversation was not, however, to involve either Gian Giordano or Julius directly. Instead, the participants were to be Felice and the Queen of France, Anne of Brittany.

Like Isabella d'Este, Anne of Brittany was a woman Felice admired and could consider a role model. Six years Felice's senior, Anne had inherited the Duchy of Brittany at the age of eleven. A natural ruler, she was married to Charles VIII of France in 1491, and had governed the country, successfully, during his absence on military campaigns in the 1490s. Although Brittany was now technically under French control, Anne contrived to rule the duchy autonomously. In 1499, she married Charles's successor, Louis XII, and continued to serve as French Regent when necessary. While Louis XII was largely ridiculed for his modest intelligence by such connoisseurs of princes as Machiavelli, Anne commanded the respect of her peers. Castiglione had described her as 'a very great lady, no less in virtue than in state and justice, liberality and holiness . . . to compare her to Kings Charles and Louis, you shall not find her inferior'.[3]

Anne herself was not in favour of French military action and was clearly of the opinion that it was her husband's desire for self-aggrandizement that led him to refuse to let French troops leave northern Italy. As powerful as she was, the decision to vacate Italy was not hers to make, and she could operate only from the sidelines. When she received Gian Giordano at the court at Blois, it became clear that she could open a politically decorous dialogue with his intelligent wife. Again, the idea that Felice and Anne could, or would, alter the course of French and papal diplomatic proceedings is not necessarily realistic. But it would do much for public relations on both sides. If the Queen of France and the Pope's daughter could deal cordially with each other, it would indicate there was the possibility of an accord between the two sides. 'Madonna Felice has been begged by the Queen of France that she begin a dialogue on the subject of peace with Louis XII,' wrote a Mantuan emissary to Isabella d'Este, in April 1511. 'The Queen of France is looking for every way to remove the King from this mission and so she is working with Madonna Felice to beseech His Holiness her father that he might wish to be disposed towards such an accord.'[4] Julius appeared willing to listen to his daughter. In late July 1511, one of Isabella's most trusted servants, Stazio Gaddi, wrote to her from Rome, 'A good end is hoped for the peace, as it is being managed by two sage women: The Queen of France and Madonna Felice.'[5]

Anne and Felice persevered over the next two years. On 29 January 1513, almost two years after the original *entente* had begun, Stazio reported that the 'Queen of France continues to seek for peace with the Pope, and has sent letter after letter in her own hand. Signora Felice, along with the Cardinal of Nantes, has been managing the affair.'[6] None the less, it would be left to Julius's successor, Leo X, from the pro-French Medici family, to bring the Vatican's war with France to an end.

CHAPTER 9

Madonna Felice is Everything

For Felice, entering into negotiations with Anne of Brittany was yet another jewel in her newly acquired crown as Rome's most powerful woman. For her, the most important issue was not whether peace with France was achieved in actuality. Instead, in this world where appearance was everything, the most pressing matter for her was that she be seen as a political player of unquestionable weight. Once again, it had been broadcast widely that her father was allowing her a diplomatic voice and she was now an internationally recognized figure. The Queen of France herself had treated Felice as an equal and had sought out the opinions and influence of the Pope's daughter. What was particularly pleasing for Felice was that much of the respect she received was precisely because she was the Pope's daughter. Her status as Orsini wife had helped legitimize her, but her power came through the recognition that she had her father's ear.

Others at the Vatican saw the power and influence Felice della Rovere wielded at court, among them Cardinal Bernardo Dovizi da Bibbiena. Bibbiena had been tutor to Cardinal Giovanni de' Medici, the future Leo X. During Julius's reign, Bibbiena served as Medici eyes, ears and fixer at the Vatican. He sent a great deal of commentary back to Florence regarding the 1511 Council of Pisa. Five renegade cardinals opposed to Julius's warmongering made up the Council, which had the aim of deposing him. Two

Maarten van Heemskerck, Borgo and St Peter's Square, 1530s

of the cardinals were French, two Spanish, and the other was Francesco Borgia, whose relative, Alexander VI, Julius himself had attempted to depose. The French and Spanish cardinals felt tricked by Julius, who had not fulfilled his promise to reward them once they had cast their votes for him at conclave to become pope. However, the Pisa Council did not succeed in its attempt to remove him, and consequently the cardinals were excommunicated by Julius. However, in the midst of their meetings, the Council's leader, the Spanish Bernardino Carvajal, wanted to involve Felice in the negotiations. 'I have been told', Cardinal Bibbiena wrote to Giovanni de' Medici, 'that Bernardino Carvajal has written a thousand pages to Madonna Felice, offering his brother as a hostage to His Holiness and promises that the council will not go against His Holiness, and other similar pleasantries . . .'[1]

Julius's desire for Felice to take a role in the negotiations with the southern clergy may be surmised by the fact that he let her dispose of the Abbey of Valdina in Sicily. The location of this office, worth 2,500 *scudi* a year, made it desirable to Neapolitan and Spanish clerics. 'It appears', commented Bibbiena, 'that His Holiness wishes the Badia to be dispensed according to the wishes of Madonna Felice.'[2] What this signified is that any cleric hopeful of obtaining the abbey for himself or an ally would need to work with Felice. They would then enter into private negotiations, not directly involving Julius, so that he could avoid any accusations of bribery. The aspiring abbot would doubtless assure Felice of his loyalty to her father, and refuse to join in any plots against him.

The extent of Felice's entrenchment at court reached the point where Julius relaxed and began to show her open affection. 'At court,' a Mantuan emissary observed, 'Madonna Felice is everything.'[3] She became a frequent presence at the Vatican Palace. 'Madonna Felice is here,' wrote Bibbiena on one occasion, 'a little bit poorly.'[4] Eleonora Gonzaga, the new Duchess of Urbino, who was married to Felice's cousin Francesco Maria della Rovere, wrote to her mother Isabella d'Este on 10 April 1511 about a dinner the Pope had held. 'Yesterday evening,' she wrote, 'the Illustrious Lady Duchess [her great-aunt, Elizabetta Gonzaga], and the Duke and I went to dine with His Holiness, Madonna Felice was there again.'[5] Julius also invited Eleonora and Felice to visit him to examine the fabulous jewels h had acquired for vertiginous sums of money. Later that year, in Septem' when Julius was gravely ill, the Venetian ambassador sent the following report home: 'The Pope is very poorly, and will allow no one to enter his chambers except his sister-in-law [Eleonora], Madonna Felice, his daughter, who is in Rome, Bartolomeo della Rovere, and the Duke of Urbino.'[6] Julius even partitioned out his estate, leaving Felice a further 12,000 ducats. He did make a recovery, however, and returned to his building and military campaigns, which left him very short of money. To help her father out, Felice actually returned the money he had passed over to her.

Even with such an act of generosity on Felice's part, there was no guarantee that Julius, whom age had made notoriously fickle and mercurial in mood, would always treat her well and with affection. While he allowed her to perform politically on his command, he grew angry if she tried to take a lead in any matters of state. She was to feel the extent of his wrath when she became involved with the affairs of Isabella d'Este's family.

CHAPTER 10

Code Name Sappho

No one Italian noble troubled Julius II more persistently than did Alfonso d'Este, Duke of Ferrara, who was consistently hostile towards the Pope throughout his reign. Fearful that Julius's invasion of Bologna might have repercussions for his own nearby city of Ferrara, Alfonso acted as an ally of the Bentivoglio and an ally of the French, and refused to obey Julius's request to desist from hostile activity against Venice. Perhaps most griev-ously of all, from a financial perspective, he also mined for salt in the town of Comacchio, which directly affected papal income from this most precious commodity in the same region. In August 1510 Pope Julius II chose to punish Alfonso by excommunicating him.[1]

Julius's bad relationship with Alfonso also affected how he viewed the Gonzaga family, the rulers of Mantua. Francesco Gonzaga and Alfonso were brothers-in-law. Isabella d'Este was, respectively, their wife and sister. Francesco was also commander of the papal troops, a position of which Julius might have relieved him, were it not that Francesco's daughter, Eleonora, was the wife of the Pope's nephew, Francesco Maria della Rovere. However, Julius saw Francesco as an unreliable and ineffectual general, and felt his ties to Alfonso compromised his military position. To ensure Francesco's loyalty to him, Julius insisted Francesco's young son Federico be held at the papal court as a hostage to ensure his father's good behaviour. Federico, who might well be the pretty, blond boy depicted at the front of Raphael's *School of Athens*, became a favourite of the papal *famiglia*, and was perhaps more indulged than if he had stayed at home. The little boy possessed great charm. The Mantuan ambassador at court wrote to his mother and father to assure them how beloved he was 'by the Pope, by Agostino Chigi [who had become Julius's financier], Gian Giordano Orsini and Madonna Felice, who willingly bestow affection upon him, and have invited him to Bracciano'.[2] On other evenings, he visited Monte Giordano.

That Julius looked on both Isabella d'Este's brother and husband with considerable distrust was not a situation that the Marchesa cared to endure. Poor relations with the Pope meant the withholding of lucrative papal rewards, cardinals' hats for her sons and nephews, access to Church benefices and the rights to the revenue on certain taxes. Isabella could not endure the thought of any kind of financial deprivation. Looking to see who at the papal court could be a useful friend to her families, she turned to the woman who had solicited her friendship half a decade earlier.

Felice was willing, indeed anxious, to be of assistance to the influential Isabella. The situation not only appealed to her taste for diplomatic mediation, it provided her with an opportunity for further advancement on the Italian political stage. In April 1511, Felice went to her father to 'see if he would consent to her giving her daughter [Julia] as a wife to one of the sons of the His Excellency the Duke of Ferrara'. Given that neither child was much more than four years old, it can be safely assumed that this was no more than a betrothal, designed as an overture to cementing an alliance between the d'Este and the della Rovere. Julius, however, was highly irritated by Felice's unsolicited matrimonial suggestion. He told her to go away and 'attend to her sewing'.[3]

It was a calculated dismissal on Julius's part: instructing Felice to return to women's work implied she was meddling in a masculine world in which she had no business. The irony, of course, is that Julius was perfectly happy for Felice to play the man when it suited him, when he needed her to dissuade the Orsini from serving Venice, or to serve as papal representative at peace talks with France. But Felice's masculine character was to be utilized only at his discretion and his command. Otherwise, she had to return to womanly subservience. Felice felt frustrated, knowing her father's appreciation of her ability and vision would have been much less inconsistent had she been born a boy.

However, Felice was stubborn and tenacious, and was not deterred by her father's response. Isabella d'Este was equally determined. So they tried again to advance their cause the following year. This time, Isabella wanted Felice's support not only for Alfonso but also for another of her brothers, Cardinal Ippolito. Stazio Gaddi, the Mantuan ambassador at the Vatican, sent both Isabella and Francesco reports on the proceedings.

Stazio wrote the more sensitive parts of his reports in code, to be translated when the letter reached Mantua. Some of the code was encrypted hieroglyphics, while in other parts an alias was incorporated to hide the identity of the subject. In some of Stazio's letters the name 'Sappho' appears. Rather indiscreetly breaking his own code, Stazio wrote at the bottom of the letter, 'I use the name of the great Sappho for Signora Felice.'4

Sappho is an especially fascinating choice of alias for Felice. Stazio was perhaps inspired by the depiction of the poetess by Raphael in the *Parnassus* he painted in Julius's library, now the Stanza della Segnatura. Raphael's rendering of Sappho has always attracted attention, as she is the only historical female figure present in the picture, among figures such as Virgil and Homer, and her name is spelled out above her. Felice had a similarly singular presence at the Vatican. Sappho was also renowned for her wisdom; the name perhaps reflected Stazio's confidence in Felice's abilities.

With Sappho as the code name for Felice, her father's code name became Lesbia, the island where the poetess had lived. 'Sappho went to Lesbia' meant 'Felice went to see the Pope'. On 17 June 1512, Stazio wrote to Isabella that Felice was

> well disposed to do good work for Europa [code name for Ippolito d'Este], and that she would do all that was possible. She has said that she will be going to Rome in four days and will most willingly exhaust herself in working for his good. She will also bring up her own interests, that is that she desires nothing more in the world than to see her daughter in the house of d'Este. In this matter, great dexterity and diligence has been used to make sure that Signor Gian Giordano is happy that she comes to Rome.5

This is the only reference that indicates that Gian Giordano, as well as Felice, might have a concern in their daughter's future marriage plans.

Isabella added her encouragement for Felice's endeavours, writing her a long and flattering letter, far removed form the capricious and dictatorial tone she often used with her correspondents:

> Your Illustrious Excellency, who is like my dearest sister. I understand from various sources how lovingly and favourably you have acted in the matters of my illustrious brothers, and I know your goodness is not only out of respect for them, but also for love of me . . . I want you to know how much I esteem your efforts and authority which I know His Holiness prizes greatly, and in every other matter I am consigning the bearer of this letter to thank you for such generosity and virtue that comes from you. I hope that you continue in favouring my brother and particularly the Cardinal, who, I understand may become court secretary. I am sure that he will act with great maturity in this capacity were he to be appointed and be obedient and faithful to His Holiness. You yourself will acquire a friend and a house that will perpetually serve you.[6]

Unfortunately for Felice's plans, Alfonso d'Este's behaviour continued to arouse Julius's ire. The Duke refused to come to the Vatican to affirm his fealty to the Pope. On 2 October 1512 Stazio wrote to Isabella, 'Last Wednesday Sappho went to Lesbia to speak about the matters of your Excellency's affairs. But she found the widow [another code name for Julius] in a great fury as the Duke was gone, and had been seen in Bolsena. Sappho could not talk with the Pope, and she has now left the palace.'[7]

But if Felice was disappointed that these negotiations could not go forward, she was absolutely crushed by another blow Julius delivered to her. He refused to let her become the governor of the city of Pesaro. Pesaro was the major port in the province of the Marche, the point of access on the Adriatic for such cities as Urbino. Until 1512, a scion of the Sforza family had ruled the city. Lucrezia Borgia's first husband, Giovanni, had been its governor and Lucrezia herself the city's countess. Perhaps Felice's interest in acquiring the city was motivated by her desire to outdo the other pope's daughter; only, this time, she would possess Pesaro in her own right. Felice did not want it as a gift. She wanted to pay for Pesaro with money she had earned from the Palo estate and through brokering political favours and ecclesiastical offices at the Vatican. If it was a gift, it might be taken from her; if it was a purchase, it was hers outright.

The other contender for this prize was her younger cousin, Francesco Maria della Rovere. In 1507 Francesco Maria had succeeded his gouty maternal uncle Guidobaldo as Duke of Urbino, and his father, Julius's brother Giovanni, as Prefect of Rome. The twenty-two-year-old Francesco Maria was feckless and dangerously volatile. He had performed poorly as a general in Julius's military campaigns and in 1508 he had murdered the cleric he saw as a rival for his uncle Julius's attentions, Cardinal Francesco Alidosi. Felice, however, was surprisingly fond of him. He had been hidden from the Borgia in Savona in 1502, and she had come to view him as a younger brother, a temporary replacement for the one she had left behind in Rome, Gian Domenico de Cupis. She actively petitioned her father to absolve Francesco Maria of the murder. Julius did so, in part because he recognized the future of the della Rovere dynasty lay with his nephew.

Felice had not taken her younger cousin, who was already endowed with so much, as a serious rival for the prize of Pesaro. On 11 October 1512 she went to her father, whose moods were increasingly unpredictable. What occurred is told tersely by the Mantuan Stazio Gadi: 'Sappho, wishing to speak with His Holiness about buying Pesaro, went to him and found him in a great rage. He greatly rebuffed her, saying he wants Pesaro for the Duke of Urbino, and spoke to her in such a way that she has left Rome, weeping.'[8]

Stazio's description of Felice's emotional state is quite surprising in its candour. Thus far in her life, Felice had performed in public, no matter what she may have felt inside, as a woman who was both proud and resilient. The greatest amount of discomfort she had ever openly displayed was her blush when Gian Giordano tried to give her a French kiss on their wedding day. For her to leave Rome in tears is an indication of the deep humiliation she felt from her father's refusal of her request. Life was frequently unfair for women in the Renaissance, but its unfairness on this occasion seemed particularly harsh to Felice. She had proved herself a more than competent estate manager, a shrewd businesswoman, an admired diplomat. All were useful attributes for becoming governor of a city. Bar her father and uncle, she had single-handedly achieved much more than any of her male della Rovere relatives, who had grown soft and lazy on papal handouts. And yet her father turned from her to her less popular and less competent cousin, simply because he was a man. If the elderly Pope remembered how much it had pained him as a younger man to have been passed over by Sixtus, despite all his hard work, in favour of his less deserving Riario cousins, then he chose not to act on his recollections. And there is certain poignancy in Felice, who so often acted as a man, being reduced on this occasion to tears, that traditionally feminine emotional response.

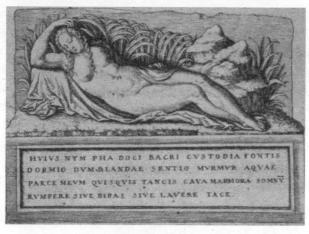

HVIVS NYM PHA DOCI BACRI CVSTODIA FONTIS
DORMIO DVM BLANDAE SENTIO MVRMVR AQVAE
PARCE MEVM QVISQVIS TANGIS CAVA MARMORA SOMNV
RVMPERE SIVE BIBAS SIVE LAVERE TACE.

CHAPTER 11

The Julian Legacy

After her father's last rebuff, Felice abandoned any further attempts to marry her daughter Julia to the son of the Duke of Ferrara, and she stayed away from the Vatican Palace. A Mantuan envoy who went out to Bracciano to see her wrote to Isabella on 5 November 1512 that Felice had assured him she had done 'everything possible to benefit the Duke of Ferrara, although little of it helped him'.[1] Several years passed without any further contact between Isabella and Felice and the Mantuan envoys. It was clear that Julius would do nothing for her brother and Isabella was not one to waste her time soliciting fruitless favours. Moreover, by late 1512, Julius was in constantly poor health. Soon, there would be a change at the Vatican and Alfonso d'Este's reputation could be rehabilitated. Five days after the Mantuan's report from Bracciano, news reached Venice that 'the Pope has shivering fits, and negotiations are already beginning for the choice of his successor'.[2]

Felice kept her own eye on her father's decline. On several occasions she paid the travelling expenses of Julius's doctor, Archangelo, to come out to her country estates when she was absent from Rome to keep her informed of his condition. He was paid well for his trouble, receiving 25 ducats (the equivalent of several thousand pounds today) on one occasion just to come to Bracciano. Julius, the *papa terribile*, was tenacious to the end and

I. J. Boissard, engraving of *Sleeping Nymph* in garden of Angelo Colocci

recovered on several occasions from what was widely believed to be his deathbed. But when he took to his bed in early January 1513, he was not to rise again. He died on 21 February.[3]

In the last days of Julius's life, Felice came to ask him for one last favour. She wanted him to make her nineteen-year-old half-brother, Gian Domenico de Cupis, a cardinal. Felice was largely motivated by sisterly affection and a desire to look after the interests of the de Cupis family. But also of great concern to her was a need to have a member of the curia whose loyalty would be to her and her alone. Felice did not know who the next pope would be, and she wanted to be sure there was someone wielding power on her behalf within the Vatican's inner circles. But while Julius had already made Gian Domenico a canon of St Peter's and a secretary at the Vatican, he refused this request. He claimed that to make such a 'young and ignorant boy' a cardinal would displease other members of the College.[4] However, Julius did re-bequeath Felice the 12,000 ducats she had returned to him the previous year. In total, in addition to her 15,000-ducat dowry, Julius had bestowed on Felice a personal cash fortune of 21,000 ducats including the money she used to purchase Palo. It was an exceptional sum for a father to leave autonomously to a daughter at this time, and made Felice one of the most independently wealthy women in Italy – if not the wealthiest.

There are no surviving letters of condolence to Felice on the loss of her father. Those who otherwise might have written to her perhaps refrained from doing so on the grounds of wishing to create a memory of saintly behaviour for Julius. Despite the Pope's growing unpopularity in the last years of his reign, unprecedented numbers came to see his corpse lying in state in the church of St Peter's. They sobbed, kissed his feet and prayed aloud, venerating the Pope's body as they would a holy relic. To draw attention at this time to the fact that Julius had left behind a daughter might have seemed indelicate. She was a reminder of the Pope's carnality and youthful venal behaviour. His life experience had encompassed the sins of the flesh.

Beyond the money Julius left her, another part of the Julian legacy lived on with Felice. She was there for all to see in the Raphael frescos on the walls of his apartments. *The Miracle of the Mass at Bolsena* was completed towards the end of Julius's reign in 1512. The miracle at Bolsena, a small hill town to the north of Rome, occurred in 1263. A German priest, celebrating Mass in the town's church, had had doubts about the truth of transubstantiation. The moment he unwrapped the host, it began to bleed, staining the cloth holding it, thereby confirming the truth of the process. This cloth, known as the Corporal, was later transferred to the nearby Cathedral of Orvieto. *En route* to Bologna to launch his campaign against the Bentivoglio in September 1506, Julius stopped at Orvieto to venerate the Corporal. He clearly associated the success of his Bolognese campaign, the most easily won battle of his military career, with his worship of the holy relic and chose to include it among the scenes decorating his apartments.

Raphael painted Julius kneeling at the altar, about to receive the bleeding host from the once doubting German priest. Below him, to his left, are male members of the della Rovere family, Julius's cousins and nephews. The clerical figures are believed to include, from left to right, Leonardo Grosso della Rovere, Raffaele and Tomasso Riario and Agostino Spinola. The secular figures, the kneeling litter-bearers, may represent Julius's nephews, Bartolomeo della Rovere, Galeazzo Riario, Francesco Maria della Rovere and Nicolò Franciotto della Rovere.[5] The family stands by to witness the miracle that Julius felt brought him so much good fortune.

On the left-hand side of the picture is a group of men, women and children. No della Rovere identities have been suggested for these men and, at first glance, the women appear to be simply idealized figures, none of them a representation of a real woman.[6] But up in the second row there is a woman kneeling at the top of the step, fixing the Pope with an earnest gaze. She is quite different from the other women painted in the picture, and there are several reasons to believe, as mentioned earlier, that she is a representation of Felice. Felice was twenty-nine in 1512; this woman could also be in her late twenties. She is dressed in black, the colour that Felice wore every day of her life. Her physiognomy, forehead, nose and chin have much in common with those of Julius himself. And the position of this figure is not unlike Felice's own position within the Vatican Palace. The woman here is by no means the most prominent figure in the fresco, not even the most prominent female figure. But her black dress is striking next to the pastels the other women are wearing and she stands out from them. Although distant from the figure of the kneeling Pope, she is spatially aligned with him, connected by a long diagonal. The hands of the figures surrounding her, ostensibly reaching out to the Pope, also serve to frame her face. She is at once visible and yet discreet, as Julius so often required Felice to be during his reign.

For many of Europe's Christians, Julius had altered the path of the Christian Church for the worse. His insatiable need for money to fund his military and artistic projects and the subsequent demands in the forms of tithes and indulgences, placed on people who would never themselves visit Rome, created a fertile environment for resentment, revolt and, eventually, the Reformation. But in Rome itself there were men who mourned the Pope's passing, humanists and artists who fully appreciated all that Julius had done for the city. His reign had brought a new golden age to the city, one that would never really be replicated. For these men, Felice became the living, breathing part of Julius's legacy, an embodiment in flesh of the world he had made. The court poet Antonio Flaminio visualized her in a poem as 'the fair Venus' and those intimate with this world instantly imagined the *Venus Felix*.[7] This second-century-AD statue is an image of a Roman matron, perhaps a princess of the Antonine family; on its base are inscribed the words 'Veneri Felici'. The statue had a prominent position in Julius's sculpture garden at the Villa Belvedere, the site of so many of his family parties. There were few who, gazing at the statue, would not have connected this *Felix* to the one who was such a frequent visitor to the Belvedere.

Among those who shared Julius's vision of Rome's new golden age was the humanist and papal secretary Angelo Colocci. A scholar of tremendous depth and learning, he was able to support his passion for collecting antiquities through his administrative position within the curia. For many years he had been a leader of the Roman *Accademia* – the wandering academy of poets, artists and writers who met to discuss matters of religion, philosophy, science, literature and antiquities. At the beginning of 1513, Colocci gave his academy a permanent home – the *Accademia Colocciana*.[8] He bought property near the Trevi fountain, one of Rome's few public sources of clean water. Colocci, too, benefited from the same spring that fed the Trevi, and installed a fountain in the garden of his new house. Water fell around a statue of a naked nymph sleeping among the reeds. She was adapted from an ancient statue of Ariadne utilized as a fountain in Julius's own sculpture garden in the courtyard at the Villa Belvedere.[9]

Although Colocci had amassed an impressive collection of antiquities, the sleeping nymph fountain, with its enviable hydraulics, became the centrepiece of his new home and academy. Had he lived, the Pope would unquestionably have been the guest of honour when Colocci threw the door of his house open to his friends for the first time in March of 1513. But Julius was no longer among them, and so it was Felice whom Colocci invited to attend instead as honoured guest, and honoured she was, in a way replete with sentiment and emotion. For Colocci's party, the Neapolitian poet Girolamo Borgia composed the 'Ecologa Felix', which can be interpreted as the 'Happy Poem', or even 'Felice's Poem'. It had a triple dedication: the late Julius, Angelo Colocci and Felice herself. It imagined Felice as a nymph in Colocci's garden. Its opening lines ran: 'Under a giant oak the prettiest goddesses gathered: Venus, the Graces, the Muses, and Pallas Minerva beside them. All to honour Felice, the nymph by the banks of the Tiber.'[10]

'Ecologa Felix' embodies many aspects of Felice's life and world. The 'giant oak' is a clear reference to the della Rovere family name and her home at Monte Giordano was by the banks of the Tiber. Borgia also seeks to imply that Felice embodies all of the great qualities of the ancient goddesses: beauty, the ability to inspire and wisdom. Later in the poem, Felice the nymph 'sings Julian praises, bringing up the benefactions of the magnanimous shepherd'. Significantly, given the preoccupations of those gathered, the poem also describes 'Rome reborn to all her primordial splendour, as he built marvellous houses and temples to imitate Heaven'.[10]

Felice received much gratification from the event at Colocci's house. It showed her that Rome's intellectuals, the men she truly admired, recognized her position within the Julian legacy. If her father was not to be forgotten, then neither was she.

CHAPTER 12

Felice, Michelangelo and the Pincian Hill

Felice's father's death secured her a revered place among Rome's humanists and access to some of the most precious items the Renaissance art
world had to offer: drawings by Michelangelo.

The frescos on the ceiling of the Sistine Chapel are the largest work
completed entirely by Michelangelo. The Chapel was a della Rovere commission through and through. The architectural structure was built during
the reign of Sixtus IV, who gave the Chapel his name. It was Sixtus who
invited Florence's most fashionable painters, including Botticelli and
Domenico Ghirlandaio to come to Rome, to paint New Testament scenes
on the lower levels of the walls of the Chapel. The Sistine Chapel subsequently became the Vatican Palace's most substantial place of worship, the
chief palatine chapel, second only to St Peter's. It was where cardinals
lived and cast their votes during conclave. Although Julius had plans for
Bramante to build a new and splendid conclave hall to rival the one he
remembered from the Avignon Palais des Papes, the design was never
realized. The Sistine Chapel was never superseded.

The Sistine Chapel was too important a space to escape Julius's attention. There was not only the matter of the family connection; there was
also the fact that by the beginning of Julius's reign the subsidence problems
that plagued the Vatican Palace had caused cracks in the Sistine ceiling.

Bronzino, *Fall of the Rebel Angels*, early 1530s, Florence, Uffizi

Julius had put Bramante to work on repairing and shoring up the vaulting. He then began to think about what he wanted on his ceiling, which was painted a traditional blue with a field of gold stars, and who he wanted to undertake this decoration. The Pope removed a disgruntled Michelangelo from sculpting his grandiose tomb project, and had him turn his attention to the art of fresco painting. The story of the frescoed ceiling is a long and complex one. It spans over four years, from 1508 to 1512, and evolves from a simple scheme of depictions of the twelve apostles to grandiose narratives of scenes from the Book of Genesis. Painted on the vaults, the spandrels and the uppermost part of the walls are the prophets, the ancestors of Christ, the *ignudi*, the beautiful naked men who are denoted as the heroes of this Julian golden age, and perhaps the most magnificent figures of all, the sibyls, the female prophets recognized by Christians and pagans.

Few were allowed to visit Michelangelo as he laboured on the ceiling over the years. He was particularly anxious to ban Raphael, who was the equivalent of an artistic sponge, and had to look at something only once to make it his own. 'Everything he learned about art, he learned from me,' the Florentine said famously, crossly and somewhat inaccurately of his rival from Urbino. And a sneak visit by Raphael into the Sistine did indeed inform the work he was doing for Julius in his Vatican apartments, especially the fresco of *The School of Athens*, in which he depicts Michelangelo in a humorous tribute as Heraclitus, the brooding, melancholic genius, leaning on a block of marble. Michelangelo could not keep out the Pope, his patron, and whatever visitors he might bring with him, including a pope's daughter, accompanying her father to what was in many ways their family chapel, to view the progress on the miraculous ceiling.

In the 1530s, Michelangelo complemented the ceiling frescos with a depiction of the *Last Judgment* on the altar wall. A span of over twenty years separates these two commissions. Julius II is the patron of the ceiling; Popes Clement VII and Paul III are the commissioners of the *Last Judgment*, painted by Michelangelo between 1534 and 1541. Many see the darkness of the *Last Judgment* as a kind of pictorial *Zeitgeist*, reflecting the horrors of the Sack of Rome that was to come in 1527, and political and spiritual uncertainty.[1] In other words, the altar wall is viewed as an entirely separate entity from the glories of creation celebrated on the ceiling.

Consequently, it seems surprising to learn that Pope Julius himself envisaged a chapel replete not only with a frescoed ceiling but with altar and exit wall decorated with themes selected by his successors. The death of Julius prevented this work from going any further, but not before, it seems, Michelangelo had made preparatory drawings, cartoons, for the Chapel's exit walls depicting the *Fall of Lucifer and the Rebel Angels*.[2] What Julius had imagined was a chapel that encapsulated and thus became the entire world, recording its beginning and foretelling its end.

Michelangelo had a complex relationship with the della Rovere family. His relationship with Julius was so volatile that it seems extraordinary he produced as much as he did for this patron. After Julius's death, he found himself constrained by the pressure exerted by the Pope's official heirs to finish his tomb. Although he had accepted payment, it was by no means easy for him to finish the task. Julius's successor, Leo X, had sent him back to Florence to work for his family there, and he was at work on designs for the Medici church of San Lorenzo. But the Florentine artist felt an obligation to Julius's heirs, or at any rate to Felice. As interim compensation, he endowed her with the relics of the most extraordinary pictorial project of her father's time as pope, the cartoons that remained from his work on the Sistine Chapel.

This gesture by Michelangelo, arguably the most supremely arrogant figure of the Renaissance, who cared very little for the feelings and opinions of others, shows he did hold Felice in some esteem. Michelangelo sought to maintain tight control over everything he produced. He destroyed hundreds of drawings he felt might blemish his reputation for posterity. He was also notoriously mean. A miser, who wore clothes and boots until they were no more than rags, he pleaded abject poverty when in reality he owned the hills of Settignano where he was nursed as a baby, and had substantial bank deposits in Florence and Rome. So for him to turn over his drawings to Felice meant there was something about her that appealed to him. Michelangelo had a fondness for women of intellectual ability. He would later have a regular correspondence with the Marchesa of Pescara, Vittoria Colonna. Felice's own reputation for wisdom made her a living relative of the powerful sibyls, the giantesses Michelangelo had painted for her father in the Sistine Chapel. Michelangelo cultivated a reputation as an outsider. Felice was by the nature of her birth an outsider but she had come to acquire a position and cultivate a personality of her own. These were certainly qualities Michelangelo admired. As were Colocci and others, Michelangelo was saddened by the death of the Warrior Pope, and he saw Felice as a memento of his golden age. These were all good reasons to give her the drawings made for the Sistine Chapel, the work of her father and great-uncle.

The history of what Felice did with these cartoons is somewhat fragmentary but compelling none the less. In 1517, Fra Mariano da Firenze produced a guidebook to the sights of Rome, both old and new. 'At the beautiful church of Trinità dei Monti', he wrote, 'is a chapel belonging to Gian Giordano Orsini with work by Michelangelo, prince of painters.'[3] In 1568, in his second edition of the *Lives of the Artists*, Giorgio Vasari, describing the *Last Judgment* that Michelangelo painted in the Sistine Chapel, writes, 'It has been found that many years before Michelangelo made various sketches and designs [of the *Fall of the Rebel Angels*], one of which was made into a work in the church of the Trinity in Rome by a Sicilian painter who had served Michelangelo for many months as a colour-grinder.'[4]

Vasari was dismissive of the Sicilian's execution of the fresco, but he notes that the work conveys 'a power and variety in the attitude and grouping of these naked figures raining from the sky and falling to the centre of the earth, counter-posing with the different forms of the devils who are most frightful and bizarre. It is certainly a capricious fantasy.'

It seems significant that it was a member of Michelangelo's workshop who carried out the actual painting, a condition possibly laid down by Michelangelo himself, who was notoriously secretive. He had loathed other painters being shown his work in progress on the Sistine Chapel – and was doubtless fearful lest any of his rivals get their hands on his master drawings.

Sadly, this chapel was destroyed in the late seventeenth century. However, a record of its frescos remains in what is probably a drawing made of them by the Florentine painter Bronzino, an associate of Vasari, depicting the *Fall of the Rebel Angels*. Its dramatically tumbling figures and naked forms are heavily Michelangesque in tone.[5] Peter Paul Rubens, an inveterate copier and adapter of Italian pictorial design, might also have stopped by Trinità dei Monti and the image that he saw there found its way into a

Last Judgment he painted, albeit one populated by predictably lush-looking, naked women. Even if Vasari found the quality of the chapel's fresco lacking, both Bronzino and Rubens, major artists of their day, found the chapel worthy of study and note. Any association with Michelangelo was always a major draw for artists wanting to hone their craft.

That Fra Mariano described the chapel as belonging to Gian Giordano Orsini might lead one to think that at the most Felice acted only as an intermediary between Michelangelo and her husband in his acquisition of the cartoons. Fra Mariano's error was not uncommon; there are several chapels in Rome that belonged to and were paid for by women that are later recorded as belonging to their husbands. But a will Felice was to write in 1518 makes it clear that the chapel was hers. The will specifies that she left 1000 ducats 'for the adornment of her chapel in the church on the Monte Pincio, which shall be used to fabricate a sepulchre and to repair the altar cloth'.[6] A thousand ducats, even minus the cost of the altar cloth, was a splendid sum, but would not have bought Felice a tomb fashioned by the hands of Michelangelo himself. However, as with the walls of the chapel, it might have purchased a design from him to be executed by another, and that might have been Felice's plan for the completion of her chapel.

Michelangelo's frescos, acquired and transferred into what she intended to be her burial chapel, formed the centrepiece of an entirely Felicitious space. Felice did not choose Trinità dei Monti as the site of her chapel accidentally. The church, replete with della Rovere family associations, was as Roverian as the Sistine Chapel. The religious order at the church was the Minims, a branch of the Franciscans, the order to which her father and her uncle Sixtus had belonged. Their founder was Francesco di Paola, a southern Italian credited with the ability to perform miracles, including healing the sick. This particular talent led the cunning Sixtus to send him to France, ostensibly to serve as healer to the superstitious and hypochondriac King Louis XI, but actually to work as a spy for the papal court. His mission undetected, Francesco di Paola became enormously popular at the French court, as spiritual adviser to Louis and later to Anne of Brittany and several French princesses.[7]

In part as reward for Francesco di Paola's excellent political service, Julius gave his order strong support. In 1506, a year before the friar's death, Julius issued a bull establishing the Minims as an order in their own right. In 1512, he began the canonization process for Francesco; it was completed by Leo X in 1519.[8] Julius also raised a significant sum of money to contribute towards the building of a church for the order, and granted indulgences for attending Mass on feast days, thereby ensuring a larger congregation than the infant order might otherwise attract. Over the course of the sixteenth century, Trinità dei Monti came to have a special appeal for the Roman elite.[9] Francesco di Paola created a branch of the 'Third Order', a spiritual group for aristocratic men and women. Significantly, the original Third Order had been created by St Francis and Jacopa dei Normanni, an ancestor of Felice. If she was a *terziara* (tertiary), Felice was not a very active member. She did not make a public show of her own spirituality. She preferred to have Mass said privately and travelled with portable altar apparatus to avoid having to attend public Mass. None the less, she did maintain ties with the Third Order, as their general came to see her towards the end of her life to ask for her help in freeing two friars imprisoned in Castel Sant' Angelo.

Felice found the Minims and their church appealing because of their association with her family. That still does not explain why she would not erect her chapel in another della Rovere church, such as Santa Maria del Popolo, or in her father's titular church of San Pietro in Vincoli. The real reason why she invested the Michelangelo part of her Julian legacy at Trinità dei Monti is that the surrounding space offered her exceptional opportunity for personal self-expression within the city of Rome.

Trinità dei Monti is situated on the Pincian Hill, at the very top of what are today the Spanish Steps. In Felice's time the church was surrounded by *vigne*, literally vineyards, though that did not mean that the land was solely used for growing grapes. Over the course of the sixteenth and seventeenth centuries, villas, such as those of the Medici (today the Académie Française) and the Ludovisi families began to dot the Pincio. The hill offered a marvellous combination of bucolic environment and splendid panoramas of Rome, with easy access to the city below. Felice della Rovere was, however, the first Renaissance figure to take advantage of the Pincio's attractions.

Significantly, it was Gian Giordano's family who owned the *vigna* behind and to the right of the Trinità church, which was situated on Orsini land. Gian Giordano had his own sympathies with the Minims, given that Francesco di Paola was so entrenched at the French court. Also located on the Orsini *vigna* was a small church. Disused and partly in ruins, it did none the less have its *campanile*, its bell tower, intact, and it became the basis for the foundation of a palace. Known later as the Villa Malta, it was to become the site where German scholars and artists, such as Johannes Winckelmann and Angelika Kauffman, gathered.[10]

Two thousand ducats of Felice's money, another part of her Julian inheritance, went towards renovating and converting the property. The investment was sufficiently large a sum for Felice to claim it as hers in the years to come, separate from the Orsini estate. For her, the establishment of such a residence had particular resonance. The abandoned church had been a popular pilgrimage site in the Middle Ages. It had been dedicated to a martyred pope, San Felice. The *chiesa* of San Felice became the *palazzo* of Madonna Felice.

This land not only had personal meaning for Felice; it carried an ancient pedigree as well, as the site of the famed ancient gardens of the late Republican Lucullus, who had famously planted exotic Asian flora. Methelusa, wife of the Emperor Claudius, was so enchanted by Lucullus' gardens that she plotted to have him put to death in order to claim them as her own. Rather than be tortured and executed, Lucullus committed suicide. Methelusa also met her own end in the gardens she had so coveted.

It can easily be imagined how such a history contributed to the prestige of the site that Felice developed. She had a palace built out of the structure of a famed pilgrimage site, adjacent to a church containing her chapel, decorated with designs by Michelangelo. She also developed the land, landscaping a garden as an area separate from the *vigna*. In many ways, the Mons Pincius became Felice's own Mons Vaticanus: a combination of pastoral landscape and palatial residence with a palatine church in the shape of Trinità dei Monti.

Money, poems and party invitations; cartoons by Michelangelo. For a woman whose relationship with her father had been so ambivalent, Felice had profited by being the daughter of the former Cardinal Giuliano. Undoubtedly, in her own way, Felice mourned her father's death. Julius had not always been very kind to her. He had not exactly nourished her filial affection towards him. He had not always given her the things that

1 Felice's father, Pope Julius II, celebrating Mass with his male relatives looking on behind him.
2 In this detail, Felice (in black) looks at him lovingly, though his gaze is elsewhere.

3 As a cardinal, Felice's father bends to his uncle Pope Sixtus IV. Also included are the pope's librarian (kneeling), Felice's uncle Giovanni, and cousins Girolamo and Raffaello Riario.

4 Felice's stepfather, Bernardino de Cupis. An early patron of Roman High Renaissance art and architecture, he taught Felice the importance of bureaucrats in the life of Rome.

5 Enemies and rivals to Felice and her father: Lucrezia Borgia (with her famous long blonde hair) and her father, Pope Alexander VI (enthroned).
6 The palace in Savona where Felice grew to adulthood. It was built by her father during their period of exile from Rome.

7 & 8 Two faces of Julius II, *Il papa terribile*: the foundation medal for New Saint Peter's by Caradosso, 1506, and Raphael's renowned 1512 portrait.

9 Castiglione, author of the best-selling *Courtier*, was the exponent of perfect courtly behaviour as well as a friend to Felice, who features in his book.
10 Machiavelli's astute political advice was useful to aspiring princesses, as well as princes.

1 & 12 The sickly Guidobaldo disapproved of Felice's headstrong ways, while his wife Elizabetta's cultivated court at Urbino was the setting for Castiglione's *Courtier*.

13 & 14 Two faces of Isabella d'Este, sometime friend and co-conspirator with Felice. As a fifty-year-old, she discarded Titian's portrait (now only known through this copy) in favour of the second version depicting her as a teenager.

15 Palazzo Sforza Cesarini, the site of Felice's wedding to Gian Giordano Orsini.
16 Marcello Foglino, *Dinner Scene*, circa 1520: a rare depiction of the dining habits of the elite of Renaissance Italy, giving a good impression of the kinds of banquets Felice attended.

17 & 18 Felice's first glimpse of life at the rural Orsini castle of Bracciano: the castle from a distance, and Antoniazzo Romano's frescos commemorating the life of her late father-in-law, Gentile Virginio Orsini.

she wanted and indeed earned. Yet Felice could say with pride that she was her father's daughter: she had many of his qualities and she knew how to put them to good use. When her father died, this thirty-year-old woman might have remembered herself at twenty, the age she had been when Julius had ascended the papal throne. A great deal had happened to her in that decade. She now had position, authority, respect and influence, not to mention a castle, and a palace of her very own.

Best of all, Felice did not have to feel any trepidation on her father's death, as she had when he became pope. Now that there was a new pope from Florence, with acolytes of his own, there were many clerics in the Julian inner circle whose influence would start to wane. But Felice's own power and prestige would not diminish. In May 1512, after several child-less years, she had at last given birth to a son, an heir for Gian Giordano. By the time of her father's death, 'Madonna Felice, the daughter of the Pope' knew another role lay ahead of her. That Felix Ruveris Ursinis might one day become *gubernatrix* of the Orsini of Bracciano was now a distinct possibility.

PART IV
Patrona et Gubernatrix

CHAPTER 1

A Trip to Loreto

On 3 October 1511, Bernardo Dovizi da Bibbiena, the Medici secretary at the Vatican, informed Cardinal Giulio de' Medici, the future Clement VII, in his daily report to Florence that 'Signor Gian Giordano and Madonna Felice have recently returned from Loreto'.[1] He did not specify the purpose of their visit, but everyone knew that Loreto was a pilgrimage location. Loreto, set on a hilltop in the eastern province of the Marche under the jurisdiction of the nearby town of Recanati, was the site of the Casa Santa, the 'holy house' where, according to legend, the Virgin Mary had lived as a girl, and in which she had conceived the Christ Child. Of course, the little stone house had originally stood in Nazareth, but the story went that it had been flown to Italy on the wings of angels to save it from the infidels. In reality, in 1291, during the crusades, knights had brought back with them a dwelling they believed to be Mary's Nazareth home from the Holy Land, transporting its stones to Dalmatia. Later it arrived by ship across the Adriatic to the port of Ancona, fifteen kilometres east of Loreto.[2]

Felice's family had a particular connection with the Casa Santa and its surroundings. Her cousin Girolamo Basso della Rovere, who had been served by her stepfather, Bernardino de Cupis, as *maestro di casa*, had been the absentee Bishop of Recanati and Loreto. He had sent Bernardino as his representative to attend to administrative matters in the two towns. The

'Motherhood', from Christofano Bertelli, *The Ages of Woman*, 1580s

maestro di casa had become popular in his master's diocese and in 1488 the people of Recanati promised that on the birth of his first son they would send a delegate to Bernardino's home in Rome to serve as 'godfather in the name of the community'[3] to stand at the baptism and present Bernardino's wife, Lucrezia, with a gift of 25 ducats.

In 1507, Julius, who had a special devotion to the Virgin, became the first pope to sanction Loreto as an official site of pilgrimage, and exploited Bernardino's ties with the area to promote Loreto. Among the commissions Julius gave Bramante was the design of a protective enclosure for Mary's house: four walls of white marble further embellished with sculptural work by the Venetian artist Andrea Sansovino. Julius's endorsement of Loreto launched its popularity. The Casa Santa's reputation grew as a place where prayers were answered and miraculous cures for any kind of bodily ailment achieved. Deep grooves are now worn into the step around the base of the Casa Santa, the effect of five hundred years' worth of pilgrims on their knees in prayer circling it.

Apart from her family connection, Felice had a very personal reason for visiting Loreto that October. She had recently discovered that she was pregnant and needed to do all she could to ensure the arrival of a boy. Time was not on her side. Popular thinking in the Renaissance was that boys were more likely to be fathered by young men with warm sperm and that it was best for the mother to be young as well. Gian Giordano was now over sixty and Felice was approaching thirty. She did, however, have recourse to the rituals, superstitions and talismans associated with the creation of a male child, which in sixteenth-century Italy was an industry in itself. Tin-glazed earthenware and maiolica bowls and trays emblazoned with the word *maschio* ('male') or decorated with strong blond little boys were especially popular. Their use by a woman during her confinement was believed to encourage the growth and safe delivery of a healthy male child. Given the belief that boys grew from all things warm, a woman was instructed to eat warm food, drink warm wine, and avoid cold things, including fruit and fish, as coldness was associated with the female nature.[4]

Felice's mother, Lucrezia, knew the difficulties of producing a son, as nine years separated Felice from her younger brother, Gian Domenico. Bernardino and the community of Recanati might have said prayers and made offerings on Lucrezia's behalf at the Casa Santa, and the De Cupis would have believed that this would have contributed to the arrival of Gian Domenico in 1492. With her own success in mind, Lucrezia might have counselled her daughter to visit Loreto, pray to the Virgin and ask her to make sure that Felice was indeed carrying a boy. The Virgin Mary, after all, had miraculously conceived a son within those very stone walls, which had been borne on the wings of angels to Italy. Later in the sixteenth century, Loreto became popular as a pilgrimage site with women from the Medici family who were equally anxious for a son. Giovanna d'Austria, the wife of Duke Francesco, endowed money, paintings and wall hangings to the church at Loreto. When she gave birth to Filippo, a special Mass was sung at the church to celebrate his arrival.

It was perhaps Felice herself who established the fashion among elite women for visiting Loreto for this specific purpose, because her own prayers were indeed answered. On 17 May 1512, 'Signor Francesco was born . . . one hour before dawn.'[5]

CHAPTER 2

Childbirth and its Aftermath

Felice gave birth at Bracciano, where she had stayed for the previous month. Labour was a perilous event that could easily claim a woman's life, as it would that of Felice's counterpart, Lucrezia Borgia, in 1519. The parturient woman had recourse to prayers to Margaret, the patron saint of painless delivery. Other talismanic tricks to prevent a miscarriage included carrying diamonds – Felice had an abundance in her possession – or an aquiline stone, a mineral whose hollow core containing small loose pieces resembles a womb containing a child. She could also place a coriander seed beneath her during labour to ensure a fast delivery.[1]

After the birth of her baby, the time Felice could spend with her son was almost non-existent. She was not present at his baptism because custom dictated the christening had to take place almost immediately after a child's birth, while the mother was still confined to her bed. If a child died before officially entering the Christian church, his soul could enter only into limbo, not into the kingdom of heaven. The future of a newborn of this time was so uncertain that immediate baptism was an imperative.

The birth of Francesco is recorded in Felice's account book. An account book seems a strange place to record the birth of a son and heir, but an explanation for the entry is provided by the subsequent record, for 20 May: 'Hieronyma, wet nurse (*balia*) of Bracciano, began her service. We

Valerio Spada, *Woman Feeding a Baby*, c.1620

have Catherina as wet nurse number two.' Catherine was a reserve in case of problems arising with Hieronyma's milk. The employment of the wet nurses needed to be accounted for in order to justify the expenditure in this list of receipts. The wet nurse did not stay with Felice. Instead, she took the newborn Francesco away from Bracciano. Only a few days after the child's birth, Felice's account book notes, 'The Signora gave funds to the husband of Hieronyma, the *balia*, for their journey from Bracciano to Vicovaro.' Felice, anxious that her newborn child should have the best start in life, had undoubtedly carefully vetted the candidates who would nurse her son. Qualities in the *balia* that she would have looked for would be the recommended age of between thirty-two and thirty-five, as the milk of younger women was believed to be weak; strength, and good-sized breasts, which should be not too large and, of course, have no sores on the nipples. Ideally, the *balia* should have given birth to a boy, as her milk would thus be stronger, and its consistency would have been checked to make sure it was pure and white.[2]

Hieronyma and her husband took Francesco with them to Vicovaro, the other main Orsini estate. The castle of Vicovaro, located to the south of Rome, had been in Orsini possession ever since Celestine III granted it to his nephew Orso. It was quite remote, the surrounding terrain more mountainous and inaccessible than that surrounding Bracciano. Traditionally, children from the Bracciano Orsini clan spent their early years in this isolated rural setting where plague was less of a threat. Plague was the disease every parent feared, and the reason why the children of the elite often lived so far from an urban parental home, with its attendant danger of disease.

Until the Orsini children were a little older, Vicovaro was the only world they knew. They were looked after by their *balia*, who, even after the children were too old to be breastfed, would stay on to take care of them. In 1520, when Francesco was eight years old, his *balia* was still on the Orsini payroll. They also learned to ride and, when they were a little older, they would have a tutor for academic lessons. Felice made regular visits to Vicovaro, and spent a few months of every year there with the children, but it was never her primary residence. After giving birth to Francesco, she spent a month at Bracciano, observing the traditional postpartum period of confinement. By 17 June she had returned to Rome and was busy petitioning her father to let her betroth her daughter Julia to Alfonso d'Este's son.

One effect of having another woman nurse her child was that Felice was fertile again almost immediately. Four years had passed between the birth of her last child and the birth of Francesco. However, five months after Francesco's birth, she was pregnant again, and on 7 July, 1513, 'Signor Girolamo was born on Friday, at half-past eight.' Despite her long-distance parenting, the children seemed to be Felice's responsibility rather than their father's. She authorized the *balia's* salary and included her among her personal staff. It was Felice who named her children and the names she gave them were associated with della Rovere men. Her daughter, Julia, was called after her own father, while Francesco was given the original name of Felice's great-uncle, Pope Sixtus IV. The name also recalled the then pre-canonization Francesco di Paola, the founder of the Minims at Trinità dei Monti, with whom Felice was very familiar. Francesco was believed to help pregnant women give birth to healthy sons; Louisa of Savoy, who had prayed with Francesco di Paola, named her son, the future Francis I of France, after him. Felice's account book records that after the birth of her son she paid for a Mass served in the Blessed Francesco's honour. Girolamo acquired his name from the della Rovere cardinal for whom her stepfather had worked when Felice was a little girl.

About a year after Girolamo's birth came Felice's fourth and final child, a girl she named Clarice. The choice of the names for all her children is significant. None of the names of her first three children had any connection with the Orsini family; they were named after her father, great-uncle and cousin. The only one to bear an Orsini name was the last and Felice did not name her to please the immediate Orsini family. Clarice was named after Clarice Orsini, the mother of Cardinal Giovanni de' Medici. Cardinal Giovanni was Julius's successor as pope in 1513, taking the name of Leo X. In the aftermath of her father's death, Felice busied herself courting Leo's favour, knowing his protection and promotion would be yet another weapon in her personal arsenal. Naming her daughter after his mother was one component in Felice's courtship of the new pope.

CHAPTER 3

The Pope' s Daughter Becomes the Pope's Friend

Giovanni de' Medici was born in 1475, the son of Lorenzo the Magnificent and Clarice Orsini. He was the Medici family's first cardinal, elected in 1488 at the age of thirteen, after his father had placed unrelenting pressure on Pope Innocent VIII. Julius had favoured him, recognizing his useful connections to the Florentine banking families as well as to France, and had placed him in several important positions, including that of papal legate to Bologna. Good natured and unfailingly cheerful, Giovanni de' Medici was popular with his fellow clerics. His election as pope at the conclave following Julius's death was approved by the great majority of cardinals. The new Leonine pope was only thirty-eight, exceptionally young for a pontiff, and he was expected to have a lengthy reign.

Leo was completely different in character from his predecessor. Neither irascible nor bellicose, he was instead a corpulent sybarite and hedonist with, among other ailments, severe gout. His sexual proclivities meant he did not fill the Vatican with female prostitutes as Alexander VI had done but there were still lavish entertainments populated by freaks and fools. He also collected an increasingly exotic menagerie of animals, including Hanno the elephant, who became a favourite at the papal court. Leo did not ascend the papal throne with the same vision of a new Rome as Julius. Leo was a Medici, and Florence, not Rome, was his city and it had

Maarten van Heemskerck, detail of steps up to Church of Aracoeli first call on his allegiance. None the less, as a Medici, he brought an exceptionally cultivated and courtly background with him. His first love was not theology but the arts, particularly literature and music, and he did not hesitate to continue Julius's schemes to build New St Peter's. Leo's obsession with Raphael, both on artistic grounds and on an unreciprocated personal level, was such that the artist and his workshop became even more firmly entrenched at the Vatican. When Bramante died in 1514, it was Raphael whom Leo appointed as the new architect of St Peter's, despite the painter's lack of architectural experience and much to the disgust of Michelangelo, who had hoped the position would be his.

Leo, as Cardinal Giovanni, had been present at Felice's wedding to Gian Giordano, earning a frown from Paris de Grassis for wearing a purple hat instead of the standard red one. His position at Julius's court had strengthened his bond with Felice. She had written to him early in her marriage, reminding him of the love they bore each other as she solicited his support for Gian Giordano's uncle Bartolomeo. Leo did have some attachment to the Orsini family. He had loaned Gian Giordano money to help him repair Monte Giordano, and he made Gian Giordano's son-in-law, the *condottiere* Renzo da Ceri, captain of the papal army. But he appeared to regard Felice as a separate entity from the family into which she had married. He shared the attitude of the curia and the humanists towards Felice, that she was Julius's living legacy, and as such was to be revered and admired. More to the point, she was an economic force in her own right, a businesswoman with whom it was in Leo's interests to be on good terms.

On 29 July 1515, the Florentine ambassador to Rome, Balar di Piscia, wrote to Leo's nephew Lorenzo de' Medici back in Florence, 'His Holiness is sending me to Vicovaro to Madonna Felice, to discuss a purchase of 6000 to 8000 *rubbios* of grain to be sent back here to Rome. He understands that is what she has.' The implication was that Felice was selling a large portion of her grain reserves to the Pope.[1] Felice even loaned money to Leo's family, advancing 2000 ducats to his brother Giuliano, Duke of Nemours.

For Leo, a woman granting him favours rather than expecting or demanding something of him was an anomaly. The Florentine Bartolomeo Cerretani commented on the nature of the women in Leo's life at court:

'There were his three sisters with their children there, and his sister-in-law, that is the mother of Lorenzo, and all were waiting to ask for and to procure the incomes from benefices and cardinals' hats.[2] Cerretani concluded it was demands such as these that reduced Leo's papacy from wealth to poverty. There was a fierce rivalry between these women as they vied for the Pope's affection and generosity. They became unpopular at the Roman court in a way that Felice never was. The worst of them, indisputably, was the greedy and grasping Alfonsina Orsini, Duke Lorenzo's mother. Although she was Gian Giordano's cousin, she and Felice always kept their distance.

Felice drew attention to the difference between herself and the women of the new papal *famigilia* by extending further favours to Leo. What pleased the pope the most was helping him to indulge in the pastime he loved most of all – the hunt.

CHAPTER 4

The Pope Goes Hunting

Leo had spent some of his youth in France, where he had developed a taste for the chase, the pre-eminent courtly activity of the north. The hunt was rarely limited to a single day, with just a few horses and dogs. Instead, a litany of servants, *cacciatori* and *falconieri* was employed, and the event could extend over several days, complete with lavish banquets and overnight stays at the hunting lodge.

The chief papal hunting lodge, which had been in use since the later fifteenth century, lay just to the west of Rome and was known as La Magliana. The wooded and hilly area contained a plethora of wildlife, including hares and wild boar. Girolamo Riario, nephew of Sixtus IV, and his wife Caterina Sforza used it, and in 1480 had organized a great wild-boar hunt in honour of the Dukes of Saxony. On his election in 1484, Pope Innocent VIII had created a *palazetto* (little palace) at the Magliana, embossed with his coat of arms, which is still visible today. He too organized hunts that doubled as diplomatic receptions, including a deer hunt for the Duke of Ferrara.

Julius II's favourite forms of relaxation involved water. He loved watching boats and he enjoyed fishing, activities in keeping with his upbringing by the sea. But he liked hunting too, recognizing its diplomatic importance, and he was committed to further development at the Magliana. The villa

Hunting Scene, Brescia, mid-sixteenth century

was on the Tiber, not far from Julius's old titular land as a former bishop of Ostia. Julius built a road from the villa to the river, allowing easy access by barge, and he hired Giuliano da Sangallo, the architect of his palace at Savona, to enlarge substantially Innocent's *palazetto*.

When he became pope, Leo was thrilled to find that he had access to a large compound comprising palace, chapel, stables and weapons arsenal, which would allow him to indulge his great passion. His huntsmen would assemble as a rowdy group in Rome prior to leaving for the countryside, and march along to a chant of 'I love hunting! I love hunting!' Leo did not enlarge the Magliana hunting lodge to any great extent but he did employ Raphael's workshop to paint frescos in the little chapel, which was dedicated to Saint John the Baptist, as well as grotesque figures and images of the Muses on the walls of the great hall of the palace itself. For Leo, La Magliana became more than just a hunting lodge, it was another papal palace, to which poets, artists and scholars would be invited to provide entertainment after the thrill of the day's chase. Most of the animals he hunted were local to La Magliana, but on occasion more exotic animals, including an elderly and infirm leopard, were imported to serve as the Pope's quarry.[1]

There were never enough wild animals at La Magliana for Leo. He even had another member of the Sangallo family, Gian Francesco, construct a *gazzara*, a little compound, to rear hawks and falcons as well as prey, deer and boar, which would later be released in order to be hunted down. Leo's voracious appetite for the hunt also compelled him to seek more extensive terrain. It was Felice who was able to assist him in his quest. She was encouraged to do so by her old business associate, her corn-broker, Giuliano Leno.

With the ascension of Leo to the papal throne, Leno had risen in power and influence, to the extent where he could justifiably be called 'the most notable capitalist of the Roman building industry'.[2] He had been appointed by Leo X as *curatore* of all the building work on New St Peter's, serving as contractor with Raphael as architect. Leno also had his own private interests, such as cloth-manufacturing in workshops on the Via delle Bottege Oscure, where he employed Jews from the nearby ghetto. His monopolies made him intensely unpopular: 'Giuliano Leno is a spy,' ran a satirical verse pinned to the ancient *Pasquino* statue, the site for poetical protest, not far from Felice's home. 'He looks to everyone for evil gain. He is a beast who has no fear.'[3]

One of the reasons for Leno's unpopularity was his substantial monopoly and speculation on grain, which drove up the price of the valued commodity in the city of Rome. Leno continued to do well from his access to Felice's ample supply of grain from Palo, but he came to realize that her estate presented further opportunities for profit for them both. Another of the tasks assigned him by Leo was to supervise the work done on La Magliana. Leno knew Leo's love of the chase as well as the danger of the livestock at La Magliana being over-hunted. He also knew that, in addition to several acres of fields, a dense forest was attached to the castle of Palo. If the papacy, and Leno himself, could profit from Palo's fields of wheat, then why not from its trees and thickets?

The idea of adding a new forest to his hunting grounds delighted Leo. The only disadvantage was the condition of the castle itself. Leo was accustomed to luxurious accommodation in which to rest, eat and drink at the end of the day's activity. The thirteenth-century castle was in a state of some disrepair. While Felice had probably intended to renovate Palo herself, she currently had no pressing reason to spend time there and thus no pressing need to invest funds in its repair. When in the country, she resided at either Bracciano or Vicovaro. But Palo's shabby state posed no problem for Leo, who was more than happy to spend money in pursuit of his own pleasure. They negotiated an accord for Palo to become a papal villa; Leo would pay for the castle's renovations in exchange for free rent. The arrangement would not affect Felice's profit from Palo's grain yield.

Leo put Leno in charge of creating a hunting lodge fit for a pope. Partly to keep costs down, Leno did not hire an established architect to work on Palo, in the way that Julius II had commissioned Giuliano da Sangallo to design the additions to La Magliana. Leno worked with another member of the ubiquitous Sangallo family, Gian Francesco, but Gian Francesco was *misuratore* – a head foreman – rather than an architect. They had no plans to undertake a radical modernization of Palo. Preserving an original, medieval appearance was Medicean design policy for country retreats. In the city of Florence itself, the Medici had built a family palace on the Via Larga, employing the architect Michelozzo to use the latest cutting-edge architectural language. By contrast, their country villas and lodges were designed to appear as if they had stood for hundreds of years. This 'antiqued' or 'distressed' appearance gave the impression the Medici were a family of established ancient feudal lords rather than of fifteenth-century mercantile arrivistes.

Leo himself would have had no great interest in seeing Palo made fashionably *all'antica*, like the ultra-modern palaces in Rome. He did, however, inspect progress on the renovation. In a letter to Felice her servant Statio del Fara reported that 'I learned that His Holiness leaves today for La Magliana and they say that he will go to see the work being done at Palo.'[4] Palo benefited from Leno's easy access to building supplies; the same materials were going into the construction of St Peter's. Leno's vast notarial archive contains such details as the shipment in July 1519 of 20,000 bricks to Palo. By September 1520 Giuliano Leno had hired 'master builders' Pietro Pasqualino of Treviso and Bucchino di Caravaggio for plaster work on the courtyard, and bricks to complete the vaulting, the windowsills and passageways.[5]

Given the plentiful array of projects Leno was supervising at the time, the work at Palo proceeded remarkably quickly, perhaps because he had a vested interest in the castle's appearance. Leno had a personal motivation for not wanting an established architectural figure to be involved with the Palo renovations. Although he was a hugely powerful figure in Rome, he was still only a contractor. His associates might have been artists or noble and elite clerics, but he did not have an equivalent status. If poems were composed about him, they were satirical in spirit. And Leno apparently desired the kinds of panegyrics written in praise of those he served, such as Leo, or Felice herself. He contrived to have himself immortalized as the architect of Palo in Latin verse, in a poem that was actually written in praise of Felice by the scholar Paolo Nomentano. Nomentano had composed verses in praise of Felice a few years earlier, along with poems to her eldest daughter Julia and stepdaughter Carlotta. In the earlier poem, Nomentano had extolled Felice's maternal virtues: 'Such a mother you are,' he wrote, 'the best and the greatest.' His later poem was about Felice, Leo, Leno and Palo: 'Our Palo, that is so lush, with its woods, and the sea, and the earth. What it is to live in such a place. How pleasing is this place. And equally so the building that is a great felicitous palace, and you have made a house for Leo with Giuliano Leno. And so they come to your castle where they can hunt stags and deer . . . '[6]

Nomentano's verses are seemingly the only instance of a poem from this time dedicated to a woman's ownership of a palace, revealing how unusual Felice's possession of Palo was. For a pope to borrow her residence made the situation all the more special. And Leno's place in her poem, as the creator of a house fit for a pope, provided him with one of very few opportunities in his life to have an equality with the cultural elite he served.

CHAPTER 5

Papal Payback

Felice received some very special rewards for assisting Leo. On 21 October 1516, Leo issued a remarkable licence on Felice's behalf, a proclamation that were she ever to commit 'any grave or serious crime', she was to be absolved.[1] The document was designed to prove Leo's protection and support of Felice, whatever the circumstances. It had considerable importance for her future life.

Leo had an even greater gift for Felice. He might have ascended the papal throne a well-liked cardinal but few popes stayed universally popular for long. Julius II, as Cardinal Giuliano, had tried to engineer the downfall of Alexander VI, and then saw, in his turn, Spanish cardinals forming the Counsel of Pisa call for his own abdication. As for Leo, in 1517 Cardinal Alfonso Petrucci of Siena actually attempted to poison him. His motivation was that the previous year Leo had expelled his brother Borghese, head of the Sienese *signoria*, from his home town. Leo planned to place the Tuscan town, an old rival to Florence, under Medici rule. The assassination plot – a surgeon was to place a poisoned ointment on a fistula on the pope's notoriously diseased anus – was discovered. On 8 June Leo assembled the Vatican cardinals and demanded to know who among them had been involved. In all, four other cardinals admitted either complicity in or knowledge of the plot.

Enea Vico, *Industry*, 1540

None of the cardinals was condemned to death, although Petrucci was strangled in prison, and his chief conspirator, Cardinal Sauli, also died in prison a year later. Leo's response to the assassination plot was to dilute the power of the members of the College of Cardinals by adding to their number. He appointed a total of thirty-one new cardinals, whose gratitude would assure their loyalty to him. They included members of his own family: his nephews Niccolò Ridolfi, Giovanni Salviati and Luigi Rossi, who appears in Raphael's portrait of Leo alongside his cousin Giulio de' Medici, who had been appointed a cardinal by Leo at the start of his reign. Other Tuscan appointees included Giovanni Piccolomini of Siena and the Florentine Niccolò Pandolfini. From Rome, Leo chose Pompeo Colonna, Franciotto Orsini, Paolo Emilio Cesi, Andrea della Valle and Francesco Armellini.

Added to this list of Romans was Felice's half-brother, Gian Domenico de Cupis. As his titular diocese, the twenty-four-year-old received the southern town of Trani. Just as his father's master, Girolamo della Rovere, rarely visited Recanati, sending Bernardino in his place, Gian Domenico rarely, if ever, set foot in Trani.

Although Julius had made Gian Domenico de Cupis a canon of St Peter's and a papal secretary, he had refused, despite his daughter's entreaties, to give him a red hat. He called him 'an ignorant young boy' and claimed his appointment would displease the other cardinals. But what Julius would not do for a daughter, Leo would do for a friend. There was nothing obvious for Leo to gain from selecting Gian Domenico as a cardinal. The de Cupis were talented bureaucrats but they did not constitute a powerful Roman family. Leo made the appointment as a favour to Felice, a recognition of what she had done for him. It was, none the less, an exceptional favour to bestow on a woman, particularly one who was not even a Medici family member. Felice's brother's appointment undoubtedly incited the envy and resentment of Leo's female relatives, who felt that they should be the only women in Leo's circle to have their sons and brothers made cardinals.

CHAPTER 6

Orsini Signora Revisited

Although Felice continued to be closely involved in events taking place at the Vatican Palace, both before and after her father's death, she also began to take on a much more active role as the Orsini Signora. Tending to the Palo estate and negotiating the sale of its grain had provided her with valuable administrative experience and proved her capable of managing the Orsini properties. Gian Giordano placed increasing amounts of trust in her, increasingly so after the birth of Francesco, for now Felice had a vested interest and legal right in the Orsini estates.

The Orsini estate account books indicate that with this responsibility came direct access for Felice to Orsini family funds. One for the years 1509–10 is clearly produced on behalf of Gian Giordano, as Orsini Lord. The next one, which records expenses between 1510 and 1514, is inscribed, 'This book contains all the money spent on behalf of Her Illustrious Ladyship, Felice della Rovere Orsini.'[1]

Some of these entries record Felice's personal expenditure. She liked to purchase brightly coloured accessories, so such items as a purchase of a 'hat for the Signora in blue silk' at 3.15 ducats are noted. Giovanni Casolaro received 2 ducats to make her velvet slippers (*pianelle di velluto*) and Catherina Spagnuola received 60 *baiocchi* for making nine towels (*tovaglie*) for the Signora. The account book also provides some of the earliest more

'The Matron', from Christofano Bertelli, *The Ages of Woman*, 1580s

intimate glimpses of Felice's life as an Orsini family member. One of her responsibilities in the month before Christmas was to 'stand at the gateway of the palace of Monte Giordano to dispense alms to the servants'. Ten ducats were allocated for this purpose on 25 November 1511. The role played by Felice here was symbolic. The heavy gate to Monte Giordano was at the top of the slope of the small hill. Each member of the staff would walk up the hill towards Felice to receive his or her Christmas bonus. Felice played her part as lady of the house, distributing largesse, in the traditional fashion of *noblesse oblige*. While the Monte Giordano staff received cash, those at Bracciano were fed a Christmas lunch, which, at a total cost of 12 ducats, actually constituted a greater expense than the alms she gave to the Roman servants.

Among the expenses for such festivities are some more gruesome outgoings, reminders of the constant presence of violence in the daily life of Renaissance Italy. In June 1514, Felice paid 140 ducats for 'the murder of Tolfia di Caroli, the homicide at Castelnuovo'. Although no other details are provided of this event, dealing with killings was an inevitable part of life as a feudal lord or lady, and one with which Felice was to become much more familiar. On this occasion, the 140 ducats was offered as compensation to Tolfia's relatives, the equivalent of a lifetime's wages of which his family would now be deprived. Felice also began to attend to other matters of Orsini estate business. She dealt with requests for assistance in obtaining justice, payments for labour and servants' wages as well as keeping account of household activities. She performed these tasks while her husband was away and to an increasing extent even while he was in residence.

Felice also embarked on some more ambitious projects for the Orsini at Bracciano. One was to oversee repairs and renovation work on the castle, which had been left unattended over the years by Gian Giordano, who had invested more time and money on his French palace at Blois. Between January and April 1511, Felice hired a team of painters, led by a man variously described as 'il Mastro Depinctor' (the master painter), 'il depinctor da Viterbo' (the painter from Viterbo), or by his given name as 'Mastro Pasturea, depinctor'. He received a monthly wage varying between 10 and 11 ducats, and he brought with him to Bracciano assistants from the nearby city of Viterbo. A great contrast to the Vatican's glamorous celebrity artists, these local artisans were hired to replenish the decorative paintwork on ceilings and beams, and brighten up the now forty-year-old frescos painted for Gentile Virginio by Antoniazzo Romano. Felice also brought in carpenters and woodworkers to make repairs to doors and windows. Such activity on her part at Bracciano indicates that she had begun to pay greater attention to her immediate surroundings. She had started to feel that the castle was her home.

The painters and carpenters hired to make these repairs were sufficiently skilled to do good, solid work but there was no requirement for them to be creative. In 1511, however, Felice brought in a much more sophisticated design team to create the first public fountain in Bracciano.

CHAPTER 7

Bracciano's *fonte*

When Italian women commissioned public buildings, they were often attracted to projects involving water.[1] There is apparently no particular reason for this but perhaps they were more conscious of its domestic benefits than were their male counterparts. In the first century BC, Phile of Priene paid for a cistern and water pipes for her city and Modia Quinta built an aqueduct. In the fifteenth century, Lucrezia Tornabuoni de' Medici rebuilt the public baths at Bagno a Morbo in Tuscany. Felice della Rovere's own commitment to personal cleanliness was such that she had a private bathroom: one room of the castle is described in an inventory as 'where the Signora bathes'. Its contents included 'a pair of fire irons, a bath made of wood', a low seat (presumably for the maid-servant assisting her) and a bench.[2] The bathroom was located next to 'the old kitchen', which might not have been in use, but which would still have had a large fireplace, convenient for heating up large amounts of water.

The residents of Bracciano were fortunate in that they, unlike the Romans, had a very large supply of fresh water in the form of their lake. The enclosed area around the castle also contained a well. There was no easily accessible water source beyond Bracciano's walls and the shores of the lake, but at the starting point of the road to Rome there was a spring.

Jean Thomas Thibault, *View of Bracciano (with fountain house below)*, c. 1810

A fountain fed by the spring would be ideal for thirsty travellers and for those who lived beyond the walls of the castle.

The inscription running across the frieze at the top of the fountain, 'Pro Pubblicatis Commoditatis' ('For the public convenience'), emphasizes that the fountain was designed to promote social well-being. Water spouts out from taps set into large rosettes, one of the Orsini insignia. A long rectangular basin collects the water, making it easy for horses to drink, and, divided into three parts, it facilitates the washing of clothes.

While Gian Giordano undoubtedly approved the fountain's installation, he was often absent from Bracciano in 1511, and does not seem to have demonstrated a great interest in the embellishment of his property. Felice was much more active in this capacity, and interested in ingratiating herself with the community whose ruler she was fast becoming in her husband's stead. The choice of the Orsini rose might not seem to be one in keeping with the woman who promoted herself as a della Rovere. However, here it was in Felice's interest to identify herself as Orsini Signora. The gift was not only practical; it was an object designed to add grace and beauty to the little town. As an act of patronage, it is in many ways a scaled-down version of Felice's father's activity in Rome.

The architecture of the fountain is as modern and up to date as anything that could be found in Rome in 1511. Many residents of Bracciano, who had never travelled to Rome, had never seen architecture the like of their new fountain. It was a simple but elegant classical design, similar to the orginal Trevi fountain in Rome designed by Leon Battista Alberti in 1453. Originally plastered white, concealing its brickwork, the Bracciano fountain was banded with Doric pilasters, from which the waterspouts protrude. The somewhat attenuated pilasters most closely resemble those at the Villa Chigi (now Villa Farnesina) built concurrently with this fountain by the architect and painter Baldessare Peruzzi for Agostino Chigi. On a number of occasions, Chigi, the wealthiest man in Italy, had loaned Julius II substantial sums of money. Julius devised a means of getting out of the payment of the loans by officially adopting Chigi. This act technically made Agostino and Felice brother and sister, and although they were not especially close they did share some business interests. In 1510, Chigi asked for Felice's help in finding lodging for a prelate, Antonio da Comopriora, and in 1513 her adopted brother signed the lease at the Orsini palace at Campo dei Fiori on behalf of a Sienese compatriot, Cardinal Francesco Saraceni.[3] In loaning Peruzzi to Felice, he was helping her achieve her desire to bring a little piece of modern Rome to fortified, medieval Bracciano. The artist had always had close connections to her family: one of Peruzzi's first Roman commissions had been from Felice's stepfather, Bernardino, at the church of San Onofrio. Nor would this be the last time in his life Peruzzi worked for Felice.

CHAPTER 8

Weaving

Slowly but surely, such acts as commissioning a fountain helped Felice della Rovere consolidate her position at the Bracciano titular estate. By 1513, she had a special staff of her own, described in her account book as '*li salariati* [the salaried] of the Illustrious Signora'. They were separate and autonomous from the other Bracciano servants. Some would travel with her as she moved from Rome to the countryside and back again; others would stay behind to act as her eyes and ears in her absence. Her salaried employees included Hieronyma, the *balia*, and her husband Philipetto, the *balio*, who looked after the children in Vicovaro. Felice also had a personal chaplain, Don Matteo, as well as *mulatieri* (mule-drivers) and *staffieri* (foot-men). Apart from Hieronyma, the only woman directly employed by Felice at this time was a personal maid, Violante di Sanframondo. Servants were still predominantly male in Renaissance Italy. This record from 1513 is also the first time the name Statio, described as her *cancelliero* (chancellor or private secretary) appears. Statio, who managed a great many of Felice's personal affairs, was to become an enormously important figure in her life.

Also included among Felice's *salariati* for 1513 is '*lo fregaro*' ('the embroi-derer') and 'Maestro Nicolo Todesco, tapeziero' ('Master Nicholas the German, tapestry-weaver'). In 1514, a fellow weaver from Germany,

Giovanni Stradano, *Household Activity*, 1587–89

Gregorio Todesco, joined Nicolo in Felice's pay, along with 'Gilio di Brusela' ('Giles of Brussels'). Europe's best tapestry-weavers were from northern Europe. Felice's hiring of three northerners to make new tapestries for Bracciano is an indication of her desire for work of the finest quality. Tapestry was the art form that interested her most. Later in the sixteenth century Michelangelo would dismiss Flemish art as work suitable only for young girls, friars or nuns. It was too busy for his taste with details of landscape, animals or flowers. Flemish art did not engage with the serious subjects of narrative art, of the kind he had painted on the Sistine ceiling. Although he directed his derision at Flemish painters, he recognized that the far greater threat they posed to the art of Italy was their inherent ability as weavers. Every real connoisseur, including Julius, Felice's father, and Leo, her friend, recognized the superior ability of the northern tapestry-makers. Leo commissioned Raphael to make cartoons for the magnificent set of tapestries that he had added to the decoration of the Sistine chapel, but it was weavers from Brussels who provided the final woven product.

Felice knew that her father recognized the value of tapestry. He had given her a set of soft furnishings, comprising '13 silk hangings for a room, 6 large carpets, 4 small carpets, 15 drapes, 4 brocaded cushions and 3 cushions of purple velvet and brocade'.[1] The silk made the hangings relatively light. Felice could take them anywhere with her and immediately make a room comfortable and luxurious for herself.

Tapestry hangings on the walls were an absolute essential in a castle such as Bracciano in winter. On high ground, with winds blowing off the lake, its rooms were draughty, and the woven fabric provided protection from the cold. The previous Orsini lords, perhaps during their expeditions to France, had acquired many grand tapestries depicting such scenes as *The Story of King Solomon* and *The Life of Saint Anthony*. However, these were now old and worn; not only were they shabby, they were also less effective as insulation.

If the tapestries Felice's three weavers made are those cited in an inventory of the contents of Bracciano made in 1518, then they produced a series of thirteen silk hangings of landscapes with exotic and mythical beasts. One featured 'a fountain with a griffin and a dragon'; others depicted a centaur and a dragon, a centaur and a leopard, and a centaur and a lion. That the same kind of design, perhaps the specialty of Nicolo

Tedesco and his team, was repeated over and over again meant that the weavers could produce more work in a relatively short amount of time.

Felice was especially fond of these tapestries. In an inventory of Bracciano from late in 1519, taken at a time when she was absent from the castle, the centaur-themed hangings are not included, suggesting she had taken them with her while she was away. She certainly appreciated the worth of the art of weaving fabulous images in silk and wool. After Gian Giordano's death, Felice sent a missive to the King of France, in which she informed him that she was prepared to relinquish to him Gian Giordano's palace at Blois, but that she wished to 'recover and remove its tapestries and all other movable goods'.[2] A palace in France was of little use to Felice. Its upkeep was costly; she had no intention of going there, and extracting rent from French nobles would prove difficult. But the palace was evidently furnished with fine tapestries, and those she was determined to have returned to her.

CHAPTER 9

Personal Reckoning

As Orsini Signora, Felice created a more harmonious environment out of the castle of Bracciano. She cultivated the loyalty of the townspeople and acquired a body of faithful servants. None the less, she still had her personal contingency plan in case things went wrong and she had to leave the Orsini household on Gian Giordano's death. The most critical issue for her was that her own property, her *beni mobili et immobili*, movable and immovable goods, be recognized as separate and autonomous from the rest of the Orsini estate. In October 1516 she took it on herself to compile an inventory of her personal belongings.

Felice's inventory reveals her carefully crafted strategy for personal survival. If life with the Orsini did not work out for her, she was still, independently, extremely wealthy. As the inventory began, she had 'brought 20,000 ducats into the home of Gian Giordano Orsini as her dowry'.[1] The usufruct, the interest, on the use of this sum was now 6,150 ducats. Added to this cash was her own personal property. The value of Palo was calculated at 9000 ducats and she had paid Gian Giordano 10,800 for the palace and land on the Pincian Hill. She was due 4,200 ducats from grain she had sold to the Vatican, and she also operated a private bank. She had lent 2000 ducats to Giuliano de' Medici, Duke of Nemours, and another 2000 to her cousin, Francesco Maria, Duke of Urbino. She had loaned a

Trinità dei Monti and Felice's Palace to the right-hand side, sixteenth century

further 2000 ducats to Giuliano Leno for his daughter's dowry. She had also lent out smaller sums: 140 ducats had gone to Portia Savelli, the widow of the Orsini Duke of Anguillara, with whom Felice had some degree of rapport. In all, between her dowry and these cash loans, Felice della Rovere was worth 56,440 ducats, which could be translated into tens of millions of pounds in today's values.

But that was not all she possessed. Felice had stored 'in many and varied places 12,000 ducats' worth of grain'. And then there were her precious stones and metals. She owned a ruby valued at 1,100 ducats; two emeralds, worth 700, one set into a ring, and a diamond ring worth 150 ducats. Cleverly, much of her jewellery was set in the form of *crocette*, little crosses. Renaissance clothing laws, known as sumptuary laws, were designed to prevent women wearing overly ostentatious clothing and jewellery, but the laws could be circumvented by wearing gems in the form of crucifixes. Felice had seven *crocette*, all made of diamonds, ranging in value from 20 to 700 ducats, the most costly being the one given to her by her father following her marriage, which had been presented to him by the Republic of Venice. Felice also possessed an array of gold necklaces and bracelets, which, with her gold medals and *paternosters* (rosary beads), were worth 1,350 ducats. In total, Felice's jewellery was worth another 4,200 ducats.

Felice della Rovere had also amassed a collection of silverware, vases, boxes and salvers worth 268 ducats. The rest of her goods did not have individual values attached to them, but collectively they formed an impressive whole. There were the hangings and furnishings given Felice by Julius, her dresses of brocaded silk and satin in her adopted cardinal's colours of scarlet and black. She also owned a particularly regal garment, clearly intended for ceremonial occasions, a magnificent crimson silk dress lined in ermine fur. By the standards of today, Felice's wardrobe might seem rather small, until it is remembered that the cost of such fabrics at this time could buy several peasants' homes.

Felice's inventory also shows that she owned two types of books. One entry simply indicates that she possessed 'many sets of books', which she had been amassing for many years now, cheaply bound and of insufficient value to list individually. There were others specifically itemized because as physical objects they were of greater worth. She owned the writings of

St Jerome, described as 'illustrated, with a silver clasp'. This illuminated book might have been made for her by the artist Marcantonio Raimondi. An interesting entry in her account book for 19 August records that 'Marcantonio da Bologna received the rest of his payment for the St Jerome, 4.15 ducats'. This Marcantonio da Bologna would be Marcantonio Raimondi, an associate of Raphael. Among his many works were prints made from Raphael's designs. These had a wide circulation and were a lucrative business. In 1524, Marcantonio landed in serious trouble when he was imprisoned on obscenity charges for making prints from Raphael's pupil Giulio Romano's drawings of sexual positions, *I Modi*. Marcantonio was probably not on this occasion providing Felice with a print, because a partial payment of 4 ducats would be excessive for such an item. However, his skills could have been put to good use creating the illustrations for Felice's copy of St Jerome. Felice's other costly books included an illustrated Suetonius, a Holy Bible, and the works of Pliny. Her castle of Palo stood close to, if not actually on, the site of a villa owned by Pliny's uncle. The last three volumes were all bound in crimson satin with silver locks and clasps, perhaps all acquired at the same time and with the same provenance.

In addition to the wall hangings, drapes and cushions that meant Felice could furnish a bedroom wherever she went, she had also acquired the furnishings for a portable chapel. Any priest who came to her to say Mass would find himself supplied with the appropriate vestments: cloak, cope, stole and maniple in brocaded silk. There was an altar cloth in the same fabric, silver candlesticks, a silver bell, a pair of silver incense-shakers, a 'little silver box to hold the hosts' and a silk embroidered 'image of Our Lady'. The only other picture Felice possessed was a 'beautiful Crucifixion in oil valued at 60 ducats'. The high value attached to this image suggests it was by a noteworthy painter. Felice did not collect paintings. She had a peripatetic lifestyle, moving throughout the year between palaces in Rome and castles in the countryside, and she liked to take her favourite possessions with her. Paintings were cumbersome to pack.

There were also a few less costly items, including 'a purse in gold worked with beautiful figures, two pieces of moonstone, one set in gold and the other plain, two strings of amber beads'. The miscellaneous quality of this part of Felice's inventory suggests these things had been in her possession for a long time, dating from the period prior to her marriage, when the gems owned by the cardinal's daughter were not yet diamonds. Now such objects were endowed with sentimental value. Otherwise, there is very little of a sentimental nature about Felice's property. Everything in her inventory was beautiful – dresses of exquisite fabric, embroidered cushions, tapestries, gems – but these were still possessions amassed with an eye to the practical. She did not collect paintings, antiquities, sculpture, maiolica – items that attracted her elite contemporaries of either sex. Such objects were heavy; they were designed to be stationary. Felice could pack all this up in a few strong boxes. She could be through the door and on her way in a very short period of time, as she had had to be as a young teenager, swept up from Rome and propelled towards Savona.

However, even if Felice's worldly goods were easily transported, such a swift getaway was not to prove necessary because she was not, in 1516, destined to leave the Orsini family. Gian Giordano Orsini was not the most active lord his family had seen, but he still gave consideration to its future after he was gone. He had no desire for his family to fall into chaos after his death, which was probable with boys not old enough to rule and no authority figure at the helm. He could look at Felice and see in his head-strong, independent wife a woman who, in over a decade of married life, had proved her commitment to his family. She had borne him two sons and she had focused her attention not only on repairing and refurnishing the castle of Bracciano but also on the public benefit of the community at large. Felice della Rovere had proved herself, in many ways, a worthy legatee. The time had come for Gian Giordano officially to endorse Felice's future with the Orsini.

CHAPTER 10

A Slave to the House of Orsini

By September 1517, Gian Giordano Orsini's health had begun to fail. He knew that it was time to vest Felice with the authority to serve as Orsini regent after his demise, while their sons were still minors. In September 1517, Felice and Gian Giordano and the children were together at the castle of Vicovaro. Gian Giordano, attended and advised by his doctor, Alessandro Sanctini, made a kind of living will. One of the Orsini chiefs of staff, Giovanni Roberto della Colle, who was present, provided a description of what occurred:

> Gian Giordano, sound in mind, but weak in body, lay in the antechamber of the palace at Vicovaro. His wife, Mistress Felice, remained with him along with his daughter Carlotta, and Francesco his son. He took his son Francesco by the hand and he said to him, 'Francesco, my son, if I die,' and here Francesco [who was six years old] began to cry, 'I must leave you, and I shall leave my wife, that is Madonna Felice, named as Lady and Guardian of the children and of the estate because she has been such a woman and such a wife, and so rightly she merits such an honour.' At this, the Lady Felice broke down and began to cry. She said, 'When you have been sick and in danger of dying, you never made such a will, and now you are healthy, God be praised, without a fever and not

Cesare Vecellio, *Roman Widow*, 1590

fading away, so, my lord, it is not necessary to say such things.' And Madonna Felice wanted to leave the antechamber, and go into the main room. Gian Giordano heard her and said, 'Donna Felice, sit down and please listen to me because there are things I want to say. I shall leave my children everything, and you, their good mother, as the new Lady and Guardian when I die.' And Madonna Felice replied, 'My Lord, I would rather die as a slave in this house than a queen of anywhere else.'[1]

Whatever depth of emotion Felice and Gian Giordano felt for each another, they had formed a deep bond acting as partners on Rome's political stage. Felice had prevented Renzo da Ceri and Giulio Orsini from serving Venice against France, which would have embarrassed her husband. She had helped him mediate between the Pope and France, and he had supported her when she wanted to marry Julia into the d'Este family. This exchange between them, as Gian Giordano lay dying, is moving, particularly for a notarial document of Renaissance Italy, which would normally be curt in the extreme. By the same token, however, it does have a staged component, because the situation was directed and acted out by husband and wife. Both Felice and Gian Giordano knew that there would be members of the Orsini family who would object to Felice becoming Lady and Guardian of the estate. She was not a member of the Orsini by blood; she was not even a Roman noble but a clergyman's bastard daughter. Consequently, Gian Giordano needed to make the proclamation about Felice's future position in the family in a way that seemed natural and yet had an attentive audience. The scene played out in the antechamber at Vicovaro was to be the last they would perform together. The record of their exchange exists because Giovanni di Roberto della Colle gave a notarized account to the Orsini lawyer, Sabbo di Vannucci, whch was independently verified, and recorded in Latin by Gian Giordano's doctor, Alessandro Sanctini. Although Gian Giordano was sick, he came out to the antechamber of his bedroom so that Felice's ladies-in-waiting could hear what he had to say and serve as further witnesses. Giovanni di Roberto and the doctor emphasized his good mental health at the time; Felice even wanted to imply that physically he was quite well. The stronger Gian Giordano was in mind and body, the greater the weight placed on the strength of his decision to leave his wife in charge when he died.

Felice's performance was also an essential part of the event. There can be little doubt that she felt genuine grief at Gian Giordano's imminent death. Whatever his eccentricities, he had been a good, and astonishingly progressive, husband for the time. Whatever his initial feelings were about taking a pope's daughter for a wife, he had come to recognize and appreciate her abilities and he gave her free reign to develop them. Felice might be excited at what was yet to come, as any prince might feel a thrill at his father's deathbed or certain cardinals at the death of a pope, but on this occasion the important thing for Felice was not what she actually felt but what those around her perceived her to be feeling. She could not appear greedy and grasping, eagerly anticipating her husband's death so that she could take over the reins of power. Instead, in tears, she had to declare that he had no need to make such a decision because he was in good health. When Gian Giordano insisted he would do so, and Felice acquiesced in his decision, she emphasized her dedication to the Orsini, the family to whom she would rather be a slave than a queen elsewhere. The suppression of her own ego was a crucial part of her performance; she must appear to have no personal interest in becoming the Orsini *Signora et Patrona*.

Gian Giordano died at the beginning of October. His death coincided with an event that would have dramatic implications for the Christian world: Martin Luther's nailing of the ninety-five theses to the door of Wittenberg Castle Church, protesting the corruption of the Church fashioned by Felice's father, Julius, and her friend, Leo. But for Felice and the Orsini, the death of Gian Giordano had far greater impact. Her husband's vocal decree to leave Felice as Guardian of the Orsini estate was supported by a plethora of legal documents and sanctions. His own will was not complicated; it reiterated what he had told Felice and the assembled company in the antechamber at Vicovaro. He left his children, Francesco, Girolamo and their half-brother Napoleone, all his worldly goods. Felice was their guardian and trustee of the estate during her sons' minority, and overnight she became one of the most powerful figures in the city of Rome, irrespective of gender. An unknown Roman correspondent recognized this, penning what was ostensibly a consolation note to her for the loss of her husband on 11 October. But the writer takes pains to assert that he himself is consoled, knowing that the Orsini were now in the hands of 'such a wise and knowing person, who is dignified by such gravity and magnificence'.[2]

Felice's governance needed to be ratified by Pope Leo X, as well as the local governing body of Rome, the Senate. Leo issued a bull in which he 'recognized Donna Felice della Rovere, the second wife and widow of Gian Giordano Orsini, as Guardian and Caretaker of his children of minor age, on the condition that she remains a widow'.[3] This last provision was the norm in Renaissance Europe; a woman would give up guardianship of her children and along with it any administrative role in her children's estate were she to remarry. Such a proviso can only have amused Felice. Marriage had never greatly interested her, and to give up the extraordinary position she had now attained for another husband was inconceivable.

The ratification by the Roman Senate highlighted the contradictions in Felice's position. She was now a woman in charge of one of Rome's two most powerful Roman families. But because she was a woman she was not allowed a role in legal proceedings, and required a lawyer to act on her behalf. On 22 January 1518, she appointed 'Galeotto Ferreolo da Cesena, consistorial advocate', to serve as her deputy at a meeting of the Roman Senate at their palace on the Capitoline hill. There, he would testify on her behalf that 'as Guardian and Caretaker of her children Francesco, Girolamo, Giulia and Clarice, she promises faithfully to administer the interests of her charges, to compile an inventory of goods, and to provide an account of her management of the estate'.[4]

Felice's official transaction with Galeotto took place 'in Rome, in the palace made by the late Gian Giordano, situated next to the church of Trinità dei Monti on the Pincian Hill', the very palace that Felice was making her own. Usually, the notarization of important legal acts, such as the handing over of Felice's dowry to Gian Giordano, or her own purchase of Palo, took place in the *Camera Magna* at Monte Giordano. But, on this occasion, Felice chose to remove herself from the Orsini seat of governance. This decision seems surprising. As 'Guardian and Caretaker' it would seem only appropriate for her to choose to do business from the Orsini Roman hub. But Felice was already adopting a habit of avoiding contact with her Orsini relations. It was just after Christmas; many of them were still in residence at Monte Giordano and many of those were resentful of Felice and the power that she now wielded.

Moreover, some Orsini were suspicious about the circumstances of Gian Giordano's death. In Venice, Marino Sanuto recorded that Gian Giordano had died in Vicovaro, without confession nor communion because the doctors had not considered him ill.[5] For those inclined towards such suspicions, Sanuto's words imply Gian Giordano's demise was not a natural one. Although no one publicly raised an accusation against Felice, there were undoubtedly several of the Orsini willing to entertain the idea that she had had a hand in Gian Giordano's departure from this world. Certainly the timing was convenient, with her boys aged only four and five, the thirty-four-year-old Felice's period in office could be a long one. Yet nothing could be proved and, in any event, Felice had her indulgence of absolution of all crime from Leo X. Yet it strengthened support and sympathy from the Orsini for her seventeen-year-old stepson Napoleone, who his relatives felt should now be the rightful leader of the Bracciano Orsini. So, for Felice, negotiating the transference of power to her from the Trinità Palace, a residence built on Orsini land, but which Felice had chosen to make her own, was a calculated statement. She had never particularly wanted to make friends with the Orsini, and she had no intention of starting now. And she could not have failed to be irritated by such pompous-sounding letters as the one written to her by Gian Giordano's cousin, Cardinal Franciotto Orsini, on 9 January of 1518: 'I advise your ladyship that you should wish to give a good example to others, and be attentive to not letting bad deeds go unpunished, so that our vassals are not tempted down paths where they might sin.'[6]

The Cardinal implies that as a woman Felice might be overly lenient and weak with the estate workers, and was inclined to be critical of her. However, Felice and Franciotto did eventually reach an accord; bound by ecclesiastical rather than Orsini connections, Franciotto realized that alienating the new govenor would not serve him well at the Vatican court. Felice, however, continued to keep her distance from the rest of the family.

CHAPTER 11

More Reckoning

Felice della Rovere Orsini knew that a new role had been created for her, and with it she had become another kind of person. Over the past decade, she had acquired respect, admiration and influence, not to mention a sizeable personal fortune. However, she had always been something of an anomaly in society, her identity as a pope's outspoken daughter was always with her, for better or worse. Now she had attained a position that Renaissance Italy could more easily understand, that of widowed regent. Many noblewomen when they became widows chose a visual commemoration of the occasion, a portrait of themselves in widow's weeds or an altarpiece in which they could be depicted as donors. Widowhood was also the time when wealthy women bought or commissioned the building of a new home. Others performed acts of charity, founding convents or giving money to holy orders. Felice della Rovere did none of these things. She already had a collection of treasured possessions, not to mention a frescoed chapel, castle and palace of her own. She felt she had no need for further visual commemoration. Moreover, she was about to become extremely busy. Most widows who became philanthropists did so because they had two things: financial wealth and time on their hands. Although Felice controlled a good deal of money, the expense of maintaining the Orsini estate was so high that there was rarely any left over. As for spare

Kitchen Interior, 1540s

time, until her sons, who were still only four and five, reached adulthood, her life was to be dedicated to running the Orsini estate. It did not leave Felice with a great deal of time for personal expression.

None the less, Felice did give some thought to her new position. With her husband recently deceased and her father dead for only five years, she considered how she too would be remembered when she died. In the midst of adapting to her new role as Orsini governor, she set aside some time to write her own will, a relatively unusual act for a woman of only thirty-five. Part of her decision for doing so was undoubtedly practical. If she were to die intestate, her own estate would become subsumed into that of the Orsini. Although her sons would benefit and, indeed, they were to receive the bulk of her inheritance, her daughters would be left with nothing from her. So Felice's will, notarized on 30 March 1518, made provisions for 'Julia and Clarice, the natural and legitimate daughters of the testator each to receive 8000 ducats'.[1] This legacy would be in addition to whatever their dowries would be from the Orsini estate.

Much of Felice's will, however, was concerned with the destination of her mortal remains, and the care of her immortal soul. She set aside 1000 ducats for the 'making of her tomb and the purchase of an altar cloth' for her chapel in the church of Trinità dei Monti. She left an additional 30 ducats to the church for the saying of perpetual Mass to her. The same sum went to Santa Maria del Popolo and Santa Maria Transpontina, for the same purpose. Santa Maria del Popolo was the della Rovere church in Rome, founded by Sixtus IV, where many of her relatives were interred. Santa Maria Transpontina on the road to the Vatican by Castel Sant' Angelo on the papal route, was fashionable and had a large congregation. Ten ducats for obit perpetual Masses went to the churches of San Agostino and Santa Maria sopra Minerva – both in the neighbourhood of Piazza Navona where Felice had lived as a child. She also left 10 ducats to San Pietro in Montorio, the other legendary site of St Peter's burial, and to San Onofrio, which her stepfather, Bernardino de Cupis, helped decorate. Felice's decision to spread her money among numerous churches across Rome ensured that her name would resonate throughout her city. It was a way of ensuring her own enduring legacy and gave shape and form to the observance of her memory.

If Felice thought a great deal about her place in the divine world, she was equally concerned with the practicalities of the earthly one. One of her first tasks as Orsini Guardian and Caretaker, as laid down by the Roman Senate, was to supervise an inventory of Gian Giordano's property. A precise record of the contents of the estate was important for ensuring that everything was intact by the time his heirs took over. Compiling a property inventory was a common duty for widows left as estate managers; a fifteenth-century Florentine fresco shows a widow standing in the middle of a room, watching as a notary records its contents. But rarely was a widow responsible, as Felice was, for making the inventory of an estate that covered several hundred square miles. This intense effort resulted in the compilation of a forty-page document detailing 'every single movable and immovable good' in Orsini possession. It was completed on 25 April 1518.[2]

No single document provides a better picture of what Felice had taken on when she became Orsini regent. The inventory opens with the contents of the castle of Bracciano, and with the items needed for its defence. These number over a thousand pieces of artillery, including cannons, cannonballs, gunpowder, mortar, sledgehammers, arqubusiers, lances, picks, ballasts, falconets (light guns) and 'five huge shields, painted with a rose', the Orsini insignia. In a striking juxtaposition, the next group of Bracciano contents listed are the furnishings of the chapel. These are very similar to those of Felice's own portable chapel, with altar cloths, priests' vestments, candelabra, a crucifix and two wooden angels. The altarpiece depicted *Christ before Pontius Pilate*, an unusual subject for an altar, and there was also 'a tiny box containing relics of the 10,000 Virgins, the Blessed Francesco di Paola and St Christina'. Given that Francesco di Paola was only recently dead, and Gian Giordano had spent much time at the French court, this relic was perhaps actually authentic, a rare instance among the oceans of the Virgin's milk and forests of splinters of the True Cross.

The kitchen contained copper cauldrons, and a large stove, winding spits, iron saucepans, spoons and knives, a gridiron, a large stone pestle and mortar, and a smaller marble one. Its first adjoining pantry housed a big salt cellar, numerous glass jars, some full, some half empty, with oil and vinegar, and a 'wooden grinding mill containing yeast'. Then there were four rooms where wine was stored, catalogued in ascending order of quality. The first contained both wine and vinegar, the second fourteen 'big bottles of Roman wine' and 'seven caskets'. The last *cantina* was where the muscatel, the best wine in the house, was stored.

Next was the *guardaroba*, a veritable treasure house of fabulous textiles. Here there were bed canopies made of crimson velvet, embroidered with the Orsini coat of arms, or of turquoise taffeta with a gold fringe. The older Orsini tapestries were stored here, along with the centaur series Felice had commissioned a few years earlier, and a large number of carpets. The first bedroom to be described in the inventory belonged to Gian Giordano. In it, laid out like a relic, was the set of armour he had received from the King of France, with body suit, arm bands, shoulder pads embossed with silver, silver gauntlets and silver collar piece.

Felice had no intention of her possessions appearing in the inventory of Gian Giordano's estate, to be misidentified as Orsini property, so there is not a trace of her here at the castle. But she did make careful note of the contents of the stables, including the 'two little bay horses belonging to Don Francesco and Don Girolamo, the sons of Gian Giordano'. In addition to the children's ponies were six riding horses, two carthorses, three baby mules and three adult animals. There were also two carts, and a 'four-wheeled cart, covered in black cow hide'. 'Thirty-two large cows and two more bulls' also lived here. Felice also listed a large pile of scrap metal, old cauldrons, spits and pans. Melted down, such goods still had intrinsic value.

From Gian Giordano's movable goods, the inventory went on to the immovable, and to the lands and palaces the Orsini owned. This section included the compound of Bracciano itself, the castle and the land. It also listed the fief of Scrophano with its fields and vineyards and the woods of Trevignano. Galera had fruit trees, Cesano meadows and Isola cow pastures. There was a large palace at Formello, and in Rome at Monte Giordano and Campo dei Fiori. The palace at Blois built by Gian Giordano himself was mentioned, and another in Naples. The castle of Vicovaro was like a small version of Bracciano. It contents were listed, but there were not so many furnishings, and they were evidently of a plainer nature. There were no luxurious wall hangings here.

A box of documents important to the Orsini family also had its place in the inventory. Here were to be found wills, concessions from Gian Giordano's maternal grandfather, Alfonso of Aragon, and privileges conceded to Gian Giordano by the King of France. Also included 'in this same box are instruments, privileges and bulls, sealed by the Illustrious Lady Felice and her notary, written in various places'. The next line stated that 'Felice, the aforesaid Guardian, has all the ingoing and outgoing expenses written down in two books compiled by her servants Carolus Galeotti and Statio del Fara'.

Documents had taken on a new importance in Felice's life. Power was conferred on her in the form of her husband's will and bulls from the papacy and the Senate. She in turn exercised her authority in the form of letters and mandates signed in her name and embossed with her seal. Where Felice differed from the Orsini men who had run their family estate before her was in her commitment to paperwork. Her roots betrayed her. She was not a noble, but the child of the curia and bureaucratic adminis- trators, with all their instincts. Without such an attitude and an inherent ability, she could all too easily have lost control of her position almost as soon as she assumed it.

CHAPTER 12

The Temporal Mother

The Bracciano estate was a small kingdom; in many ways it was a microcosm of the Italian peninsular. The fiefs, villages and compounds all had separate identities, interests and products. Land was given over to the raising of animals, to fruit orchards, to timber forests, or to the harvesting of grain and hay. It was an extraordinary task for one person to run efficiently, even if resident in one place, which Felice was not. Her year began in Rome, and she stayed in the city through the spring. In the early summer she would leave for Bracciano and then spend the late summer at Vicovaro with her children. She returned to Rome in the autumn. With such a fragmented year, Felice was heavily dependent on the abilities and services of her estate managers. She was also acutely aware that she could not simply leave the running of the estate in their hands, even if that had been her personal preference. She needed written accounts of every activity, and she herself had to oversee and personally authorize the management of provisions. She intervened in legal matters and launched judicial inquiries. She selected the appointment of Orsini officials as well as of the clergy in parishes on Orsini terrain. She also fielded endless requests for favours. Almost all of the letters she received were addressed to her as the correspondent's *Patrona et benefatrix*, patron and benefactress, implying she was possessed of some kind of charitable munificence. Running Bracciano

Antonio Tempesta, *Kitchen and Pantry: January*, 1599

was in many ways akin to becoming the chief executive officer of a large corporation – hardly a philanthropic activity. However, an element of divine absolutism came with the position and Felice was, after all, now queen of the Orsini.

Anyone familiar with the lives of bees knows that queens do not rest, and Felice's days were a buzz of activity. Wherever Felice was, her time from morning to night was occupied by a constant series of negotiations, the dispensing of orders and the granting of requests, the opening of dozens of letters and the dictation of replies. Although she signed her letters with her broad sweeping signature, 'Felix Ruveris Ursinis', she personally wrote relatively few of them by hand. Her writing skills were better than those of most members of the elite, especially women, but she was still not a professional scribe. Instead, the senior servants at Bracciano, Monte Giordano and Vicovaro stayed at her side, copying down her missives, sometimes when she was mounted on a horse, travelling from one home to another. Even when absent from one of her residences, it was important that her presence be felt. An astute servant, Francesco da Fano, wrote to her at Vicovaro from Rome that in her absence he was devoted to a portrait of her, which he 'worshipped and adored as I do my Lady Patron'.[1]

There is now apparently no trace of this portrait. However, a painting by Sebastiano del Piombo, a colleague of Michelangelo and an artist personally known to Felice, might well be this work – or at least one very like it. This portrait, produced around 1520, shows a dark-haired woman with a long nose and a determined chin. She is dressed in scarlet and black and through the window behind her can be seen a hilly landscape containing a castle on the shores of a lake. The woman has several books in front of her. The words on the one open in front of her could once be deciphered as 'I raise my eyes and close my heart', words which appear a sonnet written by an acquaintance of Felice's, the noblewoman Vittoria Colonna. In this context they are appropriate to a widow whose heart is closed, as she indicates with her right hand. But equally important for Felice's situation is that she keep her eyes open, aware of all that is going on around her.

The year 1515 had seen the publication of Niccolò Machiavelli's *Il Principe* (*The Prince*), a work still considered one of the seminal works on government. Felice did not personally know Machiavelli, as she had

Baldessar Castiglione, but it is interesting to see how closely her ruling ethos and circumstances parallel the advice Machiavelli gave to the would-be successful ruler. She became a Machiavellian *principessa*, as she had been a Castiglione *cortegiana*. Much of what Machiavelli has to say about the life of the man who ascends to such power reflects Felice's own experience. He warned that the prince would make enemies of those injured in the seizing of the principality, and Felice made a few enemies among the Orsini. He advised that minor problems be taken care of immediately, before they got out of hand; Felice always concerned herself with minor problems. He counselled frequent visits to lands to discover any problems, and Felice certainly spent a lot of time moving between the Lazio estates and her Roman palace. The weak and powerless were to be protected, as they would see the prince as their chief source of support, and servants, rather than those nearer to the prince in status, should be the ones he relied on – again, Felice's habit. Such concentrated and detailed government, stated Machiavelli, had its advantages: the ruler would become indispensable in the lives of his minions. Such was Felice's goal.

Although she was never certain that the role of Orsini governor would be hers, Felice had been preparing for the position for many years. Even as a twenty-three-year-old newly-wed she had written to her new relative, Annibale Orsini, instructing him in very blunt language to 'do what is necessary and no less' in order to help his kinswoman Dianora Orsini. She continued to adopt this direct approach when dealing with the Bracciano officials and vassals, knowing that anything less would encourage corruption, dishonesty and anarchy. When she ascended to power, Cardinal Orsini warned her not to show weakness towards the indentured servants. Felice had little need of his advice; she knew what tone to take with those who failed to show her respect.

Felice della Rovere had learned the language and cadences of the courtier's voice. Over the previous decades, she had had occasion to plead tearfully with her father and to take a somewhat obsequious position in order to ingratiate herself with Isabella d'Este. She had continually charmed and impressed the humanists and clerics of the Vatican court. Felice could be theatrical if need be: she had vowed to throw herself into the sea rather than be raped and she had wept at her husband's deathbed. But her tone of authority is what endures. Felice had to be entirely intolerant of lawlessness, which would rapidly spread were it believed she might turn a blind eye to wrongdoing. She learned that a Roman, Prospero da Castel Sant' Angelo, had been banished from the entire province surrounding Rome but was now hiding in the hilly area around Vicovaro. Suspecting a Vicovaro servant, Antonio del Covaro, of harbouring the fugitive, her stern response (referring to herself in the plural) ran: 'We want to know that as soon as you receive this letter, you will ensure that Prospero will be gone within three days, and if not, you will be fined 25 ducats.[2] Vicovaro was frequently the site of criminal activity. To Hippolito della Tolfa, the bailiff of the estate, she wrote that she understood he had ascertained the whereabouts of Pietro Paolo da Celle, who had stolen some silver. 'I expect', wrote Felice, 'that nothing will be spared in bringing him to, and dispensing, justice.[3]

Astute servants learned the benefits of appealing to her magnanimity: 'As it is not only us, but all of Italy who knows of your ladyship's benignity and complexion,' wrote the officials of the tiny fief of Incherico, 'please could you assist us in giving some help to poor Simone Rocha, who has fallen on hard times.'[4] The *massari* of Sancto Poli exhibited a very clear understanding of Felice's power when they wrote to her of the unspecified 'mistake Gaspare of this place made, which obliges us to speak of it to your illustrious ladyship. He certainly does not merit any kind of supplication or justice. However, we beg of the love you hold for this land that you might wish to consider it, and so we rely on your mercy and as our temporal mother. We are firm in your immutable humanity and benignity.'[5]

Felice might not have been a full-time mother to her own children, but her role as 'temporal mother' was certainly all-consuming. In fact she often utilized the persona of stern but loving mother who was disappointed when her 'children' displeased her. Learning that Hippolito della Tolfa had sent orders to the *massari* at the fief of San Gregorio without her permission, she told him, 'I marvel at what you thought you could do . . . considering the opinion that we hold of you, I cannot but lament that you thought you could send such a mandate without first informing our own person, so I am writing now to advise you that you should never send out orders and mandates without first ascertaining our own advice and wishes.'[6]

Felice was also equally ready to acknowledge her servants' good behaviour. While she scolded Hippolito della Tolfa for his cavalier manner in dispensing orders, she sent him praise when he acted with restraint towards a fellow servant who had wronged him. 'Having learned of the bestiality of Vincentio da Urbino towards you,' she wrote to him, 'we are extremely displeased, as we wish for our officials to be treated as if they were our very selves. But it does please us greatly that you have acted so prudently towards Vincentio, who has displeased us so greatly.'[7] Felice was clearly relieved that Gentile had not reacted violently to whatever injury Vincentio had caused him. In the subtext was the silent promise that Felice personally would deal with the miscreant.

For Felice, though, her position as governor, as 'temporal mother', was more than just about the exercise of power. Had she been a wealthy widow with time on her hands, she might well have spent her time performing good works. As it was, she enjoyed ensuring that all on her land received their fair reward, even after death. Hippolito della Tolfa aroused her ire yet again with the case of the wife of Cola da Riccardo:

> Vicario, I am marvelling greatly that such a thing has happened in Vicovaro. And at you for allowing it to happen. The case is that, according to how I have been informed, of the wife of Cola da Riccardo, who delivering a boy in her eighth month, and dying, called the notary so that she could write her will. He was forbidden from doing so by the said Cola, and so the young woman has died intestate. I can easily see that this was done with malice and contempt for the law and I wish that proceedings are taken very deliberately against Cola to serve as an example to others in the future so that no one dares to do such a thing again.[8]

Felice, who fought hard for her own rights and possessions, seems particularly angered that another woman should be denied the right to bequeath her own property as she chose.

Matters of litigation, justice and criminal prosecution occupied a great deal of Felice's time. Disputes over property and rent were common. On one occasion Gian Battista di Bracciano asked her to mediate 'in the case between Maestro Giorgio and his wife, and Liberana the widow of Bernabo Cosa, over the house once held by Bernabo and now inhabited by Liberana'.[9] In matters such as these, where she might need more information and an expert legal opinion to help her decide, Felice would call on the services of the Roman notary Prospero d'Aquasparta. He had served the Orsini for many years, had negotiated the settlement of Felice's dowry and her acquisition of Palo, and he was to become particularly valuable to her. On 18 July 1520 Cardinal Orsini wrote to her asking for leniency for Galerano di Lorenzo da Siena, who rented a garden from her. Felice, anxious not to be accused of negligence, put Prospero to work immediately to investigate the matter. He replied to her on 25 July, only a week after the original request had come from the Cardinal:

> A few days ago you sent me a letter to alert me to the dispute between Phillipo da Bracciano and Galerano Ortolano (gardener), over the rental of your ladyship's vegetable garden, and so I have been obtaining the facts from both parties. I have found out that the garden was rented by Galerano for five years, at a rent of forty *carlini* a year, and that Galerano has held it for one further year. This year Galerano fell ill and went to the country to convalesce, and he left a boy in his place with all his belongings, among which are twenty-three chickens, big and little. Galerano being absent and not having paid the rent, Maestro Phillippo went to the garden and estimated the worth of the produce without the hens and without the hay, and that was seventy *carlini*, which Maestro Philippo sold for the rent in the absence of Galerano. Maestro Philippo says he sold the hay for 14 *carlini* and after I examined him several times, the boy said he sold it for 28. According to me, those 28 *carlini* belong to this poor man, Galerano. I have not found out anything else.[10]

Such skimming and cheating were inevitable on the part of the Bracciano servants. Phillippo's act of corruption might have angered Felice but still she did not dismiss him. He was useful to her as agent and diplomat.

There were constant reminders of the violent nature of feudal life. Orsini relatives often asked Felice to pardon murderers, or those who had received the death penalty. In June 1520, Michelangelo da Campagnino, who was being held prisoner at Bracciano, escaped. On his recapture, Felice's stepdaughter Carlotta wrote to her telling her that 'the faith and trust I have with your ladyship gives me the courage to write to you to beg you to have mercy on Michelangelo, who is about to be put to death'.[11]

Felice intervened and had his sentence commuted to a fine of 100 ducats. Renzo da Ceri wrote to her about a similar matter: 'Julio Maschio, my good friend, has killed one of his sisters. I am asking you if you will bestow compassion upon him.'[12] Felice and Renzo did not get on very well. He was married to Napoleone's sister Francesca and his loyalty lay with her stepson. Felice had shown herself to be particularly hostile to crimes against women, so it is likely that she did not comply with Renzo's peremptory request. She was more likely to have given assistance to Guidone da Nepi when he wrote to her to tell about his sister 'who is at present a widow, as our enemies the Braccio have murdered her husband and I understand that they intend to abduct her and make her marry one of their own. We beg of your ladyship to extend your help in placing my sister in a convent.'[13]

Sometimes Felice's own officials advised her not to pursue judicial matters. Antonio Casulensis wrote to her about which cases were worth pursuing: 'We found one Caterina, spinster, who had become pregnant and then aborted, and killed the creature, and being in such a state we were obliged to ask who had impregnated her and her response was that first she had done it with Giovanni, and then with Stefano.' Antonio felt that too much about the case was nebulous, and it would be rather costly. He concluded, in a similarly ambiguous fashion, that 'perhaps your illustrious ladyship might wish to take up the matter with your usual immense discretion', indicating that only Felice herself could terminate the investigation.[14]

On another occasion, an unwanted child was born alive. Perseo da Pontecorvo informed her from Vicovaro about 'that girl at Cantalupo [a small fief], who was pregnant, gave birth on Tuesday to a daughter. We are asking your ladyship if we can take the child to Santo Spirito in Rome because we have not found the father, and no one wants to take care of her'.[15] Santo Spirito, the hospital near the Vatican Palace, also took in foundlings. The institution had been promoted by Felice's great-uncle, Sixtus IV; possibly this family connection would help ensure the baby a place at the orphanage.

In between matters of life and death, Felice received such written mandates as an affidavit in a suit brought by 'those men of the fief of Santa

Croce, over a dispute about creating a piazza at Castello Arcione'.[16] And there were always debts to be paid. In 1520, some pig farmers at Vicovaro wrote asking for '100 ducats owed us from the sale of our pigs in 1517'.[17] Gian Giordano had left various outstanding debts behind him. Francesco de Altanantis wrote to her several times about a credit of 2000 ducats he had given to Gian Giordano that he now wanted returned. The availability of ready cash was a constant problem for the Orsini estate.

Felice personally authorized the movement of every bushel of grain, side of meat or bottle of wine produced on Orsini land. The archive of her correspondence is littered with small chits of paper, signed 'Felix Ruveris de Ursinis', sent to those servants who headed these different areas of production and disbursement. Bernardino Cannovaro, addressed as *in cantina*, 'in the wine cellar', at Bracciano, received a great number of such missives. Felice issued Bernardino with instructions to send a bottle of wine to Bernardino Sarto in Rome, a tailor 'who has worked for our family' and a bottle of 'our Bracciano wine, to the pig-herders who are watching over our pigs'. Nerone, the head pig-herder, received separately 'a bottle of Maremmesca wine', suggesting wine from the Maremma region was of better quality than the Bracciano estate's own vintage. Felice ordered that the mother of Priest Menimo of Bracciano was to receive an unspecified amount of bread and wine, and the labourers at Isola an assortment of wines. 'Silvestro, *balio* of Francesco, my son, is to receive two *cavalli* [a unit of measurement equivalent to the saddlebags a horse could carry] of wine from my vineyard, which shall be part of my sons' rations.'

Felice knew the exact contents of her cellar. She told Bernardino to send her 'all the Greek wine [malmsey] in the cellar, which amounts to twenty barrels'. When making requests for the cellar's best wine, Felice was always clear to state that it was for her own consumption and that of her children: she told Bernardino to 'send two barrels of the best wine in the cellar that we wish for ourself and our children'. When the time came for the grape harvest, she sent a personal representative to oversee it, one not connected with the Bracciano estate and thus less susceptible to bribery or corruption. She told Bernardino, 'Francesco d'Arpino, our servant, is coming, who shall be in charge of the *vendemmia* [harvest] . . . and he shall be given obedience and his orders obeyed as if he were our very self.'[18]

Bernardino exasperated Felice when he did not follow her instructions precisely, or immediately, particularly when it concerned provisions for herself and her family. Her cross little notes give an insight into family meals: 'Bernardino, we are astonished that you have still not sent the wine'; or 'We received from Polo Parmesano nine loads of wine and two lambs, which have arrived dead'; on 6 June 1520, 'Bernardino, yet again we are writing to you to send the cheese you have yet to send, now we also want you to send three lambs.' This time Bernardino immediately complied with her request. A day later, Felice wrote a note to confirm the receipt of 'three lambs, fifteen rounds of ricotta, two sausages . . . brought by Alessandro Genovese, consigned by Nardo Cannovaro, and received in good condition'.[19] She also acknowledged receipt of a 'a bag of leaves for worms'. Silk worms ate mulberry leaves; Felice was perhaps experimenting with silk production.

Nearly all the meat, lamb and veal, grain, wheat and barley, and fruit, in particular figs, consumed by Felice, her family and staff was produced on Orsini land. There were some exceptions, such as fish that did not come from the lake at Bracciano. One Christmas Eve, in Rome, they bought crab legs from Niccolò Ridolf's shop. An agent, Perseo di Pontecorvo, was charged with obtaining fish from the port of Gaeta, halfway between Rome and Naples. Perseo wrote to her to tell that his brother at Gaeta had helped him negotiate the sale, as 'everyone knows that the Gaetani can be cheats'.[20] He sent three kinds of fish: pike, mullet and trout.

If the majority of Orsini foodstuffs was home grown, then the opposite was true of the textiles Felice needed. Some linen was woven from flax grown at Bracciano. Another note Felice wrote to Bernardino from Rome told him, 'We are in great need of chemises. So we need you to send three yards of linen for us to have in hand as quickly as possible.' Another occasion saw a minor Orsini relation, Giovanni, writing a receipt to Bernardino for five yards of linen on the commission 'given to me by her illustrious ladyship'. But sheets or undergarments made of linen were not the only needs generated by Felice's family. There was also a huge demand for silks and satins, in particular for her own clothing, and for furnishing the Orsini homes. Luxury textiles were not always easy to find, and so a large network of staff and agents was always at work in pursuit of its acquisition. Such fabric was an investment in itself. The high prices it fetched meant that dowries were often at least partly comprised of yards of silks and satins. Secondhand clothes sometimes have a stigma attached to them. In Renaissance Italy, however, an exquisite and beautiful weave was a work of art in itself, and it did not necessarily matter if such fabric had once belonged to somebody else. The secondhand cloth trade was a substantial industry.

Felice had always worn black, so she already had several black dresses for her transition to widowhood, but she still regularly acquired more. In August 1520 Francesco d'Ancona wrote to tell her that 'Signor Ippolito ordered me to send you from my expedition to Bologna the three yards of white silk and the three yards of the black silk that is the most beautiful possible, as you yourself told me. The cost is 24 *carlini*.'[21] The city of Bologna was developing an expertise in the production of black silk, a particularly expensive commodity. The Spanish economy did almost as well from its monopoly on the logwood tree on Caribbean islands, which produced rich dark black dye, as it did from the silver the Spanish mined in the New World.

Francesco d'Ancona also bought material in Venice, home of Italy's finest textiles, which were brought back to Rome by a mule-driver who was paid 0.45 *carlini*. Valerio Antonelli wrote to tell her that he had found 'Russian damask of great beauty, black, blue and yellow'. Blue and yellow were the della Rovere colours; Felice might have wished to accessorize her widow's habit with her father's family colours, perhaps in the form of a bodice, or undergown. In January 1522, her 'affectionate servant' Antonio di Salmoli told Felice that he had sent the 'silk of many colours' she had ordered. Even the family lawyer, Prospero d'Aquasparta, was not exempt from receiving requests from her for purchases: in one letter Felice asked him to send a request to another servant to obtain 'thread of every colour' for her.[22]

Felice ordered silk veils, appropriate to her widowed status, specially from *veletori* (veil-makers) in Rome. Her young sons did not wear silks and damasks, but clothes of sturdier and warmer fabric, such as serge and chamblet, a blend of wool, silk and linen. This was for practical reasons; there was no point in making doublets and jerseys for small boys living in the country out of delicate fabric that would quickly be worn through or outgrown. Vicovaro, high in the hills, was extremely cold in the winter.

Felice's daughter Julia, aged thirteen, asked her mother on 3 October 1520 to send her 'velvet dress and jacket, as there is an intolerable cold here'.[23] As a young girl, Julia had grasped the importance of clothes. A year earlier she had written to her mother, 'I thought it best that your ladyship know that Signor Girolamo has no more shirts, so you might want to send the lawn for five shirts.' A few days later, she sent her mother the request for some velvet clothes and wrote to ask her for 'two yards of lawn and an ounce of gold thread', suggesting she wanted to make an embroidered chemise – intended more probably for herself than for her younger brothers.

CHAPTER 13

Statio

___

No one on Felice's staff worked harder for her obtaining what she needed than her servant Statio del Fara. Statio had been in Felice's employment since at least 1513, when he appeared on the list of her personal *salariati* as 'Statio, cancelliero'. He was well educated; his letters are written in a most exquisite hand, and his loyalty to Felice and commitment to his job were unquestionable. He took the issue of expense very seriously indeed:

> Through Vincenzo Staffieri I have sent you two pieces of chamblet, and one of home-spun serge. They both exceed the six yards that I wrote down, but because your ladyship has not responded to my letter regarding this I am sending you all the chamblet and the serge and you can measure off what you want . . . Your ladyship wrote to me to order Signor Girolamo's overshirt and doublet which amounts to 6 *palmi* [0.2234 metres] of serge, and with the lining, which comes to 6 *carlini,* it's 8 *carlini* in all. The shoemaker is asking for 4 *julios* for Madonna Julia's slippers and shoes, but I believe he would be content with 3 and a half.[1]

The *julio* was the ducat introduced by Felice's father, Julius II, with his own portrait engraved in profile.

Statio's days were a frenzy of activity. Like most large Roman palaces,

Market scene, fifteenth century

Monte Giordano had shops on its ground-floor level, rented out to butchers, saddlers and apothecaries. This commercial practice dated back to the *insulae* of ancient Rome, and is still common to modern apartment blocks in the city. But most of Statio's responsibilities would take him into the Via dei Banchi, the street just behind Monte Giordano, which was the heart of Rome's shopping and financial district, home to stores and banks since the Middle Ages. It was there that Statio would haggle and fight with the silk merchants and the shoe-makers, determined to get his mistress the best prices, and receive praise and credit for his thrifty ways.

Perhaps because of the length of his service with her, Statio had achieved a comfortable relationship with Felice. This is evident from his style of writing to her, which is unusual between a servant and a member of the nobility. His letters can show something of a flair for the dramatic. On one occasion he wrote to her, 'I am sending you ten *palmi* of velvet. The merchant told me that it was the best, and that one should not dress in anything else. I have faith in him at the moment, but if it does not satisfy you, I will quarrel with him so terribly that I will almost wring his neck.'[2] When Felice did not immediately send him the money from Vicovaro and Statio needed to pay for the serge for Girolamo's shirt and Julia's shoes, he first wrote to her household manager there, Hippolito della Tolfa, asking him to 'solicit our lady to send me the money'. The household expenses were mounting up, and so when that approach did not appear effective, Statio, in the body of a much longer letter to Felice, informed her, 'Your ladyship knows that I have been in Rome nine weeks now and I am counting out every expense from the purse. Your ladyship knows what it is to live and spend money in Rome, in such a way that I am now finding myself in a real calamity, and I could never have believed that I would see my ruin. I do not say this to contradict your will in any way. My obligation and debt to you are such that I would spill my own blood for you for your goodness towards me.'[3]

Felice clearly allowed Statio to write to her in this way without fear of reprisal. She appears never to have sent him the kind of sharp rebuke that Hippolito della Tolfa, his counterpart at Vicovaro, sometimes received. Statio did much more than just shop for Felice. He served as her linchpin when she was absent from Rome. He sent her all the latest gossip, which ranged from who had come to Monte Giordano to what was going on at the Vatican and the latest international scandals. 'Let me tell some news,' Statio reported gleefully to Felice in 1517, 'which came in a letter from Venice. The Great Turk [Selim I] has a very beautiful Christian slave with whom he is in love. One morning he gave a fine meal for all the court, and she was present, elegantly dressed with magnificent clothes and jewels. At the end of the meal he asked all if she was most beautiful. They were all stupefied and agreed.' Statio had a novel solution to the problem of the dangerous and powerful infidel, whose empire was expanding rapidly: 'All we have to do', he concluded, 'is to wait for a man like her who can conquer the kingdom.'[4]

When Statio was not speculating on international events, fighting with merchants, or declaring he would shed his own blood for Felice, he distributed licences for the acquisition of another valuable commodity that Felice controlled: wood. Wood was used for the making of furniture, the heating of the home, and even as currency in its own right, bartered for other commodities. The 1518 inventory of the Orsini estate indicated which fiefs had forests attached to them, including Trevignano, Galera and Isola. The woods were mainly of oak trees, for this was the ancient land of the Sabines, which even in 64 BC, as the Greek writer Strabo described, 'produces acorns in great quantities'.[5] In other words, for over fifteen hundred years, the land Felice now ruled had always been the land of oaks, the land of the Rovere.

Care had to be taken that the woods were not over-felled each year. Not only would they take a long time to restock, opportunities for hunting would also be reduced. So the woods were patrolled by Orsini servants, and anybody who wanted to chop wood had to have permission in the form of a licence stamped with Felice's seal. A sample blank licence gives an indication of the form this permission would take: 'Felice della Rovere Orsini allows the bearer to chop wood in the holding of Isola, reserved for the bearer and two pack horses for the duration of one month. We order and command our bailiff and the guards not to harm the bearer because the bearer has paid to chop down trees. Validated in Rome, 1531.'[6]

Not surprisingly, such licences were in great demand. Even Felice's half-sister, Francesca De Cupis, wrote to her, grateful for having received 'the licence for wood'. In January of 1521, perhaps because it was particularly cold, the *ministra* of the Sisters of the Pietà wrote to Felice with the following request:

Our lady benefactor: The faith which we have in you, and our own great necessity gives us the strength to avail you of our needs and to beg you, for the love of God, that you might wish to concede gracefully in allowing us to go to your forest at Galera or Isola for some logs of wood, to be carried away by the one animal we possess. This would be doing us a great charity, for which we would be eternally obliged, if you would deign to send the licence of authorization for your bailiff. As always, we recommend ourselves to you.[7]

In addition to these impoverished nuns, there were many high-ranking clergy who sought licences from Felice, among them Cardinal Bernardo da Bibbiena. In the reign of Felice's father, Bibbiena had been secretary at the Vatican to the Medici cardinals. Felice and he had always had some peripheral contact and she sometimes appeared in his reports back to Florence. But during the reign of Pope Leo X, Bibbiena had become a figure of much greater importance and influence. He had been the boyhood tutor of Giovanni de' Medici, who was now Leo X. He had become Leo's most trusted adviser. Leo had made him cardinal deacon, had given him his own former titular church of Santa Maria in Domnica in Rome, and a suite of rooms in the Vatican Palace, because Bibbiena could not afford a palace of his own. Raphael, before his death, was to have married Bibbiena's niece, who is now buried next to him in the Pantheon. Bibbiena now wanted to acquire wood from Felice, and Felice's servant Giovanni Battista della Colle reported to her on 16 January 1520, that, 'Monsignor Reverend of Santa Maria in Portico recommends himself to you. He begs that you would send him a bull to let him chop wood in the forest at Galera.'[8]

Unfortunately, when they went out to Galera, Bibbiena's men ran into difficulties. The Cardinal wrote personally to Felice, 'You would give me much grace if you could let me send three of my mules to Isola. I do not know why, but my men fought with those at Galera, and they do not want to go back there again.'[9] According to Statio, whom Bibbiena visited in person, the men of Galera had 'torn the licence into shreds'.

This was not the only time that problems occurred between curial servants and the woodsmen. The Romans, dressed in the livery of their cardinal employer, fancied themselves a cut above these peasants and undoubtedly put on airs not appreciated by the countrymen, even if they did come with authorization from Felice. Felice herself was absolutely furious at the way in which the head woodsman had treated the servants of Alessandro da Nerone, who was the *maestro di casa* of the Pope himself. They had refused to let Nerone's men take away the wood they had chopped down. When she heard what had occurred, Felice wrote to Statio to tell him to let the head woodsman know exactly what he had to do: 'Tell him to send out again all the wood they took from the mule-drivers of His Holiness, under the command of Alessandro Neroni, His Holiness's *maestro di casa*, at the expense of the head woodsman, and with this, show him how he has displeased me with his insolence.' To confirm that the curia would continue to be allowed to take wood, she added, 'And now send a licence to Pietro Oromabelli [a papal secretary], so that he can send mules for the wood from my forest.'[10]

For Felice, providing papal servants with goods they needed was a means of ensuring her continued position and influence at the Vatican. Support from the papacy was her best protection against any attempts by the Orsini to challenge her leadership. She also came increasingly to rely heavily on her half-brother, Cardinal Gian Domenico, who had grown from an 'ignorant young boy' into his sister's most loyal and trusted servant.

CHAPTER 14

Family Matters

Felice della Rovere had risen far above the ranks of the bureaucrat's family in which she had spent her earliest years, but she never left them behind. The de Cupis had provided her with stability and affection when those elements were lacking in her life. Such a bond was unusual. Few illegitimate daughters of the elite were allowed to bond with their mothers. They were frequently removed at an early age from this maternal orbit, brought up with their father's family, or placed in a convent. Yet Felice had always returned to her mother's home. Despite the fact that Felice was now Rome's most powerful woman, her mother Lucrezia still fretted over her as if she was still a young girl. Learning that her thirty-four-year-old daughter was afflicted with toothache, she wrote to her, 'I learned that you have a pain in your teeth, which upset me. I beg that you warm up a bit of vinegar in a well-heated pitcher, and a pinch of salt, and three or four laurel leaves, and hold it as long as you can in your mouth, and then it will not hurt.'[1]

Despite her motherly concern, Lucrezia understood the protocol of writing to the daughter who was now the Orsini Signora. She addressed her as 'most illustrious lady' and signed herself, 'your most obedient Lucrezia'. Securing a cardinalship for Gian Domenico was the best way Felice could raise her maternal family's status to one commensurate with her own.

Pasquino statue decorated with 'Pasquinades'

Gian Domenico understood very well how and why he had become a cardinal, and where his loyalties and duties lay. He appears in very few ecclesiastical records for almost a decade after his appointment as cardinal and was not an active member of the curia. The reason for his low clerical profile is that his regular position was as his sister's *aide de camp*, a fact widely recognized in Rome. In satirical verses pinned to the Pasquino statue, Giuliano Leno had been mocked for his greed but Rome's cardinals were easy targets as well. Gian Domenico was derided for being 'dear to his mother' or for 'the love he bears his relatives', references to Lucrezia, with whom he lived, and Felice, who had made him a cardinal.[2]

The individuals in question had little regard for public opinion. After she became Orsini *gubernatrix*, Felice quickly marshalled Gian Domenico and his sister Francesca as her aides. They knew Rome well and spoke the same language as the city's bureaucrats and merchants. Consequently they and their mother had an easy rapport with Felice's high-ranking servants and with Statio del Fara in particular. Statio mentioned Francesca and Lucretia frequently in his letters, suggesting an easy informality existed between them: 'Madonna Lucrezia dropped in on her way home. She asked me how Signor Girolamo [her grandson] was, and it gave her great pleasure to learn from me that he was well.'[3]

Statio often worked in conjunction with Francesca, who frequently served as Felice's agent in the acquisition of textiles and other objects. Just a few years younger than Felice, she was married to Angelo del Bufalo, a high-level Roman bureaucrat who would eventually receive the appointment of *maestro di strada*, commissioner of public works. Angelo gave Francesca connections that were useful to Felice. He was also a notorious philanderer. The churchman Matteo Bandello's *Novelle* of 1554 tells the story of 'Imperia, Roman courtesan . . . loved by an endless number of great and rich men. But among those who loved her was Signor Angelo del Bufalo, a man who was valiant, humane, genteel and extremely rich . . . he kept her in a very honourably furnished house, with many male and female servants continually in attendance upon her.'[4]

Consequently Francesca was frequently to be found in the company of her mother and brother, undertaking commissions for her sister, rather than at her 'humane and genteel' husband's side. She had a good eye, and was remorseless in seeking out hard-to-find luxury items. 'I am dutifully letting you know that I have done what you commissioned me to do regarding those items made of gold, as well as the little cross. And if your ladyship has need of lawn, let me know as I have found some that would serve your ladyship well that is beautiful, and well priced.'[5] On another occasion: 'I am sending you the ribbon about which you wrote to me. I have searched all of Rome, and this is the most beautiful I could find, as it is the end of the summer, and every merchant has sold the best that he has . . . If your ladyship does not like it, I can take it back and I shall see what I can do.'[6]

Statio also gave reports on Francesca's purchases: 'Madonna Francesca has found two *canne* and two *palmi* of Venetian *pavonazo* [highly sought after peacock-coloured silk].'[7] Another message from Statio reads, 'I received your mandate from the 11 June which authorizes Madonna Francesca to obtain silk for the boys' caps and the silk for Madonna Carlotta. This morning the aforesaid Madonna will undertake to acquire what your ladyship specified in your memo.' Sometimes Felice's mother assisted too; Statio informed Felice in another letter that 'I am sending you three *canne* of the dark cloth (*panno perso*) and I believe you will be well satisfied with it, as it was acquired by Madonna Lucrezia and Madonna Francesca, who made comparisons, and found it to be the best. It cost 8 ducats and it was all paid for by Madonna Lucrezia and Francesca.'[8]

If Francesca's job for Felice was to seek out the best fabrics at the best prices, then Gian Domenico's was to do everything and anything where his ecclesiastical position and influence would be of use. For example, as cardinal, he could bring to Leo Church-related requests from Felice that it might be inappropriate for her to make herself. On 9 August 1520, Gian Domenico wrote to his half-sister, 'Gian Jacopo your vassal came here to see us, saying that you wished for an indulgence to be granted to the church of Santa Maria del Fiore in Bracciano. We have sent the request to His Holiness and when he authorizes it I shall have it expedited to Bracciano.'[9]

Absolutely indifferent to the protests against indulgences by Luther, the northern heretic, and his growing band of followers, Felice intended her request to be for the benefit of the community of Bracciano. An indulgence awarded to those visiting Bracciano's church meant more travellers would stop at the little town on their way to Rome from the north and boost its economy. It might be noted that Gian Domenico wrote of *when*, and not *if*, Leo would grant Felice's request.

A more personal matter of Felice's that demanded her brother's assistance was with regard to her palace at Trinità dei Monti. As Orsini regent, Felice rarely expressed interest in the acquisition of new objects, and she was by no means a typical patron of the time. While by necessity she spent a lot of money on good-quality textiles, she did not, as Isabella d'Este did, purchase elaborate glassware or maiolica. Felice was satisfied with crockery and uten-sils of the most ordinary and serviceable kind, as is indicated by a letter from her servant Alexander, in August 1524, in which he informs her that he is sending 'a quantity of white beakers, 18 saucers, 11 dishes, 2 large plates, 2 half-plates, 2 candlesticks, a jug and a salt cellar'.[10] This type of pottery was of the plainest sort to be found in sixteenth-century Italy, with a simple white glaze and perhaps some decorative lines in green and blue. The disparate pieces suggest they were to replace ones that had been broken, perhaps by her children, as the wares were being sent to Vicovaro.

Only occasionally did Felice acquire anything for herself of a more frivolous nature after she assumed the Orsini regency. A rare moment of personal indulgence came with a letter sent from Naples in 1518 from Eliz-abetta di Mare, who was related to the Savelli, the Roman noble family. Having learned of Felice's request for 'a fan made of peacock feathers', she was bringing one with her to Rome.[11] This exotic fan was still at the castle of Bracciano at the end of the sixteenth century, clearly still deemed a rare and beautiful object. Felice liked fans, the only form of ventilation available at this time. Later she paid one golden ducat for one fashioned by a Roman craftsman from black feathers.

What mattered most to Felice were her residences, because of their immense intrinsic value – financial, social and political. She might not have restored Palo herself, as she had no immediate need of the castle after the death of her husband and in fact the Pope had done it for her, but there were certain matters at the Trinità Palace that needed to be resolved, not the least of which was access. Today, the Pincian Hill, on which the church and convent of Trinità dei Monti and Felice's palace, which partly com-prises the present-day Villa Malta, are situated is entirely urban, connected to the city by a dense network of roads. But in 1520 these were among the few inhabited buildings, built on land that was otherwise wilderness or used for vineyards. The hilly topography made the palace difficult to reach, even for those on sure-footed mules. The grand Spanish Steps leading up to the hill were not constructed until the eighteenth century. Until then, what is now the most popular route to the Pincian Hill, Rome's most glamorous steps, was just a slope and it was frequently very muddy.

Felice needed a new road built to make access to her palace easier from the city below. One direct route would have been to run a road in front of her property, down the hill. This route, however, would cut across the grounds of the convent of Trinità dei Monti, and the friars objected to such a proposal. Felice decided that if the matter were to be dealt with as quickly as possible, she needed to avail herself of an influence respected not only by the friars but also by the *maestri di strade*, the officers of public works in Rome, who could have the ultimate power of veto over her plans for a road. While she herself was absent from the city in the summer of 1520, she called on the College of Cardinals. Her brother, Gian Domenico, the Cardinal of Trani, brought in further clerical support to help his sister realize her ambition, and subsequently sent her the following detailed report on 27 June:

> Dearest sister. This morning, the Cardinal Reverend of S.T. [possibly San Teodoro] and Monsignor the Reverend of Quattro Santi [Lorenzo Pucci] and I met to go over our differences with the convent of Trinità. We went up to the Trinità to see the place where you want the street. There we met the *maestri di strade* and the Reverend Phantano di Senis, the tutor of the heirs of Maestro Felice di Brancha [who had owned the vineyard behind Felice's property] and with the other master builders we really looked the place over.
>
> There are three ways of building the street, and three possibilities. If the street is made as a wide road, the *maestri* say that it will cost more. And Phantano de Senis says that Maestro Felice's heirs would not be happy with blocking up the vineyard to make a public route, so you would need to compensate them for the damage. Making the street towards the cow pasture would cost less than going though the vineyard. The *maestri* say that would cost 200 ducats.
>
> The third way is to buy the vineyard from the heirs of Maestro Felice, whose price is 2000 ducats. The friars say they would pay 800 and you

19 & 20 The inner workings of Bracciano: the castle's courtyard, and the fountain house that Felice possibly commissioned from the architect Peruzzi.

21 *Venus Felix and Amor* was a prized part of Julius II's collection of ancient statues at the Villa Belvedere;
the reference in its title to his daughter's name cannot have passed without comment by visitors.
22 Sebastiano del Piombo's portrait of an unknown woman, dressed in black with a white veil, is possibly
an image of Felice.

3. Following the death of her father, Felice found an ardent supporter and even a business partner in Pope Leo X.

4. Cardinal Bernardo Dovizi da Bibbiena, Leo's boyhood tutor and close adviser, commented on Felice's activities at the papal court. She in turn supplied him with wood from the Orsini forests.

25 More Medici friends and enablers: Pope Clement VII wholeheartedly backed Felice in her struggle against Napoleone, her stepson.

26 Following Napoleone's murder, Felice petitioned Cardinal Ippolito de' Medici daily to restore the Orsini estates to her family.

7 The seafront castle of Palo was a spectacular acquisition by Felice, paid for by funds donated
y her father.
8 The medieval palace of Monte Giordano was the major Orsini seat in Rome, but it was Felice
ho saw to its renovation. She commissioned an up-to-date facade by Peruzzi, following the damage
 used in the Sack Rome.

29 Della Rovere cousins: Francesco Maria was one of Felice's favourite relatives, but he repaid her kindness by casting aspersions upon her legitimacy.

30 His wife Eleonora helped house Felice and her family during their exile from Rome after the Sack.

The Lives of Felice's children: Titian's erotic *Venus of Urbino* was presented to Guidobaldo della Rovere his wedding to Julia Varana, but his true love was Felice's daughter, Clarice.

A Pre-Raphaelite vision of the kind of bloody encounter that took place between Felice's headstrong n Girolamo and his half-brother, Napoleone.

33 Felice's presence was used to sway
Michelangelo to complete her father's tomb.
The figure of Rachel is perhaps a tribute to her.

34 Felice's bold and masculine signature:
'Felix Ruveris Ursinis', ('Felix of the Oak and the Bear').

would pay the rest, which is more because you would have the part that has a beautiful fountain. So your price would be 1,200 ducats, which would get you the vineyard and you could then have the exit and the street where you wanted. It is true that the vineyard is a bit dear, but it is worth it for the convenience. Certainly your ladyship is much obliged to the Reverend of S.T. and Santi Quattro Coronati who have acted with the greatest love and affection towards you as if they were your own brothers. And because in the vineyard there are certainly ancient walls, the Reverend di Santi Quattro Coronati thoughtfully mentioned that you could make some barns out of the ruins at little expense. As to the price, I told them that your ladyship is at present ill supplied with cash; in fact you do not have a penny. Phantano says that with regard to the price he can wait six months and perhaps more . . . [12]

Three days after Gian Domenico's meeting at the Trinità, the ever efficient lawyer Prospero d'Aquasparta wrote to Felice, 'Monsignor Trani and also Cardinal Orsini have communicated to me the difference you have had with the friars of the Trinità over the entrance to your garden, and that finally on Sunday they went there to adjudicate. Although I am not notarizing the sale of the garden it will pass through my hands. At this hour I have sent for the notary who will process the sale, and who will inform me of everything.'[13]

Thanks to a team of industrious cardinals working on her behalf, led by her half-brother, Felice got what she wanted. The Bufalini Map of Rome of 1557 indicates that the road to Felice's palace was indeed built using the vineyard she purchased from the heirs of Maestro Felice di Brancha. A winding road exits the property to the east.

Like Palo, the Trinità dei Monti Palace came to have its own cachet with the curia. In 1518, Leo X's younger cousin, Cardinal Giulio de' Medici, had begun the construction of the Villa Medici, now the Villa Madama, located out to the north-west of Rome on Monte Mario, by the Milvian Bridge. The villa was designed by Raphael, inspired by Pliny's description of his villa in his *Natural History*. In doing so, architect and patron relaunched a passion for the suburban Roman villa beloved by the ancient Roman emperors and their acolytes. In due course, his own family would also build on the Pincian Hill but, in the meantime, there were other members of Leo's family who envied Felice's possession of the Trinità Palace. In June 1524, Leo's nephew, Cardinal Giovanni Salviati, wrote to Felice, addressing her familiarly as his 'sister'. He told her that 'having resolved not to leave Rome this summer in order to take care of certain matters, I have been thinking of being accommodated in some delightful place that was remote from other dwellings in Rome, where I could go for pleasure and recreation in these times where there is the threat of plague, and I have been seeing in my mind your beautiful rooms at the Trinità. I thought I would request accommodation there, given your absence, seeing that I am addressing someone of your humanity and courtesy, and for the good friendship which exists between us.'[14] His request came as no surprise to Felice, for Salviati had already approached his fellow cardinal Gian Domenico a few days earlier regarding his interest in the palace. Gian Domenico immediately alerted Felice, telling her that he had assured Giovanni 'the rooms were well furnished'.[15] The Cardinal would pay rent, and Felice had a constant need of cash, so both she and Gian Domenico were anxious that the influential Florentine cardinal might take on the Trinità Palace as a summer let.

Although Gian Domenico wrote that he had stressed Felice's lack of ready cash to those selling the *vigna* only two weeks earlier, he had secured her a loan of 2000 ducats with an interest rate of 13 per cent, money perhaps already earmarked for other plans.[16] The Italian elite was always notoriously short of money, and they constantly traded loans between themselves to cover any temporary embarrassments. Felice always welcomed any opportunities to make more money. She was neither avaricious nor miserly because she always spent very quickly any money she had on household needs, clothing or servants' wages. Despite her initial reluctance to use Monte Giordano as her primary seat of governance in Rome, it was important for Felice's own self-image as governor that she repair the shabby state into which it had fallen. In January 1519, Statio wrote to tell her that 'Antonio Puccino and I have been measuring up the outer door of the antechamber, and getting in the wood for the loggia, and to make up the doors and windows'.[17] Felice's 1519 account book also mentions an expense of 40 ducats for making 'the window in the sala grande'.[18] In some small way, Felice was attempting to restore the image of Monte Giordano as it had been back in the fifteenth century, under the patronage of Cardinal Giordano, or at the very least to make it cleaner and tidier.

Felice also chose to part with those Orsini residences she felt were more financial liabilities than assets. She was willing to hand over the palace Gian Giordano had built at Blois to King Francis I, as she saw that it served little purpose to keep it in the family. In 1520 she also sold a fifteenth-century Orsini palace in Naples to the Count of Nola. The matter of cash had begun to press hard on her, because she now had the matter of dowries to concern her.

CHAPTER 15

Dowries and the Great Queen

In October 1519, Felice had arranged the marriage of her stepdaughter Carlotta to Giovanni Pico, the Count of Mirandola. This decision was not one she could make on her own. Because Carlotta was only her step-daughter, she needed the acquiescence of Carlotta's now eighteen-year-old brother Napoleone, Renzo da Ceri and Felice's main ally among the Orsini, Cardinal Franciotto. Felice wanted to ensure that Carlotta's hus-band was not too powerful a figure, as that would not only require a very large dowry but might also run the risk of providing the Orsini with an over-influential ally against her. At the same time, family prestige demanded a spouse of some rank and stature. The terms of Carlotta's dowry were negotiated at Bracciano on 28 October 1519: '16,000 gold ducats, of which 12,000 are the legacy of her father, 1000 are promised by Donna Felice, another 1000 in ornaments, *corredo* [trousseau] and jewels, and 2000 will come from Napoleone, Abbot of Farfa, on the profits of the Abbey'.[1] Sixteen thousand ducats was not a vast dowry, only a thousand more than Julius had provided for Felice herself. But the Count of Miran-dola had difficulty in extracting it from the respective parties. In January 1520, Felice's servant Philippo da Bracciano wrote to tell her that he and Statio were trying to renegotiate the terms of the dowry payment on her behalf, which they felt were 'too narrow'.[2] In 1525, six years later,

Detail of *Fountain of Youth* frescos, Castle of Bracciano, fifteenth century

Napoleone had yet to pay his provision of 2000 ducats to the Count.

With Carlotta married, Felice immediately turned her attention to her own daughter and eldest child, Julia. Felice had considered betrothals for Julia since the child was four years old, including the son of Alfonso d'Este, and the son of the Duke of Nemours, Giuliano de' Medici. In the end, however, she looked to the far south not to the north for Julia's husband. She found a suitable candidate in the Calabrian principate of Bisignano: its ruler, Pier Antonio da Sanseverino.[3] Felice's contact with the Prince probably came through his brother-in-law, the Count of Nola, to whom she had recently sold the Orsini palace in Naples.

Ordinarily, the marriage of a daughter saw only the exit of money from her family in the form of her dowry. In this instance, however, Felice had the opportunity to turn a profit. What the Prince of Bisignano wanted as much as a wife was a cardinal in the family. Felice's rapport with Leo X was well known and the Orsini *gubernatrix* was widely respected. Felice could assist the Prince in securing the Sanseverino family the honour and influence they lacked. On 9 August 1520, Gian Domenico wrote to Felice, 'In the last hour a gentleman came here who asserts that he is the secretary of the Prince of Bisignano who charged him to find you to discuss the matter of the betrothal to Madonna Julia. We have offered as a dowry 40,000 ducats on your part and the agreement that Signor Antonio, the uncle of the Prince, will be made a cardinal. I told him that only the Pope makes cardinals, but that your ladyship would do everything possible, given the love that His Holiness bears towards you.'[4]

However great Leo's love for Felice, a cardinal's hat was too precious a commodity for him to give away for nothing. But he was prepared to consider a proposal that would be to his material advantage. Leo was as big a spender as his predecessor, and more than willing to accept funds to swell the coffers that paid for, among other things, Raphael and his work at the Vatican and New St Peter's, as well as the Pope's hunting villas and lavish parties. Nor was any secret kept of the deal negotiated by the Pope, the former Pope's daughter, and the southern Prince. Such an accord only confirmed the view of the north's emergent Protestants of the Catholic Church's inherent corruption.

In March 1521 the Prince of Bisignano arrived in Rome. Baldessar Castiglione wrote to Mantua to tell the Gonzaga court, 'The Prince of

Bisignano has arrived, and has been most fondly embraced by His Holiness, and he has made the betrothal which in so doing means he will take Madonna Felice's daughter. The Pope has a petition from Madonna Felice which declares if the betrothal succeeds, he will make a cardinal of Signor Antonio Sanseverino.'[5] The Venetian Sanuto was much more explicit about how the Pope and Felice would profit: '[The Prince] will give the Pope 25,000 ducats, 8000 of which he will receive now, in cash, and he has promised to give 16,000 to Madonna Felice.'[6] The Prince's family was delighted with the match. His sister, the Countess of Nola, wrote to Felice to express her happiness at the betrothal. 'It is', she wrote, 'as if he had taken the daughter of a great queen.'[7] For her part, the 'great queen' expressed her happiness by appearing in public in a white veil.[8]

The Prince of Bisignano paid a high price for a cardinal's hat for his uncle. In order to marry Julia Orsini, he broke a betrothal to the sister-in-law of the Viceroy of Naples, for which he had to pay a fine of 26,000 ducats to his liege lord, the Holy Roman Emperor and King of Spain, Charles V. Sanuto reported, 'He will need to live with little expense, in order to pay such a debt.'[9]

'Living with little expense' was not something to which the Prince of Bisignano was accustomed. After his marriage, he and Julia frequently petitioned Felice to advance them instalments of her dowry. Julia wrote regularly to her mother, long, largely indecipherable letters. She often sent her mother the same kinds of requests she had made when she was a young girl at Vicovaro, for clothes and shoes. 'Now that I must dress in white clothes,' she wrote, 'please could you send me two lengths of white silk twist, and two all-white large headscarves.'[10] Julia's letters give little sense of Felice's eldest daughter possessing an inner life, although she was under a certain amount of pressure to produce a son. Julia gave birth to two daughters, the first named after her husband's mother, Eleonora, and the second after Felice. Letters Felice received from the Prince's secretaries described the first little girl as 'most beautiful, all the house takes joy in her'. With the appearance of a second daughter, in July 1525, the Duchess of Nerito, the Prince's aunt, wrote to Felice, saying, 'The Princess has again made a girl; let us hope that in a year we will be blessed with a boy, and not be discontented with a girl as they are at times useful for the house . . .'[11] Bisignano himself, however, wrote with pride to Felice, telling her, 'The Princess has made a beautiful baby girl, and to this one I have attached the name Lady Felice, after you.'[12] 'Lady Felice' was the first in a succession of girls to be named after the daughter of Julius II, who thereby succeeded, for a time, in feminizing what had hitherto been an exclusively male name.

Julia's marriage to the Prince of Bisignano had secured Felice a substantial cash sum, and allies of her own in southern Italy. But the southern alliance opened up the floodgates of Felice's enmity with the Orsini men. 'The Orsini are unhappy with the marriage of the daughter of Gian Giordano with the Prince of Bisignano, and Signor Renzo da Ceri most particularly,' wrote Sanuto.[13] They were angered by her decision to grant her own daughter a dowry from Orsini funds much more than twice the one her stepdaughter Carlotta had received. But none was angered more than her stepson Napoleone. He was incandescent with rage that Felice had used her influence with Leo to procure a cardinal's hat for her daughter's new family – a hat he thought should have been his.

CHAPTER 16

Napoleone

For many chroniclers of the Orsini house, Felice della Rovere earns no credit for her considerable abilities as regent. She is little more than a wicked stepmother, plotting and scheming to prevent Napoleone, Gian Giordano's eldest son, from succeeding to his rightful inheritance.

When Felice della Rovere entered the house of Orsini, there was a tacit agreement that were she to have a son he would be the heir to the lordship, thereby deposing the incumbent heir, Gian Giordano's son Napoleone, born in 1501. This situation was not unusual; the same provision would have applied had she married the Lord of Piombino. But several of the men of the Orsini house, in particular the *condottiere* Renzo da Ceri, who was married to Napoleone's sister Francesca, viewed the provision with suspicion and resentment. Gian Giordano was ttwo decades Felice's senior; they knew the likelihood was that he would die before her sons were old enough to govern. This interloper, the bastard daughter of a pope, would take over. And when she did, she made it plain that she had no interest in their counsel. Nobody resented this more than Napoleone Orsini. He was eleven by the time his brother Francesco was born, old enough to be conscious of having been disinherited, with all its attendant disappointment and humiliation. As compensation, Felice's father Julius had endowed Napoleone with the Abbey of Farfa, although the boy was not required to

Lucas Cranach, *Pope Descends into Hell*, 1518

take holy orders. Farfa, located to the south of Rome, was one of Italy's largest monastic benefices, a holding of over eighty square miles. When Leo became pope, he granted Napoleone, as abbot, an additional income of 1000 ducats a month.

Was Felice really a wicked stepmother, determined to deprive the eldest son of his rightful inheritance? She certainly did attempt to have Napoleone excluded from provisions relating to the Orsini estate; some documents regarding the disbursement of Gian Giordano's property show that Napoleone's name was clearly added only later to those of Felice's two sons. From Felice's perspective, Napoleone had received more than adequate compensation for the loss of a future title. Farfa encompassed almost as much terrain as did the Orsini estate, and she was reluctant for him to receive anything else. She also did not want him near her own sons. The boy was fast growing into a headstrong, aggressive and unstable young man, and she perhaps feared he might contrive a means of eliminating her own children, his competition for the Orsini inheritance. Felice insisted that Napoleone live at Bracciano, isolated from her boys at Vicovaro. (The 1518 Bracciano inventory shows that the seventeen-year-old's bedroom was decorated entirely in black.) However, her attitude towards Napoleone's sister Carlotta was different. Carlotta stayed at Vicovaro along with Felice's children. She and her stepmother exchanged cordial messages both before and after her marriage. Felice had commuted the death sentence of Michelangelo da Campagnino after being petitioned by Carlotta and in her will of 1518 she left her stepdaughter a bequest of 3000 ducats. To Napoleone she left nothing. On one level, in stripping Napoleone of his power, Felice was striking a blow for her past. This illegitimate woman had turned the tables on convention. She had an unprecedented degree of power over a legitimate male, and she was not afraid to wield it.

Felice knew that, as a Machiavellian-style *principessa*, any kind of conciliatory gesture she made towards her stepson would be taken by him and the relatives who supported him – Renzo da Ceri, Mario Orsini, Roberto Orsini – as a sign of weakness. They would not hesitate to use it to try to take advantage of her and depose her. Compromise, as far as Felice was concerned, was not an option. But nor could Felice ignore Napoleone. He might not succeed his father as Lord of Bracciano, but he had not been disinherited entirely. He was entitled to his share of the estate's produce and, when his brothers reached their majority, to some part of his father's patrimony. So Felice adopted a policy of trying to keep her relationship with her stepson one where she was most emphatically in financial control. Napoleone was obliged to pay yearly taxes on the Abbey of Farfa to the papacy. As a minor, these were actually paid on his behalf by Felice, so she was kept fully informed of the state of affairs at Farfa. She kept a sharp watch on his access to goods from the estate. When he wanted to obtain linens from Bracciano, Felice, on her way from Rome, wrote somewhat exasperatedly to Daniela, her maidservant, 'My dear Madonna Daniela, go immediately to the linen chest, and send to Signor Napoleone: four table cloths for himself and thirty napkins; four credenza covers and four hand towels; and do send them to him very quickly, and do not look for my signature because I am having to dictate this letter from horseback.'[1] The implication here is that Napoleone was not above forging a permission slip from Felice in order to take what he wanted.

Although not greatly interested himself in estate administration, Napoleone was angered by his stepmother's interference. He became known as *l'Abate* ('the Abbot') but he had the genes and the instincts of a *condottiere*. By the age of seventeen, Napoleone had begun to live as a kind of brigand, accompanied by a band of vassals picked up from the Orsini estates, staying at whichever castle Felice was not occupying at the time. On one occasion, when Felice was away from Vicovaro with her younger son, Napoleone turned up at the castle with his mistress. Her servant Benedetto di San Miniato wrote to assure her that he had turned them away. Napoleone also became convinced that Felice was removing things from Bracciano to which she had no right. Her servant Christoforo wrote to her from Bracciano in May 1521 that 'the Abbot has insisted on making an inventory of everything that is in the room where we keep the best things'.[2]

But it was Felice's decision to help her prospective son-in-law's family acquire a cardinal's hat that really ignited Napoleone's resentment. He made no secret of his fury, as he felt that any cardinal's hat she was able to negotiate should be his. It was not in Felice's interests to make her stepson a cardinal. At that period, there was only one Orsini cardinal, Franciotto, and he tended to be conciliatory towards Felice because he did not want to lose his alliances with the other College of Cardinals' members who were her supporters. A second Orsini cardinal might make him less amenable towards her. Felice had no intention of tipping the balance of power at the College too far towards the Orsini, making it easier for the family to unite against her. And she would have made no personal profit as she had from the Bisignano negotiation. Baldessar Castiglione reported back to Mantua, informing the Gonzaga court that 'the Abbot presumed that it would be him. Now he has gone to Bracciano and he is being terribly threatening.'[3]

At that time, Napoleone could do little more than threaten, because Felice was assured of Leo's love and support. But on 1 December 1521 Leo died suddenly of pneumonia, having caught a cold watching bullfights at La Magliana. The following month, the College of Cardinals elected a Dutch pope, Hadrian of Utrecht, who had been the boyhood tutor of the Holy Roman Emperor, Charles V. Hadrian chose to keep his given name and became Pope Hadrian VI. It was a winter election and Hadrian's reign cast a wintry chill over the life of Rome. He had no ties to Rome and no love for the city. He was instinctively thrifty. He put the building of New St Peter's on hold. Construction work was halted, weeds began to grow through the stones, and the church came to appear as great a ruin as any of the ancient basilicas in the Roman forum. Raphael had died the previous year, and instead of supporting his school of talented students and associates, the new Pope favoured northern artists, such as Jan van Scorel, from Hadrian's home town of Utrecht. Scorel was deemed as no more than mediocre by the Roman cognoscenti.

But no one felt the chill of the northern Pope's reign more than Felice della Rovere.

CHAPTER 17

The Taking of Palo

Unlike his predecessor, the new Pope had no ties to Felice and no interest in developing any. For Hadrian, Felice was no treasured memento of Rome's golden age. She was, rather, a symbol of papal corruption, a reminder of the carnality of one predecessor and the greed of another who had conspired with her to sell offices. Consequently Hadrian had no intention of support-ing her. Conscious that Felice was now without a papal protector, Napoleone, supported by his greatest ally, Renzo da Ceri, wasted no time in flexing his muscles and trying to frighten her into granting him concessions.

Renzo da Ceri had been Leo's military commander and he advised Napoleone how to attack Felice. It was a delicate matter, as they could not do anything to jeopardize the safety of her young sons, who were Orsini heirs after all, and damaging Orsini property would be the equivalent of attacking themselves. But they did identify a point of vulnerability in Felice's castle of Palo, which, following Leo's demise, was currently unoccupied. As Orsini men, it was an outrage that the castle, which had once been Orsini property, should now be in her sole possession. It was a point of honour for them to reclaim it, on the grounds that it was not hers by right.

On 13 January 1522, the Urbino ambassador in Rome, Gian Maria della Porta, wrote to his master, Felice's cousin, Francesco Maria della Rovere, 'Madonna Felice has received news that the Abbot has gone to take Palo with the complicity of Signor Renzo. She is very unhappy and afflicted more than ever . . . She bought Palo with money given to her by Pope Julius.'[1] Felice had confided her fears to Gian Maria as a friend. She mentioned nothing of what had occurred in the letters she wrote simultaneously to Francesco Maria herself, knowing that she must not appear to have lost control in any way. Instead, she discussed with him some of the final details of the restitution of his estates, for if Leo had been a good friend to her, he had not been a good friend to Francesco Maria. As general of the papal troops, Renzo da Ceri had led an attack on Urbino to oust Francesco Maria and place Leo's nephew Lorenzo in his place. Francesco Maria had only just returned to the Duchy of Urbino. Attempts to reach an accord between the Medici and the della Rovere were now made. One suggestion was to betroth Lorenzo's infant daughter, Catherine de' Medici, to Francesco's infant son, Guidobaldo. Catherine was by then an orphan and in fact, in January 1522, she was placed in Felice's care, until the betrothal fell through. As Felice wrote to Francesco Maria, 'Maestro Ridolfi came to see me last Monday on behalf of the Cardinal of Cortona, and demanded that I give back the baby girl.' A rueful second letter remarks, 'These things are being managed by persons of much higher rank and respect than myself.'[2]

Despite her attention to other matters, Felice did take certain precautions. For example, she left her most valuable possessions in the care of the Abbot of the church of San Salvatore in Laura, adjacent to Monte Giordano in Rome, in case Napoleone should attempt an attack in Rome. Napoleone continued his campaign. On 22 February 1522, when Felice was absent from Bracciano, Napoleone paid a visit to the castle. Gian Maria reported, 'The Lady Felice is very unhappy, troubled because one of her dearest servants at Bracciano has been imprisoned in Rome, and he has taken the castle, and she is worried because all the most important accounts and documents are there. Recently the Abbot has made threats around the estates in the cruellest manner possible, saying he will bring death to all of those who are her servants.'

If Felice worried in private, she did not express her anxiety publicly; this was important for her public persona, her *bella figura*. She was aware that Napoleone did not have the manpower, nor, as yet, the experience to prolong such an offensive indefinitely. She was proved right. After a couple of months, Napoleone's forces weakened and fragmented. Palo was returned to Felice's possession, and he was forced to abandon Bracciano.

If Napoleone expected such tactics to have an effect on his stepmother, he was to be proved wrong. Felice had been standing up to the Orsini for over a decade now, and she was not about to change her ways. She continued writing to him in the same firm tone, demanding to see records of the accounts at Farfa and receive any revenue she felt rightfully belonged to the Orsini estate and not to him personally. After one request in June 1522 that Napoleone evidently found too much to bear, he exploded, sending her in return a letter full of invective and righteous self-pity:

Illustrious Mistress, my Honourable Mother. I received your letter and response to me. Truthfully, ever since the death of my father, I do not seem to be a brother of the sons of Signor Gian Giordano, but a true bastard. Everyone can see that you have enjoyed and taken not only my paternal patrimony but the ecclesiastical one as well. For the two years that I have held my abbey I have seen you take the fruit of it. When you came into the house of Orsini you received many benefits, and were elevated and exalted, that you cannot deny. But other women who came benefited and exalted our house, such as my mother, who exalted and benefited the house in a way I do not need to tell you. She brought with her 33,000 ducats, and the favour of such a king as was her father who raised our house to the heavens. I mention this dowry and other things, because it is well known that you can take pleasure in the possession of your dowry and other things. I have been deprived of my paternal state and my mother's dowry, and these are my displeasures and bad tidings, which injure me. And what brings me sadness is that I have been forbidden to live with my brothers. They are alienated from me and I from them, instead of feeling the charity and love there should be among three brothers.

And then you accuse me of absorbing all of the estate, when in fact it is to the contrary, that I have only 30 ducats a month, which reduces me to eating the snails in the valley, whereas you are assigned the usufruct of your dowry, and you hold Palo apart and with it its produce . . . I have always thought there is more hate than love in you to me, and Signor Renzo concurs. You know how he has worked on our behalf and has borne the love of a father towards me and my brothers. Leaving him aside, you have said that you have been a good mother to me. I have been a good son to you and patiently I have tolerated all these injustices.

As for the Abbey, the holy memory of Pope Julius may have given this benefice to the house of Bracciano, but he gave a lot more to the other barons' houses, benefices and bishoprics and cardinals' hats, and other things that make this estate look like nothing . . . '[3]

Other members of the Orsini family privately shared Napoleone's opinion of Felice, that she was a mere prelate's daughter who had brought no illustrious bloodline with her and who had exploited the house of Orsini for her own ends. But to put such thoughts in writing was a dangerous breach of decorum. Felice now had documentary evidence of the depth of her stepson's resentment of and hatred for her, proof of the extent of his fury, which was now approaching madness.

Over the summer of 1522, Napoleone continued to cause trouble for Felice. She had taken into her care Francesco Maria's niece, Bartolomea Varana, who had just lost her brother, Sigismondo. 'I believe that poor Madonna Bartolomea will consume herself with endless tears and affliction,' wrote Felice to Francesco Maria. 'I am full of maternal love and compassion for her.'[4] But she also feared for Bartolomea's safety. With Napoleone on the loose, none of the Orsini properties was secure. Gian Maria della Porta wrote to Francesco Maria on 3 September 1522, 'Madonna Felice has sent me word that Madonna Bartolomea must leave, as she is afraid that the Abbot will attempt to come and ravish her, and she does not want to run this risk.'[5] There was a sufficient vestige of feudal attitudes in sixteenth-century Italy that were such a rape to take place, Napoleone would have the right to claim Bartolomea as his own. So Bartolomea was removed from Felice's care. Despite the turbulent times, she clearly remembered the months she had spent with her cousin with great affection. A few years later, she wrote her a charming letter, excited about the young husband chosen for her, Gaspare Pallavicino, who was, Bartolomea told Felice, 'of no small importance, and intelligent, literate and musical, and he seems handsome to me. I think you would be pleased for me.'[6] She also wanted Felice to send her the same kind of white and gold embroidered slippers Felice had given her own daughter Julia when she got married.

The following year, Napoleone changed his tactics. He had travelled to Venice, from where, he wrote to his stepmother on 4 May 1523, 'Because my father, God rest his soul, destined me to become a priest, and recognizing that it is not useful for the house that I do not have the literary principles, and neither does it honour me, I have decided to remain for a few years in Padua [the seat of a university].'[7] Felice wrote Francesco Maria, who was Captain of the Venetian Army, 'My son the Abbot has written me in the past few days about being in Padua, with the desire to pursue a course of study, and finds himself there with little family. He has ordered four of his servants to go there, and they are setting out on horseback. I ask your lordship to allow them safe passage. Nothing else occurs to me at this time.'[8] Felice's letter is mild and neutral, seemingly solicitous for Napoleone. But Francesco Maria was now apprised of her stepson's movements, and could keep an eye on him, in case, as was more than likely, her stepson the Abbot was up to no good.

CHAPTER 18

Papal Reprieve

In October 1523 Hadrian VI died, much to the relief of the Roman elite, after a reign of twenty very long months. Prior to the Pope's death, Felice had some small revenge on Hadrian VI, who had stood by while Napoleone wreaked havoc with her life. Her servant Bernardino di San Miniato wrote to her on 26 August 1523 to inform her that 'this morning the Reverend Cardinal Ermellino sent for me in order to apprise your illustrious ladyship that His Holiness would like to rent Palo in the same way that it was held by the holy memory of Pope Leo. I replied that your ladyship could do nothing as the Reverend Cardinal of Trani [Felice's brother] had taken possession of it.'[1]

Hadrian's enduring legacy was that he was to be the last non-Italian pope until the twentieth century. The Northern Pope had inflicted gloom on the city of Rome, and many in the College of Cardinals wanted to see a return to the golden days of Julius and Leo. They chose Leo's cousin Giulio as their new pontiff, Pope Clement VII. Ultimately, the election of Clement was to bring disaster to Rome but, in 1523, he seemed to bring back a bygone era to the city. Felice was relieved. She knew that her long-standing friendship with the Medici family would serve as good defence against the volatile and dangerous Napoleone.

As Francesco and Girolamo grew older, Napoleone started to agitate for

Maarten van Heemskerck, *Detail with Cardinal on a Mule*

the early declaration of their majority. This, of course, would terminate Felice's tenure as Orsini regent. The younger his brothers were declared adults, the weaker they would be, and the easier for Napoleone, with the support of the family, to dominate. In early 1525 he drew up a draft of provisions regarding the estate, in which he proposed that 'the proposed minority of the sons of the Signora should end on the fourteenth birthday of Signor Girolamo'.[2] Fourteen, even by the standards of the day, was young for a boy to be declared an adult. Napoleone also wanted Felice to pick 'one place as her residence where the Abbot will not go, reserving Bracciano as the communal residence', which would serve to isolate her. He proposed that should the 'Signora be obliged to leave for any reason the governing of the estate, she should elect one of the Orsini in her place'. For Felice the most sinister of all his suggestions was unquestionably that 'the governance of Madonna Clarice shall be deputized communally to all three brothers'. In 1524 Clarice was ten years old. Napoleone was proposing that Felice's youngest child be wrested from her, and he be given authority over her.

Felice turned to papal arbitration to suppress Napoleone's schemes to oust her from her seat of governance. At the end of October 1525, a lengthy 'chapters of ordinance between Donna Felice della Rovere, and her children, signed by them in the presence of Pope Clement VII', was presented in the Sala Regia, an audience hall of the Vatican Palace.[3] The lawyer who prepared it was the ever efficient Prospero d'Acquasparta. It was, not surprisingly, overwhelmingly in Felice's favour. Clement gave Felice another four years as 'sole and unique administrator of the estate', so her sons would not come to their majority until they were seventeen and eighteen, and would have more time to mature. In that period of time, Felice could get Clarice safely married. These *capitoli* also forbade Napoleone from bringing armed men with him to Bracciano. While he could live at one of the Orsini castles, he had to accommodate himself at his own expense, and not that of the estate. Although, 'in the event of illness' the Pope recommended that Felice allow Cardinal Franciotto Orsini to govern in her place, she could, with Napoleone's permission, elect another 'qualified person who was not from the house of Orsini'. And if Napoleone refused, Clement still reserved the power to arbitrate himself. This allowed for the option of Cardinal Gian Domenico de

Cupis governing the Orsini in her absence, a situation Felice would of course prefer.

Clement also agreed to some provisions to benefit Felice personally, beyond her role as Orsini trustee. He decreed that as Felice had invested 2000 ducats of her own money in the palace at Trinità dei Monti, the palace should be considered hers, even if it had originally been a part of the Orsini estate. Additionally, with regard to the Orsini holding of Galera, 'a seat which, it is hypothesized, was a part of Madonna Felice's dowry, and given to her for her marriage, and so shall remain in the hands of Madonna Felice'. That there was no surviving document to support this 'hypothesis' and that Galera was not included in the 1516 lists of Felice's possessions suggest that this was a private donation from Clement to Felice. Given that a large number of cardinals who depended on Galera's forests for their wood, it was an arrangement by which the Vatican could continue to profit.

Napoleone realized that the *capitoli* authorized by Clement rendered him completely powerless for the next four years. It was a great victory for Felice. She knew, however, that the negotiation had in no way lessened the enmity of *l'Abate*, who now hated the Pope almost as bitterly as he hated his stepmother, a hatred that was to colour and shape the next decade of her life.

PART V

Dispossessed and Repossessed

CHAPTER 1

At Prayer

The year 1527 marked Felice's tenth anniversary as *gubernatrix* of the Bracciano Orsini. 'I would rather die as a slave in this house than a queen of anywhere else,' she had told the ailing Gian Giordano when he conferred the position on her and reminded her of her duty to the family. She had intended her declaration to be disingenuously rhetorical but a decade later Felice was in fact both queen and slave. She exercised more authority over more individuals and more terrain than any other woman in Italy but there were no holidays from her responsibilities, no respite, no letting go – not even for a moment. There was always Napoleone or an Orsini cousin eager to step in and take advantage of her perceived weakness to wrest control of the family from her. In the interim period, she had also lost her most trusted servant: Statio del Fara, who had died in 1524. Right up to the end, Statio had been devoted to her. The last letter he wrote to her told her how he regretted that his 'fever makes me unable to serve your sweet presence and I feel the affliction even more from your absence, deprived as I am of the company of the wisest and most virtuous lady that I have ever seen, or heard nominated. You are an ornament and glory, and neither our land nor this unhappy country can provide another example of such excellent ways, chastity and every virtue, which you possess, and every Roman is obliged to you for our well-being and our honour.'[1] Following Statio's

View of Rome showing Monte Giordano and Palazzo De Cupis, sixteenth century

demise, Bernardino di San Miniato came to serve Felice and her family as long and as faithfully, but without the same kind of piquant intimacy.

Felice came increasingly to keep the de Cupis family, her mother Lucrezia, half-brother Gian Domenico and half-sister Francesca, as close to her as possible. They had never sought, unlike her della Rovere and Orsini relatives, to belittle or undermine her. Much of their fortune depended on her but there was genuine love between them as well. If Felice could ever relax, it was in their presence. Gian Domenico, thanks to the income from the cardinalate Felice had secured for him, had turned the family palace on the Piazza Navona into a magnificent residence, with a staff of a hundred and fifty servants. It was near enough to Monte Giordano for her to keep an eye on the Orsini, and Felice preferred to spend her time in Rome at the Palazzo de Cupis, with its familiar memories of her childhood. Letters arrived addressed to her *in Agone*, the original name of the Piazza Navona. Even when they left Rome in the summer, the de Cupis family was solicitous for her well-being: Gian Domenico wrote to her from a summer house at Campagna: 'We were glad to get your letter letting us know that you and the children are well. Madonna Lucrezia has been a bit indisposed, but it is nothing else other than old age. We have left Rome for Campagna, and we hope that you will come and stay with us at our house. You do not need to give us notice, you know the rooms that are here, take the ones in which you will be most comfortable. Truthfully, it is not only our house that is here to serve you, but our hearts as well.'[2]

In addition to the solace Felice found in her maternal family, she took comfort from prayer. In one of her account books listing smaller daily expenses such as cough syrup, soap, slippers, gloves, oil of camomile and lily, is a preponderance of wax candles. Over and over again, entries appear such as 'four *carlini* were spent on wax candles for the prayers of the Signora', 'five were spent on wax candles for the prayers of the Signora', or 'a pound of wax candles were bought for the prayers of the Signora'.[3] Beeswax candles, which did not have the noxious odour of those made of tallow, animal fat, were expensive. Their expense is justified in Felice's books because they were acquired to accompany her prayers. The records of purchases of costly wax candles increased to the point where sometimes she was lighting over a pound a week at her orations. These brief entries reveal a very private Felice, one kneeling in the dark, lit only by the flickering votive candles, asking for divine guidance as she negotiated her ever increasing challenges and obligations.

Despite the regular time she spent at prayer, like many others in Rome in 1527, Felice della Rovere would come to wonder whether God had abandoned her.

CHAPTER 2

The Fall of Rome

Felice's personal demons were ferocious, but they were to pale in comparison with those unleashed on Rome in May 1527.[1] The Sack of Rome by the Holy Roman Emperor Charles V's troops began on the morning of 6 May 1527 and lasted well into the following year. The first-hand accounts that exist of the raping, robbing, pillaging and murder by these 'barbarous hordes' are chillingly vivid. 'In the streets,' wrote Luigi Guicciardini in his history of the Sack, 'many nobles lay there cut to pieces, covered with mud and their own blood, and many people half dead lay miserably on the ground. Sometimes in that ghastly scene a child or man would be seen jumping through a window, forced to jump to escape becoming the living prey of those monsters and finally ending their lives horribly in the street.'[2]

What had Rome done to warrant such an invasion? Whatever their transgressions, its citizens were largely blameless. Few could have anticipated that this savage attack on Rome would be the outcome of the antagonism between Charles V and Pope Clement VII over a matter that meant little to most Romans. There had been a longstanding feud between the Emperor and the French King, Francis I, over territorial rights in the Burgundian provinces and occupancy of Milan. Francis and Charles sought to buttress their claims by alliance with, and allegiance from, the Pope, the Holy Father. Alliance with the Emperor, who controlled over half

Jerome Cock, after Maarten van Heemskerck, 'Death of Bourbon', 1555 of western Europe, was in the papacy's, and thus in Rome's, best interests. But in making his choices, Clement VII did not act as Pope; he acted as a member of the Medici family. Honouring a history of matrimonial ties between the Medici and the French royal family, Clement severed an old alliance with Charles to make a new one with Francis.

Charles, angered by Clement's treachery, sent thirty thousand soldiers into Italy late in 1526. His troops, led by the Duc de Bourbon, consisted primarily of Spanish and German soldiers, the famous *Landsknechts*, augmented by some Italians. The Bourbon Duke envisaged a few skirmishes in northern Italy as enough to make Clement change his mind and switch his loyalty back to Charles. The Emperor would pay his troops and they could return home. The Duc de Bourbon's victories were indeed substantial. He even felled the last of the great *condottieri*, the Medici Giovanni delle Bande Nere, whose mercenary soldiers, the Black Bands, were the best in Italy. Nevertheless, despite military losses, Clement did not capitulate. Nor did Charles V pay his troops and the soldiers, rendered ferocious by starvation, continued the march south.

Two of Felice's relatives also played a part in bringing the Sack upon Rome. Her cousin Francesco Maria della Rovere, the Duke of Urbino, was Captain General of the Venetian troops, the most substantial of the armies assembled to block the Imperial invasion. Clement gave him command of the troops of the entire papal Holy League, who were employed to keep back the Emperor's army. But Francesco Maria did not behave as might have been expected of a general fighting on his home territory. Rather than pressing his advantage and acting aggressively to rout the invaders, he avoided meeting the Imperial troops in armed combat. When he did advance, he almost immediately ordered the retreat of his own men. Guicciardini voiced his scorn for Clement's appointment of Francesco Maria as his general: 'What did Clement think would happen?' he asked. 'His immediate predecessor [Leo] had taken the Duke's estate; when he [Francesco Maria] was finally able to show his contempt and hatred for the Medici family, was it likely that he would conceal it, or give up before he saw that family ruined and destroyed?'[3]

Greatly assisted by the Duke of Urbino's strategy of revenge on the Medici, the Emperor's soldiers advanced closer and closer to Rome. At the beginning of May, they reached the Aurelian walls, on the upper slopes of the Janiculum Hill, above St Peter's.

Francesco Maria della Rovere, one of Felice's favourite relatives, facilitated the Imperial troops' arrival at the gates of Rome. Renzo da Ceri, one of her more troublesome Orsini cousins, allowed them into the city. His actions, though, were the result of incompetence rather than malice. 'The Pope had no time to search for troops in the areas where good and courageous ones were to be found,' explained Guicciardini. 'Consequently he was forced in furious haste to arm about three thousand artisans, servants and other simple people.' This army of scullions would scarcely have been sufficient to hold back the Imperial forces, but 'more often than any other officer, Signor Renzo declared his opinion that the enemy could not last two days outside the walls because of their lack of food'.[4]

The enemy, however, had no intention of remaining outside the walls. The Aurelian walls were weak. They had undergone little major reinforcement since the days of ancient Rome, and had received only perfunctory attention in preparation for this siege. This time, it was another of Felice's associates who was at fault, as this task had been placed in the hands of Giuliano Leno. Bourbon, prior to the assault, made a speech designed to rouse his soldiers' mettle. Not only did he remind them of 'Rome's inestimable wealth of gold and silver', which would be theirs for the taking; he also told them, 'When I look into your faces I plainly see that it would be much more to your liking if waiting for you in Rome were one of those emperors who spilled the blood of your innocent ancestors . . . You cannot avenge the injuries of the past; you must take whatever revenge you can.'[5]

Spurred on by the idea of revenge on the ancient Roman Empire, the Imperial assault began. Bourbon, in an effort to encourage his men further, made a foolish decision. He took the front line and so was one of the first to be killed, shot by an arrow from a papal arquebusier. His death meant there was no leader to control the fury and rage of his soldiers as they stormed the city. The pathetic Roman guard was powerless to stop them and simply fled. Having penetrated the city walls near the Vatican, the Imperial troops made their way through Trastevere, over the Ponte Sisto, the ancient bridge restored by Felice's great-uncle Sixtus, and into the heart of the Roman *abitato*. Many of the Spanish soldiers had participated in the taking of the New World, and in the sack of the Aztec capital of Tenochitlán. They now applied those devastating and ruthless methods of conquest to the Eternal City. They imprisoned the inhabitants of the homes they captured and no type of torture was too extreme if it meant their prisoners would reveal where they had hidden their treasure. Afterwards, the Iberians torched the properties. By the evening of 6 May much of Rome was ablaze.

Noble families had gathered together for protection in Rome's larger palaces, believing in safety in numbers, but such safety was by no means assured. Felice's wealthy neighbour, Domenico Massimo, was killed by the Imperial troops at his palace on the Via Papalis, the ceremonial route Julius II had taken pains to improve and maintain. So were Domenico's wife and children and along with them many other noblemen and women who had sought shelter at the home of Rome's richest man. 'Just imagine with a heavy heart', wrote Scipione Morosino to his brother Alessandro, the chamberlain of the Duke of Urbino, 'those poor Roman noblewomen witnessing their husbands, brothers and children killed in front of their very eyes – and then, even worse, that they themselves are murdered.'[6]

Where was Felice della Rovere as Rome was destroyed? She could have avoided the Sack entirely. In April, she had received an invitation from her daughter Julia's sister-in-law, the Duchess of Nerito, to tour the southern province of Calabria. But Felice had not taken up this offer as she was reluctant to leave Orsini lands, fearful of disturbances breaking out in her absence. Ironically, her worst fears were to be realized without a trip to the south. She and her children, Francesco, Girolamo and Clarice, were all trapped in Rome as hell descended around them.

CHAPTER 3

Hostages

Felice's name had always encouraged word play. Her correspondents always wished her *felicità*, or called her a *domina felix*. Yet never had her name been as apt as it was on the day of the Sack. Her current distaste for staying at the Orsini palace of Monte Giordano probably saved her life and those of her children. Monte Giordano was one of the first Roman palaces attacked by the Imperial soldiers, the Orsini family being traditional supporters of the French, the Emperor's great enemy. By the end of the first day of the Sack, the invading troops had stormed the great gate of Monte Giordano, and set the family compound on fire. A poet, Eustachio Celebrino, declared in verse that, 'Monte Giordano was set ablaze and burned to the ground.'[1] Celebrino did use some poetic licence as damage to the palace was not so severe but there is little doubt that had Felice and the children been inside the palace, they would have met the same fate as their Massimo neighbours.

As the Sack began, Felice and her children were all together at the Palazzo de Cupis with Lucrezia, Gian Domenico and Francesca. As grand as the de Cupis palace was – Gian Domenico had continued to enhance the house his father had built – it had not been designed as a stronghold and lacked fortifications. Felice and her family knew it would not withstand any kind of a siege. They had to act quickly if they were to save

View of Palazzo dei Dodici Apostoli, sixteenth century

themselves from the invading troops as the battle cries and the shouts of terror from the victims grew closer and closer. Although many of Clement VII's cardinals had scrambled to be by his side, and were now with him at the fortress of Castel Sant' Angelo on the Tiber river, Gian Domenico knew that his first loyalty was to his family. Together, they decided that they would stand a better chance of survival if they did not try to escape as one group. They could move faster and would be less conspicuous if they grouped themselves by gender. Gian Domenico and Felice's sons, Francesco and Girolamo, went as one group; Felice, her mother, sister and daughter as another.

Gian Domenico did not initially take his nephews very far. They simply crossed the street to find refuge at the palace of his neighbour, the Flemish Cardinal Henkwort, adjacent to the German church of Santa Maria dell' Anima. Gian Domenico's reasoning for seeking refuge from Henkwort was entirely logical. Henkwort was the most distinguished northern prelate in Rome and so presumed to be immune from attack by his countrymen. Nor was Gian Domenico alone in his thinking; many others had crowded into Henkwort's home.

Unfortunately, neither the *Landsknechts* nor the Spanish soldiers had any respect for geographical ties when there were riches to be had. For them everyone in Rome was Roman and 'the Spanish and the Germans, be they priests, or officials or courtiers, were all sacked and taken prisoner, and sometimes treated more cruelly than the others'.[2] The soldiers went systematically to the other cardinals' palaces, to those of Cesarino and della Valle, who were also Imperial sympathizers. Not only did they strip their homes of all their riches; they demanded ransoms from those sheltering inside. Henkwort was no exception. 'All the cardinals' homes were sacked,' the Cardinal of Como explained to his secretary, 'even those who were Imperialists. The house of della Valle was robbed of more than two hundred thousand ducats, as was that of Cesarino, those of Siena and Henkwort more than a hundred and fifty thousand, and they made hostages of those inside with ransoms of thousands upon thousands of ducats.' The hostages paid the ransoms, or *composizione*, in whatever wealth they had on them, supplemented by promissory notes. Yet payment of ransom was no guarantee of personal safety. The soldiers killed many of their victims after extracting their money.

When the Imperial soldiers came to Cardinal Henkwort's palace, Gian Domenico paid 4000 ducats as security for himself, Francesco and Girolamo. But he quickly realized that such a payment would not ensure their safety. Gian Domenico had not spent the last ten years of his life working to protect his sister's and her children's interests to let them, or himself for that matter, die on an Imperial sword. He must also have been very afraid of what would happen were the enemy to learn that Francesco and Girolamo were heirs to the Orsini lordship. So he decided that he and the two teenage boys would escape from Rome. 'Letting themselves down by a rope, they exited Henkwort's palace and the city of Rome,' wrote Como. 'They went many miles on foot, and encountered many dangers.'[3]

Their journey was a long and circuitous one, for the countryside was swarming with Imperial soldiers. But a man with two teenage boys could travel in disguise relatively easily. They acquired a mule, and passed as *mulatieri*, the ubiquitous mule-drivers. Gian Domenico rode the mule and the two boys went on foot. They made first for lake Nepi, which had been designated a safe stop, free from Imperial soldiers. Their ultimate goal was the sea, and boats to freedom, and so the port of Civitavecchia north of Rome was their planned destination. A week after setting out, they finally reached the port, where 'they are now', reported the Cardinal of Como, 'safe among us'.

Of all the great palaces in Rome, 'only the house of the Marchesa of Mantova, Isabella d'Este, who was staying in the great palace of the Santi Dodici Apostoli, built by Papa Julio, remained unharmed'.[4] It was Felice's great fortune that Dodici Apostoli was the place where she chose to take her mother, daughter and sister.

Isabella d'Este had come to Rome to secure a cardinal's hat for her younger son, Scipione, and she had rented the Dodici Apostoli palace from the Colonna family for the duration of her visit. She was perhaps less alarmed than others by the threat of the invading troops as her nephew by marriage was the ill-fated Duc de Bourbon and serving under him as chief lieutenant was her own son, Ferrante. Isabella was confident of a considerable degree of protection. Moreover, Dodici Apostoli was, as the Cardinal of Como noted, 'extremely well fortified, with bastions on every doorway', and difficult to penetrate. Isabella sent out word that she would offer shelter to any noble who could make it to the palace. By the end of the day of

6 May, 'more than a thousand women, and perhaps a thousand men' were inside Dodici Apostoli.

The initial journey for Felice and the other women was as harrowing as it had been for Gian Domenico and the boys, if not more so. They were much more vulnerable than the men, as their group comprised two women in their forties, one in her sixties and a fourteen-year-old girl, and they could not move as quickly. They had to make their way through the narrow streets from Piazza Navona up behind the Via Flaminia (present-day Via del Corso), the location of Dodici Apostoli. Throughout Rome, women like them were being raped and murdered. But this was not the first time in Felice's life that she had had to resolve that she would not be taken by Spaniards, and they reached the palace her own father had built almost half a century earlier in safety. They were shrewd enough to dress plainly, realizing that ornate costume would draw attention and betray their noble status. One commentator described them arriving at Dodici Apostoli wearing only 'simple gowns'.[5] However, beneath these simple gowns they had concealed Felice's fortune in gems. Her decision, made years earlier, to collect only what could be easily transported, had proved wise. The assembly of Roman nobles and foreign emissaries passed the night at the palace, listening to the destruction of a city. Many beat on the great door of Dodici Apostoli, begging for entrance. Others attempted to break it down, but the portal did not open for them.

The following day, business negotiations began with the invaders, transactions that suggest that Isabella's offer of shelter might not have been entirely altruistic and that shelter did not come without a price. The first Imperial officers to arrive at the palace were Ferrante Gonzaga, along with his cousin, Alessandro Novolara Gonzaga, a captain of the Emperor's army. They recognized the financial value of the assembled company, and they called the Emperor's Spanish lieutenant, Alonso da Cordova. 'He entered,' wrote Como, 'saying he was in need of a good drink, and he began to make calculations, not of how much the Marchesa and her goods were worth, but of all the others. He demanded no less than 100,000 ducats, declaring that they could easily afford such a small sum.'[6]

But the assembled hostages were not Renaissance business men for nothing, and they haggled with Cordova about how much they could pay, beating him down, narrated Como, 'to 40,000 ducats, and then with an additional 12,000, which in total made 52,000 ducats. This was paid in money and silver, and of the thousands that were missing, in bank credits. Of the first 40,000, half went to Alessandro Novolara, the other half to the Spanish captain. Of the 12,000, 2000 was given to four *Landsknechts* and the other 10,000, some say, was secreted away by Don Ferrante. We do not know if this is true, but if it is, it would have been very dishonest.' The hostages were, after all, Ferrante's mother's visitors, and it is hardly polite to extract 10,000 ducats from one's overnight guests, no matter what the circumstances.

Not everybody could afford the same amount. Felice stood security for others for small and large sums. She contributed 150 ducats for the ransom of the Genoese Pietro di Francesco, and promised 2000 ducats on behalf of her nephew, Francesca de Cupis's son, Christofano, who was of far lesser standing than herself. How much she paid for herself is unknown, although undoubtedly it would have been several thousand ducats. She gave up her jewels for ransom, including her most treasured possession, the diamond cross her father had given her after her marriage, for the equivalent of 570 ducats.

Felice's long-standing relationship with Isabella d'Este allowed her the privilege of being among the first to go. The Marchesa of Mantua was anxious to leave Rome, although such an exit was not deemed prudent until 13 May owing to the continued carnage in the street. The Sack of Rome was by then over a week old.

Outside the fortified walls of Dodici Apostoli, the streets of Rome had become human abattoirs, depositories of rotting flesh. It is hard to imagine how sickened Felice felt. Rome was her city, on which her father had lavished loving care, a city of which she had become a symbol of its golden age, a city whose future was represented by her sons. What future could she see now among the dead bodies and the burnt-out houses, especially when she had no way of knowing whether her sons were dead or alive?

CHAPTER 4

Escape from Rome

The party's journey to the Roman walls was a relatively safe one as Isabella's son Ferrante supplied them with an escort. Travel beyond the walls was another matter. Gian Maria della Porta, the *nuncio* for the court of Urbino, another member of their party, gave a graphic account of their journey:

> Finally we left Rome accompanied by Signor Ferrante Gonzaga, who took us all the way to the road to Ostia, from where we were to take a boat. But as we arrived there, the wind changed, and we were obliged to spend the night sheltering by the city walls, in greater danger than had we stayed in Rome. The following day we could go no further than the Magliana [the papal villa built by the river, from where they could sail to the coast]. Finally yesterday it pleased God to take us to Ostia, from where we are hoping to leave as soon as possible . . . [1]

An hour before midnight, the group sailed from Ostia to the port of Civitavecchia, which they reached in the small hours of the morning. Boats were in great demand at the port, but this was an occasion on which Felice could be the one to give assistance. The Genoese sea captain Andrea Doria was in charge, and he gave Felice the deference due to the woman who had once been Madonna Felice of Savona. He helped Isabella get ships to take

View of Boat Sailing down the Tiber, sixteenth century

her and the considerable quantity of possessions she had acquired in Rome back to Mantua.

Felice had to wait for the arrival of Gian Domenico and her sons before she could do anything, and her relief was immeasurable when they finally appeared at the port. Now that they were all finally out of Rome, she could take in the extent of their plight and her own helplessness. Here she was, a woman in charge of vast estates in the Roman *campagna*, and it was too dangerous for her to go to any of them. All were prime targets for the Imperial troops. They were burning much of the surrounding countryside in order to deprive the Romans of food supplies. This action only compounded Rome's pre-Sack food shortage, brought on by the huge numbers of pilgrims who had come to the city in 1525 for the Papal Jubilee.

Greater than Felice's fear of Charles V's army was her fear of Napoleone. The rage of the imperial troops would eventually burn out but Napoleone's never would. In March 1527 Napoleone had been arrested for entering into anti-papal negotiations with the Spanish viceroy in Naples and had been imprisoned in the Castel Sant' Angelo.[2] But Napoleone, along with other prisoners, had escaped from the Castel when the Sack began. All had taken a vigorous part in the killing and looting, unconcerned that it was fellow Romans they were attacking. Felice knew he would not hesitate to take advantage of Rome's anarchic state to pursue her and her children if he could, to take them hostage or even kill them. She was also sure Napoleone would feel confident that he would be free from the threat of any papal reprisal. Pope Clement VII had reneged on the payment of most of a 400,00 ducat ransom to the Emperor. The Pope had then fled to Orvieto, 126 kilometres to the north of Rome. Orvieto was a nearly inaccessible hill town, easily defended, with the added benefit of a papal palace built during the late Middle Ages. Hidden away in the hills, Clement was in no position to offer the protection he had given Felice in recent years.

Felice knew her only option was to flee far from Rome, and she considered where she might find suitable accommodation, perhaps for a lengthy period. She might have gone to Mantua with Isabella d'Este, or to the island of Ischia, off the Neapolitan coast, where the noblewoman and poetess Vittoria Colonna was offering shelter to a number of Roman nobles and humanists. Instead, Felice turned to her blood relations, her cousins in

Urbino, Francesco Maria della Rovere and his wife Eleonora Gonzaga. The della Rovere cousins were a logical choice. Felice was on good terms with them, and she had made numerous efforts on Francesco's behalf over the past years. She was also aware that neither Francesco Maria nor Eleonora was currently resident at Urbino. Francesco Maria, however nominally, was still commanding the Holy League from a camp outside Viterbo, some fifty miles to the north of Rome. Eleonora divided her time between her parents' home in Mantua and Venice. So Felice had good reason to believe that they had room to spare at their ducal palace. And like Orvieto, Urbino was high in the hills. Felice and her family would be far from the reach of Napoleone.

Felice and the de Cupis family split up once again. This time, Felice took her three children, and her mother, sister and brother stayed together for the journey to Venice. At Civitavecchia, Felice commanded a ship robust enough to undertake the long sea voyage from the Tyrrhenian Sea to the Adriatic coast. The family sailed south. They rounded the heel of Italy, and then sailed north until they reached Pesaro, the largest port in the Duchy of Urbino. The devastated city of Felice's birth was left far behind and she could finally feel she and her family were out of danger.

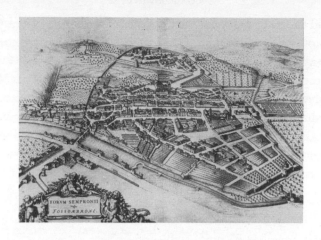

CHAPTER 5

Fossombrone

Even today, Romans often make the Marche, the province containing Urbino, a summer retreat. Its hilly peaks, which are not quite mountains, are still verdant when all else is parched, and the landscape is wilder and more densely wooded than the cultivated fields of the northern Lazio. For the Orsini *gubernatrix* and her children, this country was to be a similar kind of retreat, a haven.

By the beginning of June 1527, Felice and her children had settled in Urbino. From his battle camp at Viterbo, Francesco Maria wrote to her to ease her lingering fears. He assured his cousin that she was not to worry. 'I think of your children as my own,' he wrote. 'You are now in a safe place and the Abbot [Napoleone] will not be able to get to you.'[1] In return, Felice wrote a series of grateful letters to her della Rovere cousins. Each expresses her thanks more fervently than the last, and are a far cry from the businesslike missives she wrote in the first person plural to her servants. The first letter announced that she and her children could never fully express the obligation they felt to their highnesses. The second, to the Duchess, told of her gratitude for the kindness of all at court, which was such that, Felice claimed, 'a hundred tongues could never tell of it'. The third, again to the Duchess, was even more fulsome:

View of Fossombrone, late sixteenth century

I would like to be able to show my mind's conception of the expression of my obligation, and that of my children to his excellency the Duke, and to your ladyship. So much humane action never ceases to invoke in me a continual sense of obligation: what gentility and rare virtue you have shown towards me, your servant, and what memories I retain of it. And what merits even more praise is that I know that your demonstrations to me are not those of a lady and benefactress, but of a sister. Only God knows how you can be rewarded for your goodness. My tributes to you could never be sufficient were I to live for a thousand years.[2]

Three letters expressing more or less the same sentiments, however heartfelt, might seem more than sufficient. However, Felice was aware that more and more refugee Roman nobles were drifting towards the expansive Urbino court, seeking assistance. She was apprehensive that the della Rovere dukes might feel obliged to help these displaced nobles too. After all, Francesco Maria's military tactics had contributed to their predicament. Felice had no desire to suffer the indignities of overcrowding; the period she had spent at Dodici Apostoli with two thousand fellow Romans had undoubtedly been enough. So she constructed this last letter to Eleonora with the aim of reminding her cousin that her obligation to Felice was one bound by the special ties of blood and not simply charity. Felice knew she was due, and should receive, preference.

Felice's solicitations proved effective in helping her obtain what she wanted. So rather than reside in a palace potentially filled with any number of Roman neighbours, she contrived a relocation to an Urbino fiefdom in which she could create an establishment for herself. The della Rovere offered her a palace of her own in the small hillside town of Fossombrone.

Fossombrone is about thirty kilometres to the north-east of Urbino, in the foothills of the Alpe de la Luna. It was one of the ancient settlements in the province of the Marche, deriving its name from its original Latin title, 'Forum Semprone'. The town, now rather sad and dusty, was acquired in 1445 by Francesco Maria's grandfather, the great duke and *condottiere* Federigo da Montefeltro, from the Malatesta, the famed tyrants of Rimini. Federigo had built a small palace at the top of the town known as the Corte Alta, the 'High Court'. In the second part of the fifteenth century, Fossombrone served as an attractive retreat for the Urbino court. It was reasonably close to Urbino itself, yet isolated enough to be quite private. It was renowned for its pure water and good air, so might be said to be the ideal environment for a woman and her family attempting to recover from the traumatic ordeal of the Sack of Rome.

Francesco Maria's and Eleonora's frequent absences from Urbino meant that the Fossombrone residence was also not in regular use. The Urbino court chamberlain, Raphael Hieronimo, spent the month of August making ready apartments at the Corte Alta for Felice. He supplied Fossombrone with ample quantities of straw mattresses, wood and wine, as well as 'molti tappetti' – tapestries to cover the walls and provide insulation, for the hill town was cold in the autumn and winter months.[3] Three months had passed since the Sack of Rome when Felice moved to Fossombrone at the beginning of September. Her main goal was to construct a semblance of normality and stability for her children. When she was younger than they were, Felice had experienced at first hand the fear of arriving in a strange and hostile-seeming environment, when she had moved from Rome to Savona. So she attempted to search for a tutor in Latin and Greek for them, and wrote to associates to see if they could help. However, as Aloysio da Lode, whom she had enlisted in her quest, wrote to her in October 1527, 'The confusion of everything is such that I can find no one.'[4] Even the humanists were in hiding.

Girolamo, her *condottiere* in the making, wanted to ride, and Felice took pains to find a good saddler to repair an old saddle to her son's exacting instructions. She received a letter from one Hieronimo da Cerbo in Monte del Cio, who wrote that a saddle had been refurbished in accordance with Girolamo's wishes. The leather had been retooled and it now had a seat lined with white musk fur; the cost would be 2 *scudi*. 'Your ladyship's saddle,' the saddler concluded, 'with the additions you wanted for the pommels and girth, costs 3 *scudi*.'[5]

Clothing for the children, especially for Clarice, was another priority. When Felice arrived at Fossombrone, she wrote with gratitude to Eleonora, acknowledging receipt of 'your ladyship's letter and along with it the undergown, white damask and sarcenet taffeta that you, in your immense goodness and kindness, have deigned to send Clarice my daughter, and your most devoted servant'.[6] Felice also took advantage of Cardinal Gian Domenico's residence in Venice, the textile capital of Italy, to acquire other supplies. The minute details of a letter he sent her with regard to this matter belie the fact that only a few months previously both had been fleeing for their lives and were now, technically, refugees. 'The other day,' wrote Gian Domenico, 'you wrote to me to send you the material for two silk hooded cloaks. I wrote back to you asking what colours you wanted, and you told me to pick whatever I thought was best. So I am sending you two cloaks of purple lined silk, two serge jerkins, and some pink silk, because you also asked for something for Madonna Clarice, and I thought it best to send her a piece of pink.'[7]

Felice skilfully contrived to create her own establishment on the della Rovere estate. Conscious that she was still a guest of her cousins, staying at Fossombrone at their expense, she was shrewd enough to ensure that her presence continued to be welcomed. Her management of the Orsini estates had taught her useful lessons in thrift and parsimony, and she was to behave no differently on borrowed land. In November 1527, Eleonora Gonzaga, anxious about the expense of so many refugees, wrote to Raphael di Hieronimo to ask him to supply her with a list of 'le boche', the 'mouths' for which the Urbino court was currently responsible. 'Mouths' implied not only the cost of food but also the cost of clothing, the expense of servants and the stabling of horses. Raphael wrote to Eleonora that there were many – over two hundred – and more besides, because two further 'courts' had been established. In addition to Felice's at Fossombrone, there was another at Pesaro under the governorship of another compatriot from Savona, Marco Vigerio, now Bishop of Senigallia. But the style and habits of these two courts, Raphael reported, were very different. As he explained,

> The aforesaid Signora [Felice] is very well measured in her choice of dishes, but the Governor insists on a lavish table, and demands no fewer than twelve or fourteen young chickens a day, whereas the Signora only eight, and they are dear. When it comes to meat, she takes the usual meat that we serve at table at our court, but the Governor wants white bread for everybody, and veal and castrated animals. If he does not get that he starts threatening our officials with prison, or the rack . . . soon we shall not find a single servant who wants to stay there.[8]

By contrast, the Urbino officials liked staying at Felice's economic yet evidently pleasurable court at Fossombrone. Felice had always treated the high-ranking Orsini staff well. She respected their abilities, and had no reason to behave any differently towards her cousins' staff, especially when she was more dependent on their good will. Raphael di Hieronimo also seemed to prefer Fossombrone to the Urbino palace itself, as he frequently wrote letters to his mistress addressed from there. The Urbino *nuncio*, Gian Maria della Porta, who had escaped the Sack in Felice's company, also spent time at Felice's court. The pair were long-standing friends. Felice had confided her fears to him about Napoleone when her stepson had taken Palo, feelings she would not acknowledge to his master, Francesco Maria.

The atmosphere generated by Felice at Fossombrone evidently appealed to Eleonora Gonzaga when she came to visit her cousin in the autumn of 1527. This was perhaps the first time when the Urbino Duchess could visit a palace in which a woman was completely in charge. Even Eleonora's headstrong mother, Isabella d'Este, had always had to act in relationship to a man, first as the wife and then as the widowed mother of a duke. Felice's table might have been relatively humble, but the court Felice created at the Corte Alta had an alluring grace and simplicity, in keeping with the tranquillity for which Fossombrone was famous. It attracted Eleonora, perhaps particularly so after the more ostentatious courts at Mantua or Venice, where she had spent much time, and seems to have inspired her to develop her own establishment at Fossombrone. Early in January 1528 she charged Gian Maria della Porta with seeking out a property in the town that could be developed into a fitting residence. He advised Eleonora to purchase the three adjoining houses now known as the Corte Rossa, a name derived from their red-painted window frames. The Urbino court architect, Girolamo Ghenga, subsequently set to work renovating the houses.[9] Much of the spring of 1528 was spent readying the Corte Rossa for Eleonora, and it seems appropriate that it was Felice, as Fossombrone *châtelaine*, with her experience in supervising building renovations, who was on site to oversee and advise on the project.

CHAPTER 6

The Exiled

Fossombrone clearly proved a haven for Felice after the horrors of Rome. Yet however delightful the refuge may have been, there were many reminders of the attendant anxieties of the outside world. Even in times of plenty Felice had invariably been addressed in letters as 'patron and bene-factress' from those anticipating her help. Now that title came to have even more resonance. There was a constant stream of correspondence from those asking for her assistance. Giuliano Leno, the man who had once con-trolled almost every monopoly in Rome, who had cavalierly disregarded the need to fortify the walls of Rome as the Imperial troops approached, was now in reduced circumstances in Perugia. Leno, who had negotiated transactions with Felice worth thousand of ducats, now asked if she could send him fifty.[1]

Felice did what she could and if there was nothing she could do herself, she tried to put those in need in touch with others who could help them. Her efforts were not always successful. Her servant Giovanni Egitio de Vicovaro wrote to her, 'I went with your credentials to the Reverend Orsini and I told him of the great necessity that has finally reduced me to beg from his Reverence. He replied to me that he himself is in great need and necessity, for his estate has been totally ruined. He has not even a sack of grain left.'[2]

Jerome Cock, after Maarten van Heemskerck, 'Landsknechts at Castel Sant' Angelo', 1555

Felice received many tales of the hardships suffered in Rome. One such letter, from December 1527, came from the Bishop of the Ligurian town of Monterosso, who flatly told her that 'it is impossible to live in Rome; there is no bread of any sort, and nothing for the people to eat'.[3] Other communications arrived regarding property stolen in the Sack and now recovered, although often with a hefty ransom attached to it. The Bishop of Mugnano wrote to her from the island of Ischia, where he was benefiting from the extended hospitality of the poetess Vittoria Colonna. The Bishop was pleased to inform Felice that he had been able to recover a jewel belonging to Nicolò Orsini, Lord of Monterotondo and Mugnano. This jewel, worth 50 ducats, had been a baptismal gift from Felice to one of Nicolò's children, and it had been cherished by its owner not for its monetary worth but because the donor had been Felice.[4]

Many of Felice's correspondents had lost everything, but one to inspire little sympathy was Isabella d'Este. Felice had barely arrived in Urbino when Isabella wrote to her, lamenting that a boat containing many of the artefacts she had acquired in Rome had gone missing. Isabella was sure that Andrea Doria, the Genoese naval captain in command of the harbour and fleets at Civitavecchia, had ordered the boat commandeered at sea so he could steal her treasures. Felice was upset by Isabella's smear on her countryman and responded, 'Prior to my departure from Civitavecchia, Maestro Andrea Doria came to find me in the rooms where I was, and he told me about your belongings, the same truth that he wrote to you, that they, along with some servants, had been taken at sea by the Moors. Your illustrious ladyship can be most certain that if I knew otherwise, and if he was my son, I would tell you the truth.'[5] Felice's words to Isabella have a rather reproachful tone. Many had died in the Sack and Isabella's fretting over what amounted to little more than a weekend shopping trip for the Marchesa seems at best frivolous and at worst distinctly hard-hearted.

A year later, Isabella wrote again to Felice in a manner that suggests she was anxious to win her over:

My dearest sister, I feel that the troubles we experienced together in Rome forged a new bond of friendship between us, and I greatly desire news of you as we are good sisters. And it is many days since I have heard from you. As I do not have a great deal else to write to you, let me tell you that, thanks to God, I have recovered the belongings of myself and my family, the ones I believed had been lost at sea at the hands of the Moors. They were discovered in a ship sailing to Venice under the command of a Venetian gentleman Cazadiavolo. This Cazadiavolo had also found the beautiful tapestries of the Pope [those in the Sistine Chapel made from cartoons by Raphael for Leo X], which my son Don Ferrante rescued from the Spanish by paying 500 *scudi* for them . . . [6]

Isabella took some pains in her letter to extol Ferrante as a saviour of papal patrimony. Ferrante's greed, sanctioned by Isabella, in taking ransom money from Roman nobles had had a direct effect on Felice. Isabella knew what Ferrante had done and had indeed been complicit in it. At the palace of Dodici Apostoli, Felice had put up 2000 ducats as surety for her nephew Christofano del Bufalo and the del Bufalo family had yet to produce this sum. Ferrante wrote to both Felice and Gian Domenico de Cupis to remind them of this debt, but gave the letters to his mother to send on. Isabella wrote to him remarking that she 'cannot believe that Maestro Angelo [Christofano's father] would not pay his debt; even though he is reputed to be a gentlemen, we are obliged to find him the world's vilest man. Your letters have been sent to Signora Felice and the Cardinal of Trani.'[7]

Isabella also went to work on Ferrante's behalf to extract the money from Felice's extended family. Perhaps the 'bonds of friendship' prevented her from writing directly to Felice, but she did write several times to Gian Domenico. In one letter she reminded him of the 'services my son has done to you and to Signora Felice' and in another that she hoped he would resolve the issue as she did not wish for her son 'to have any reason to resort to any terms with yourself and Signora Felice'.[8] Gian Domenico did pay the debt, and Isabella was then nothing but charm, writing to him that she hoped he would excuse Ferrante for the manner in which he had approached someone 'of your grade and dignity', and that it was being obliged to negotiate in such a way with the Spanish that had pushed him to such extremes.[9]

If Isabella did not write to Felice directly, then Gian Domenico made sure Felice knew what had occurred. For Felice, Isabella's behaviour served to end a friendship that had lasted over twenty years. She knew how wealthy the Gonzagas were. Their exploitation of the Romans in such a time of financial desperation was utterly despicable. Yet Isabella was too powerful and too useful a person, especially given the ravaged state of Rome, for Felice to be able to sever links with her entirely. However, while Isabella wrote to Felice as her 'dearest sister', Felice in return used the formal language of patronage which emphasized the distance she felt between them. In a letter she wrote to Isabella following the incident with the del Bufalo family, Felice revealed nothing of her personal life; nor was there any suggestion that she held any affection for Isabella. 'My lady and benefactress,' wrote Felice to Isabella in 1529, 'I must thank your illustrious ladyship for the order you sent out for possession of the church pension of Santo Stefano di Povi to be given to Maestro Vincentio Caroso, gentleman of Rome, who is my creature, and I would be most obliged if you would write to the priest and ensure possession is maintained for Maestro Vincentio . . . and with reverence I recommend myself to you. Your servant, Felix Ruvere d'Ursinis.'[10]

Nothing in the tone of this letter suggests that Felice and Isabella shared a history, one that had once involved plans for Felice's daughter and Isabella's nephew to marry, or their daring escape from Rome. Felice would have preferred not to have to write to her at all. It was difficult for Felice to be in a position of obligation to Isabella, even if it was on behalf of another, when she was so accustomed to being the *patrona et benefatrix*. And while she enjoyed the peace and tranquillity of Fossombrone, she longed to return to the states that she governed.

The Imperial army vacated Rome in the autumn of 1528. Many Romans waited not just for the soldiers to depart but for the plague to die down as well before they returned. Felice herself was unable to leave for Rome until the late summer of 1528. She had to wait for more than disease to leave her city. She had the added disadvantage of being haunted by the spectre of Napoleone.

Freed from gaol in Castel Sant' Angelo, her stepson, predictably, had taken advantage of the anarchic situation, as well as of Clement VII's lack of power, to take full control of the Orsini estates. He had established Bracciano as his headquarters, from which he was fighting his own personal war against the Imperial army, primarily for personal financial gain. He even took to piracy, holding up Spanish ships on the Tiber. Napoleone's activities drove the Imperial army, an unlikely ally for Felice, to launch an attack on him. She received a communication from a secretary, Giovanni Egiptio da Vicovaro, in July, informing her that Napoleone had been 'broken, with the loss of forty horsemen'.[11] Undaunted, he went north, to serve as a mercenary soldier in the Tuscan revolt against Medici rule.

It was only at this point that it was deemed safe for Felice to consider leaving Fossombrone and finally returning to Rome. Napoleone had gone; the Imperial troops had gone; the plague was over, and a humiliated Clement VII had paid a vast ransom to Charles V to secure his return and peace in the city. In the same letter, Giovanni Egiptio informed Felice she would receive a licence from Pope Clement VII, allowing her entrance into monasteries that would offer her accommodation on her way back home. Mules were hired for the journey, although Felice was to prove tardy in paying for them. One Angelo Leonardo da Calli would be obliged to write to her a year later demanding 25 *scudi*, a not inconsiderable sum, for the mule she rode when she left Fossombrone.[12]

CHAPTER 7

The Return to Rome

Felice rode on the hired mule into a Rome that was all but destroyed. The gleaming city created by her father, Julius II, had vanished. In its place were blackened buildings, such as the Palazzo Massimo, whose residents were now all dead. The remains of less opulent houses had been dismantled for firewood in the bitterly cold winter of 1527. The population was decimated by violence and its aftermath, disease. Anybody looking at Rome could ask themselves, with good reason, how it differed from the city as it had been at the end of the Middle Ages. It says much for Roman resilience, a determination not to let the progress of the early sixteenth century be for nothing, that when its leaders did return, they immediately and effectively set to work restoring the prestige of their families and returning their city to its former glory. None the less, here and there, signs of the destruction can still be found. Underneath the beautiful pavement of Palazzo Massimo, rebuilt in the 1530s by Baldessare Peruzzi, lie charred floor tiles, a memento of the time the palace was set alight in May 1527.

Felice spent the next few years attempting to re-create her life as it had been prior to the events of May 1527. There was much to be done, much to be replaced, from replacing clothing lost in the Sack to the repair of the badly damaged Orsini palaces. This period was not an easy one in Felice's life and the events of 1527 had taken an emotional toll on her. Her servant

People in front of ruined buildings in Rome, sixteenth century

Perseo di Pontecorvo wrote sympathetically to her in the August of 1529, 'I have heard that you are physically well, but that your soul is afflicted from these great troubles. I can say nothing but that I have the greatest sorrow for you, as well as for myself and that all we can do now is to be patient. I beg that you have the will to govern as well as you possibly can, with all your wisdom.'[1]

However emotionally scarred Felice might have been, she had no option but to return to work, and there are indications that even if she was mentally depressed, she had no intention of entering into a physical decline. In the same month as she received the letter from Ponticorvo one of her woman servants, Camilla, wrote in response to Felice's request for a teeth-cleaning recipe. Camilla's instructions were to 'boil rosemary with spring water, and with that, wash the teeth and gums every morning, then repeat, and this is the way to keep the gums healthy. To keep the teeth clean and white, take coral, pumice stone and radish and mix them into a powder, and in the morning rub them on to the teeth. Then take a bit of vinegar and wash it round your mouth, and this will make the teeth white and clean and refreshed.'[2]

Felice also had a number of outstanding debts as a result of the Sack. She owed 4 *scudi* to the mariner who had taken her from Ostia to Civitavecchia, although he had to wait until December 1531 to receive his fee. She needed a vast amount of new clothes for herself and her children. As her account book shows, a Roman merchant, Donato Bonsignore, did very well out of the family's losses. 'An authorization was made up for Bernardo de Vielli who has to give 50 ducats to Mr Donato Bonsignore, which is in part payment for the 105 ducats for the requirements created by the Sack of Rome.' 'An authorization was made for Donato Bonsignore to come to receive 20 *scudi* for the many clothes Signora Felice wishes to take from the said Donato.' 'An authorization was made up for Donato Bonsignore, merchant in Rome, for 12 *scudi* and 10 ducats, 12 *scudi* to Mr Riccio, tailor, for the fabric taken by order of the Signora, which is for two yards and three palm lengths of raw silk to line a dress for Signora Clarice, and more to line and border two ladies' dresses, and a *scudo* to Lorenzo Mantuano for a half-palm of scarlet silk for a stomach piece for Signor Hieronimo.' 'Two yards of satin and raw silk were taken from Donato Bonsignore for Signora Clarice's under and outer garment for 5 *scudi*.' The greatest expense for a single item of clothing for Felice came in Jaunary 1532, when 'an authorization was made up for Bernardo de Vielli to pay Faustina de Cola da Nepe 20 *scudi* to give to her husband in payment for the dress made of damask that he will make for Signora Felice.'[3]

Rome was still experiencing severe food shortages. In March 1531, Felice wrote a letter to Antonio da Corvaro, to whom she had written harshly in the months before the Sack, admonishing him for hiding a Roman fugitive. This time, however, she addressed him warmly as 'mio amantissimo', and thanked him profusely for sending a package of provisions to Rome: honey, chestnuts, and a barrel of snails.[4] The snails say much about the hardship of the time. Customarily the food of the poor, they were no longer to be scorned.

Felice was actually in a more fortunate position than most when it came to access to food supplies, thanks to the grain grown on Orsini farmland, as well as her own harvest at Palo. The grain shortage in Rome was dire. Even before the Sack, grain reserves had been low. The Jubilee of 1525 had brought thousands of pilgrims to the city and they had demolished existing grain supplies. During the Sack, not only had the soldiers taken for themselves most of what was available, they had also fired much of the surrounding countryside, destroying young crops. In consequence, the price of grain rose exponentially and now cost as much as 20 ducats a *rubbio*.[5]

The high grain prices operated to the advantage of those who had grain to sell. Indeed, the inflated price was the means by which Felice was able to bring about her family's economic recovery. Her own servants had always received part of their wages in the form of grain, but it now became part of the payment given to outside help, such as Francesco Sarto, the tailor, who visited Felice's home to sew for her. He received 'one *scudo* and an authorization to go pick up a *rubbio* from Galera, on account of the sewing of the clothes he did for Signora Felice'.[6] And it was grain that helped Felice pay for the damage done to her Roman properties during the Sack.

CHAPTER 8

Rebuilding

Despite her evident ambivalence towards the palace of Monte Giordano
and her reluctance to spend any more time within its walls than she could
possibly avoid, Felice recognized its importance – physical, economic and
symbolic – to her sons' patrimony and their prestige in Rome. Monte
Giordano had suffered considerable damage during the Sack. The Orsini
French connection was well known and the palace had been one of the first
targets of Imperial attack, set ablaze on the first day. To leave the burned
and blackened exterior unrestored would be to preserve a symbol of the
Orsini family's humiliation and defeat. However, this need to repair the
damage also gave Felice the opportunity to dissociate herself further from
her Orsini relatives. Monte Giordano was not one single integral palace,
but a citadel-like settlement of several adjoining buildings situated around
a courtyard, each belonging to different branches of the Orsini family. The
Bracciano Orsini had always occupied the largest wing, but now Felice
chose to ensure, through architectural devices, that from the outside her
family appeared as removed as possible from the rest of the Orsini clan.
After the completion of the renovation in the 1530s, Felice spent much
more time in Monte Giordano than she had in the previous decade. It was
as if, having placed her own seal on its fabric, she was finally comfortable
within its walls.

View of Campo dei Fiori, Orsini palace with clock tower in background, sixteenth century

Fittingly, the architect Felice probably employed in this enterprise was the one she had commissioned to design Bracciano's *fonte*, Baldessare Peruzzi. Poor Peruzzi had suffered badly at the hands of the Imperial troops. Vasari wrote:

> Our poor Baldessare was taken prisoner by the Spaniards, and not only lost all his possessions, but was also much maltreated, because he was grave, noble and gracious in demeanour, and they believed him to be some prelate in disguise, or some other man able to pay a fat ransom. Finally, however, those impious barbarians having found that he was a painter, one of them, who had borne a great affection for Bourbon, caused him to make a portrait of that most rascally captain, the enemy of God and man, either letting Baldessare see him as he lay dead [Bourbon was laid out in the Sistine Chapel] or giving him his likeness in some other way, with drawings, or words.[1]

Peruzzi was one of the architects who contributed to the renewal of Rome. He designed a beautiful scheme for the renovation of the palace belonging to the wealthy Massimo family, who had lost not only their home but many family members in the Sack. Prior to the Sack, in 1525, he had converted the upper storeys of the ancient Teatro Marcello into a palace for the Savelli family, who also owned the Colosseum and rented its upper storeys to hermits and mystics. At the Teatro Marcello, Peruzzi designed a façade for the Savelli, which, with its strategically designed details, would provide optimum legibility when viewed along the narrow street on which Teatro Marcello stood, thereby augmenting the Savelli's visual presence in the city. He accomplished this effect through a simple but ingenious optical device: inflating the scale and relief of the façade's window details. A similar strategy is employed on the upper storey of the Bracciano wing at Monte Giordano, which is also situated on a narrow street. Peruzzi's architectural design gave visual definition to the part of Monte Giordano where Felice and her family resided. It provided a dramatic break, which is still visible today, between the Bracciano palace and the other Orsini buildings within the complex. When the latter were repaired, it was in the late-medieval style of their original design. This emphatic visual separation, at least as far as Felice della Rovere was concerned, served not only aesthetic purposes but social and political ones as well.

For Felice, renovating the palace at Monte Giordano was important for family pride and self-esteem. Renovating another Orsini palace on the market place of Campo dei Fiori was critical for economic reasons. Embedded within the ancient fabric of Pompey's Theatre, the Campo dei Fiori palace had been the original Roman residence of the Orsini. However, for as long as Felice della Rovere had been attached to the family, the Orsini had rented Campo dei Fiori to cardinals as yet insufficiently wealthy to afford a palace of their own in Rome. The let provided a twofold advantage: income as well as the good will of a cardinal who could become another ally at the papal court.

Campo dei Fiori, which was both market square and residential area for merchants and cardinals, had been an easy target for the Imperial troops who had destroyed some of the palaces flanking the piazza, including the one belonging to Cardinal del Monte, the future Pope Julius III. The damage to the Orsini palace was not so complete. Its ancient foundations had, after all, withstood more than one assault by foreign invaders, but the palace still needed repair. Felice della Rovere did not commission an illustrious architect to undertake its renovation. She probably did not feel the Campo dei Fiori palace, which was a glorified boarding house, needed a new and decorative façade in the way Monte Giordano did. Instead, she hired Ambrosio da Lodi, a *muratore*, a more humble builder, to repair the damage to the palace walls. Ambrosio worked full time for Felice for two years, receiving monthly payments of one or two *scudi* 'for the work on making the walls of the palace at Campo dei Fiori'.[2] Felice also employed Ambrosio at Monte Giordano, making door and window frames.

Despite the damage to the Campo dei Fiori palace, it was still a viable let. Property was at a premium in Rome as so much housing had been rendered uninhabitable during the Sack. Felice had an eager and potentially useful new lodger in the form of the Archbishop of Matera, Cardinal Andrea Matteo Palmieri, a long-standing acquaintance. There was a record of him having loaned her 190 ducats in 1525 to pay for soldiers serving as bodyguards to Girolamo to protect him from Napoleone. Palmieri, from Sicily, which was under Spanish governance, had been one of seven new cardinals appointed by Clement VII in November 1527 as a good-will gesture to Charles V. With no palace of his own in Rome, the new Cardinal was in need of substantial accommodation. Renting Campo dei Fiori to him gave Felice access to the Imperial camp should she need it. In accordance with the mandates from Clement that Napoleone be informed of all activity regarding Orsini property, Felice duly wrote to him. His reply was predictably contrary: 'I received your letter in which you inform me that I must be content that our house at Campo dei Fiori is to be had by Cardinal Palmieri. I reply to you that I cannot be content as I promised it to another and I do not wish to be less than my word, and God knows how much I have sacrificed in other matters for love of you and my brothers. Nothing else occurs to me. I recommend myself to you.'[3] Felice appears to have gone ahead, despite Napoleone's protests, with the let to Palmieri.

Although she was prepared to rent Campo dei Fiori to a Sicilian who had helped her in the past, Felice must have had ambivalent feelings towards the Spanish themselves. They had wrought untold damage on her property and possessions at Trinità dei Monti. The convent of Trinità dei Monti had some association with the French crown – the friars who resided there were Franciscan Minims. Their founder, Francesco di Paola, had gone to France in the late fifteenth century as a spy for Sixtus IV. He had stayed at the French court as confessor to the French queens and Louisa of Savoy named her son, the future Francis I, after him. Some French money had gone towards the building of the Minims' church in Rome. This French tie had made Trinità dei Monti a prime target for Spanish rage. But it was not the French who were to suffer but the Italian friars, not to mention Felice herself. When the realities of the Sack hit home, Felice had arranged to have the precious objects and valuable papers she kept in her palace adjacent to Trinità transferred to the church. As many had done, she believed that Rome's holy places would be safe from attack. She was to be proved very wrong.

CHAPTER 9

At the Trinity

Felicewas in Fossombrone when she learned of the horrors unleashed at Trinità dei Monti. In July 1528, Benedetto di San Miniato, now her chief *maestro di casa* in Rome, sent her a report of the state of the convent he had received from a Genoese friar who had gone to stay at Trinità just before the Sack occurred: 'This friar tells me he is a loyal servant to your ladyship, and being at the church he was able to tell me all that happened to the young friars and their father. Of the friars only thirty-three remain alive; the others are dead, either martyred, or from fever and plague.' There was certain irony here, Trinità dei Monti, with its secluded hilltop location, was usually safe from plague, and had served as a refuge during previous outbreaks of the disease. Benedetto went on to tell her, 'The convent received much damage. The Spanish invaded the sacristy and sacked the convent very badly, burning, setting the woodwork, doors and windows alight. And the Genoese friar tells me that the Spanish took away the papers and other things belonging to your ladyship.'[1]

The Spanish also went on to ravage Felice's own adjacent property, the garden, the vineyard and the palace itself. On her return to Rome, Felice had set about a comprehensive renewal of the Trinità dei Monti property. In September 1531, 'Maestro Menico Falegname [carpenter] da Formello was given one *scudo* to buy hinges and other things to make beautiful doors

View of *vigne* around Trinità dei Monti

at the Trinità.' 'Menico da Formello was given five and half *scudi* for hinges, a lock and key for the Trinità.'[2] For the outdoors, she hired an entirely new team of gardeners, who erected a new vineyard and re-created the pleasure garden, which had been the subject of admiration by Felice's guests in earlier years.

The other treasured possession of Felice's that the Spanish stole and then desecrated was her diamond crucifix, the one given to her by her father and which she had given up as ransom that night at Dodici Apostoli. She had written from Urbino to the Bishop of Mugnano, who had been so skilled at locating the jewel she had given as a baptismal gift to the Monterotondo Orsini, hoping he could help her find the crucifix. He professed to have heard nothing about its possible whereabouts. Much later, in November 1532, she would receive a letter from an Italian, Giovanni Poggio, in Madrid. Poggio had discovered its location, and he was prepared to broker its return to her. He wrote:

> I found myself in these parts the other day with the Viceroy of Navarre, the brother of the late Alonso da Cordoba [the Spaniard responsible for assessing the ransom of those nobles at Dodici Apostoli] whom your ladyship will remember for the time he was in Rome when Rome was sacked. He came to discuss business with me, and told me that Don Alonso his brother had told him at the time of his death that he held a diamond crucifix belonging to you valued at 570 ducats, and that the said cross has lost two diamonds. If you wish to have the crucifix restored to you, you can pay him the 570 ducats, less the value of the two diamonds. The price, as your ladyship knows, is estimated on the value of other similar items . . . All I desire to know is whether your ladyship would like me to proceed in the recuperation of the cross.[3]

Felice's cross had had a life story of its own. It had been a diplomatic gift, offered by the city of Venice to Pope Julius. In presenting it to his daughter, the Pope had used it as a token of reconciliation, where it became the prize piece in Felice's jewellery collection. She in turn had had to use it as ransom, handing it over to Cordoba. The Spaniard had then gouged out two of the cross's individual gems, using them for wages or bribes, desecrating the cross for purely practical reasons.

Badly as she wanted to see her cross removed from the hands of the unconscionable Spanish, and returned to her, its rightful owner, by late 1532 Felice was suffering from severe financial constraints. Heavy responsibilities, both past and present, meant she did not have the ready cash to retrieve this prized possession.

CHAPTER 10

A Memorial to the Past

If Felice was unable to secure the return of a memento of her father, she was more successful in helping to ensure the completion of a memorial to him. The Sack had made this urgent, for the church of St Peter and the Vatican Palace had been particular targets for Imperial destruction. Storming the Vatican Palace, the German soldiers used their daggers to score into the famous frescos painted by Raphael in Julius's apartments the name of Charles V and mocking anti-papal sentiments such as 'You should not laugh at what I write. The *Landsknechts* have run the Pope out of town'; or, quite simply, 'Babylon'. These graphic reminders of their desecration are still visible today. In the meantime, the Spanish plundered Julius's tomb in the choir of the Petrine church. The prelate Pietro Corsi lamented, 'Entry was made even into graves and rich tombs . . . the diamond ring and emeralds were wrenched from fingers. Who could take such liberties with you, Julius, greatest of popes and best father of fathers? . . . [From you] the unpacified Iberian has not feared to despoil the right hand of its signet ring after you were buried.'[1] Other reports claimed that after robbing the pontiff's tomb, the Spanish soldiers played ball with his skull. Of all the insults the Imperial troops had heaped on the papacy, the plundering of Julius's tomb and the desecration of the body of this father of new Rome were seen as among the most heinous.

Print of Michelangelo, *Tomb of Julius II*

The tomb in which Felice's father had lain was always envisaged as temporary. The Warrior Pope of Rome's golden age had, only a year after his election as pontiff, begun to plan his final resting place. The aim was, in the words of Vasari, 'to surpass every ancient and imperial sepulchre'. In 1505, Julius had invited Michelangelo to design a tomb that would be no less monumental than the Mausoleum of Halicarnassus, one of the seven wonders of the ancient world. For Michelangelo, too, this was an opportunity to outdo the ancients. He conceived a free-standing chamber, embellished with monumental sculpted figures, to be placed in the choir in the church of St Peter's, which had been designed in the fifteenth century by Rossellino and completed later by Bramante. However, Julius was distracted by other projects, in particular by Bramante's design for New St Peter's, and froze the funding for his tomb. Angered, Michelangelo quarrelled with the Pope and departed for Florence. In 1508 he accepted Julius's invitation to return to Rome to paint the ceiling of the Sistine Chapel. But the earlier project was still close to his heart: the composition of his Sistine ceiling, laterally banded with heroic figures of the prophets, the sibyls and the *ignudi*, the naked heroes of the Golden Age, is derived from his first conception of Julius's tomb.

The Julian tomb was to become Michelangelo's *bête noire*. In 1513, a year after Julius's death, the artist signed a contract with the representatives of the heirs to Julius's estate to continue work on the monument. Although she was included among the Pope's heirs, Felice was not among those listed in this document. The extent of her activities in the political and business world notwithstanding, her gender prevented her from signing this legal document. Instead, the signatures were those of her cousins, Nicolò and Francesco Maria della Rovere. Felice did, however, negotiate on her own behalf with Michelangelo, and it was at this time that she acquired his cartoons from the Sistine Chapel for the frescos decorating her own chapel at Trinità dei Monti.

Despite the new contract, relatively little work was produced during this period by Michelangelo towards Felice's father's tomb, and the design was radically modified from the artist's earlier grandiose vision. Among the few sculptures for the project Michelangelo did manage to complete at this time was the figure of Moses, which would eventually become the tomb's centrepiece. Michelangelo had a new master, Pope Leo X. When

Leo confiscated Francesco Maria's land and titles, he also assumed the right to employ Michelangelo. This made it possible for the Medici pope to send Michelangelo back to Florence to work for his family on their church at San Lorenzo. Although he had mixed feelings about his new employment, Michelangelo remained there throughout the 1520s. On the one hand he was excited to be given the opportunity to complete one of the great churches of his native town. However, his designs for the façade of San Lorenzo were never realized and the church remains without a façade to this day. He would also claim that he had been 'tearfully wrested' from working on Julius's tomb, and he was undoubtedly upset at his removal from Rome, and thus from his ultimate ambition, to be the architect of New St Peter's. He was not to achieve this ambition until 1546 when he was appointed architect on the death of Antonio da Sangallo the Younger.

In Rome, with Julius's temporary tomb desecrated, the need for a memorial to commemorate him became imperative, both from a practical and a symbolic standpoint. If Rome were to be renewed, then the patron of Rome's most recent golden age had to be honoured in a fitting manner. Given the extent of the physical and emotional damage that the Spanish had wreaked on Felice, it was appropriate that she seek to mend this rent the Iberians had made in the fabric of her family history.

In December 1531, Felice, accompanied by representatives of the Duke of Urbino, went in person to Pope Clement VII to discuss the completion of the Julian tomb. Clement, mindful of the damage done to the prestige of the papacy by the Spanish desecration, was prepared to listen to their petition. Serving as Michelangelo's representative at this meeting was the painter Sebastiano del Piombo, who wrote a report of the proceedings to the artist in Florence. Sebastiano was himself anxious to convince Michelangelo that completing the tomb would be the right thing to do. He was careful to inform Michelangelo that 'La Signora Felice' had been present at these negotiations, and he encouraged Michelangelo to agree to return to the project. 'You should see the happiness of the Signora Felice,' Sebastiano wrote of the reaction of the daughter of Pope Julius at the thought the tomb might yet be completed.[2]

Securing Michelangelo's commitment to complete the Julian tomb was not easy. There was the matter of money – Michelangelo claimed that the

8000 *scudi* Francesco Maria della Rovere had paid him following Julius's death was not enough. In the end, he and Francesco Maria agreed to scale down the design for the tomb. Its intended site was changed to San Pietro in Vincoli, Julius's titular church when he was a cardinal. Clement had to grant his permission for Michelangelo to return to the work. The Medici Pope was reluctant to release Michelangelo from Florence, where he was now working on the chapel attached to San Lorenzo. But with an understanding that Michelangelo would direct others to do the actual work, thereby freeing him to continue at San Lorenzo, Clement was more agreeable. On 20 April 1532, a new contract was drawn up between Julius's heirs and Michelangelo. The signing took place at the Vatican Palace; Clement was present, and so was Felice.

To what extent Felice's involvement in the proceedings was the spur to Michelangelo's agreement to complete the tomb cannot be determined. However, at the very least, she personified Rome's past golden age. She was, after all, the Warrior Pope's direct descendant and his only child. It might then be more than coincidence that, following Felice's intervention, the only statues to be completed personally by Michelangelo were the figures of the two Old Testament women, Rachel and Leah. These women, within the framework of the tomb, were deemed to represent respectively the contemplative life and the active life. The human scale and appearance of the sculpted women is radically different from the Amazonian goddesses adorning the Sistine ceiling and the Medici family tombs. Real women posed as the models for these figures. It has been suggested that Vittoria Colonna, who corresponded on spiritual matters with Michelangelo, might have been his inspiration for Rachel.[3] Yet given that this is Julius II's tomb, a much more appropriate and compelling identification for Rachel is another female friend of Michelangelo, Felice della Rovere, the Pope's own daughter.[4] Michelangelo's Rachel is clothed in a hooded robe, veiled in a way redolent of the kinds of widow's weeds Felice would have worn. She gazes upwards, a heavenward glance appropriate to the contemplative life. Yet she is also looking up to the top of the tomb, where a sculpted figure of the pontiff reclines. Rachel's gaze is as much filial as celestial.

One might also see traces of Felice in the figure of Leah, who represents the active life. If Rachel is a daughter, then Leah is a mother, 'an incarnation of abundance and fertility, the solidity of her heavy matronly body . . . increased by the river of folds tumbling down from her girdle to the ground'.[5] Felice's own fertility had ensured a Julian line. And if she was *patrona et gubernatrix*, giving birth to four children undeniably made her *matrix* as well. Rachel's gaze looks to the past, to Felice's father; Leah's body embodies the future, a future created by Felice herself.

It was the future that had become Felice's most pressing concern. Through the renovation of family palaces and Michelangelo's continuation of his work on her father's tomb, she had made remarkable progress towards repairing her family's heritage. Her family's future, however, still demanded her close attention.

CHAPTER 11

Clarice

Felice della Rovere shared many of her father's characteristics: his insurmountable stubbornness, intense tenacity and focused single-mindedness.
Yet she came to differ from him in one great respect. Julius, like all men of
his age, saw his legacy as a memorializing of self. To that end, he had commissioned all those towering buildings at the Vatican Palace emblazoned
with his name. While she was younger, Felice had fashioned herself in his
image. She had acquired a castle and palace of her own, a chapel decorated
with Michelangelo designs, and she had left money for nearly every
church in Rome to say Mass for her when she died. But as she grew older,
she began to define her legacy in terms of her identity as a mother.

Felice's daily life, the necessary and perpetual attention to the affairs of
the estate, would suggest that motherhood was not always a high priority
for her. She might not have spent every part of every year with her children, but she was a constant presence in their lives. The Vicovaro servants
sent her frequent reports on their well-being. 'The children are healthy,
learning, studious, cheerful and virtuous, and hoping for your happy
return,' one letter from Alessandro at Vicovaro reads.[1] The children themselves also sent her letters, some written in careful hands clearly produced
in a daily lesson; one sent by Julia, Francesco and Girolamo in 1520 is
typical: 'Mater Optima. We are very well and hoping to learn the same of

'Unmarried Young Woman', from Christofano Bertelli, *The Ages of Woman*, 1580s

you.'[2] Felice also kept her children on a very tight budget and did not spoil or over-indulge them in any way. Julia had to write to her for extra clothing, or for fabric to make garments. Nor did Felice always respond to their requests on first asking, as Francesco and Girolamo made clear in a letter of 1524: 'Illustrious Mother. We have told you over and over again that the velvet on our saddles is no good any more because it is so old, so please, for our love, will you help us to have it repaired.'[3] By 1530, Felice's major concern was to see her children settled. She wanted her daughter Clarice married and her sons, Girolamo and Francesco, ready and able to take over the running of the Orsini estate.

Felice had placed on hold the matter of a husband for Clarice after the Sack of Rome. In the months prior to the Sack, she had entered into negotiations with the Farnese family to secure Ranuccio, the son of Cardinal Alessandro Farnese, for the fourteen-year-old Clarice. Several members of the Orsini family were actually in favour of this alliance and the match would have been a shrewd investment; Alessandro Farnese was widely tipped to become the next pope. In 1534, he did indeed ascend the papal throne as Paul III. Felice's efforts came to nothing, however, the turmoil of Rome putting paid to her plans.

After the Sack, with Rome still a wasteland and the political and economic climate so unstable, Felice had no desire to marry Clarice into any family with ecclesiastical or Roman ties. She was also anxious about her daughter's personal safety. She felt Rome was still too volatile a place for a young girl, and she was particularly afraid of any action Napoleone might take against her. Following Napoleone's enforced removal by papal troops from Bracciano in 1529, Felice had received a warning from a servant: 'Napoleone is melancholic and disordered, and wishes now for the matters with your ladyship to be remedied not only with property but with blood itself.'[4] There was also the possibility that Napoleone would take Clarice hostage. If she were to be raped by one of his allies, the man could legally demand and be given the right to marry her, the same fate Felice had feared could have befallen Francesca Maria's niece Bartolomea if she had remained with Felice. Napoleone knew that Clarice was Felice's weakness; this was the reason he had once proposed that he be allowed a voice in determining her future. Consequently, in order to protect her, when Felice returned to Rome she left Clarice at

Pesaro, at the della Rovere court run by the gluttonous and spendthrift Marco Vegerio. Clarice was still there in 1530.

Clarice was the most engaging and the most intelligent of Felice's children. She was her uncle Gian Domenico's favourite, his *bambolina* ('little baby doll'). She took matters of education far more seriously than her siblings. When, as children, the others wrote to Felice from Vicovaro, they usually asked for things for themselves, Julia for clothing, the boys for saddles. Clarice, at eleven, wrote to her mother, 'We are all well, healthy and strong. We continue to do our lessons, and I beg of your ladyship to recommend me to the Reverend Monsignor [Gian Domenico] and to my Madonna Lucrezia, and Madonna Francesca and M. Angelo and M. Christofano, and I beg of you, if for love of me, you would have a cloak made for Father Menico [a priest at Vicovaro].'[5]

At Fossombrone, when Felice had attempted to find a teacher in Latin and Greek, the tutor was intended not only for Girolamo but also for Clarice. Clarice was far more concerned with her lessons than was her brother, whose ambition was to become a *condottiere*, and who disdained formal education. While Girolamo writes his letters in a next to indecipherable, almost illiterate, scrawl, Clarice writes in a clear and elegant hand. Her mother continued to pay for a tutor for her while she was resident in Pesaro. In addition Clarice had a music teacher there, Fra Francesco, who later travelled to Rome, with a letter of presentation for Felice from Clarice. 'Fra Francesco', she wrote, 'is a worthy man and has taught me how to play. He is coming to Rome, so please could you give him some money, for I do not have a penny.'[6] When she did return to Rome, in late 1531, her education continued. The entry 'Maestro Babuccio, tutor of Signora Clarice' appears in Felice's account books.[7] Clarice was by then seventeen, and formal education for girls often finished once they knew how to write their name and read. This suggests Clarice and her mother were both at pains to develop her intellectual ability.

Clarice also took the threat of Napoleone very seriously. She was attentive to rumours about his movements and passed on whatever she heard to her mother. She sent her word from Pesaro of a young man 'dressed in a red cassock and hat, riding a black horse, coming from Venice and now about thirty miles from Rome, who is said to be one of Napoleone's men'. They feared that he might be acting as a scout for Napoleone, although

Clarice added, 'I doubt that this one is coming to start up something against us, since Napoleone is still in Venice.'[8]

It is hardly surprising that this engaging, accomplished and thoughtful young woman would win the admiration of those who visited the court at Pesaro. Yet nobody expected her cousin Guidobaldo, the son of Francesco Maria della Rovere, to fall madly in love with her.

Guidobaldo was sixteen when he first fell in love with Clarice. For two years, he carried a torch for her as only an ardent adolescent can. Love rarely, if ever, entered the matrimonial equations of the elite, and Guidobaldo's father did not intend to use love in his matrimonial calculations for his son. He wanted him to marry Julia Varano, the daughter of the otherwise heirless Duke of Camerino, who would bring the estate, which adjoined the Duchy of Urbino, and title with her as her dowry. In 1532, Guidobaldo begged permission to marry Clarice, turning to his mother for support when his father ignored his pleas. He wrote Eleonora a letter in which the words simply tumble out:

> For two years now I have spoken at length, begging you that in giving me a wife, it would seem that in this act the principle matter is to satisfy me, given that I carried, and still carry such a love for the lady Clarice, due to her qualities, and her manners. To let me have her would give me such extreme happiness, and not to have her would cause me such infinite sadness, so I beg you with all my heart, if you have any regard for my sanity and health, satisfy and concede me this favour, knowing that in her is my all, perhaps if you wish to have any care of me, knowing that otherwise this will be my ruin, and I am certain that I will be sorrowful for ever.[9]

Guidobaldo's father Francesco Maria wrote a blistering letter to him in response:

> Against all my expectations I understand you persist in wishing a marriage with the line of Signora Felice. Against my deliberate wishes you continue in this dishonourable practice, and because you seem detached from reason, I shall make it clear to you that as servants of our past we do not take in marriage the bastards of our house. And if you do not seek to honour and exalt your house then do not at least

debase it. Morcover, if the present condition of the house of Orsini does not discourage you then you might remember how Renzo da Ceri [as Leo X's General] sought to ruin our state, and if you had known the plainly crazy Gian Giordano you would be ashamed of proceeding so.

In another letter he also reminded Guidobaldo that marriage to Clarice would attract the enmity of Napoleone and he would be persecuted 'not only for your property, but for your very life and soul'.

Felice had always stood by her cousin. She had supported him after he had murdered Cardinal Alidosi, Julius II's adviser, in a fit of jealous pique and she had helped him get back his lands from Leo X. They had always corresponded in a warm and cordial manner. Not so very much earlier, he had told her that he thought of her children as his own. Yet there was a baseness and a snobbery at the heart of Francesco Maria that prevented him from making an alliance with his bastard cousin's lineage. Guidobaldo attempted a spirited defence of Felice, Clarice, and their line, declaring that the Orsini were far more noble than the Varano family. But his father refused to listen.

It was Felice herself who decided matters. She perhaps blamed herself for leaving Clarice unsupervised at a busy court. She had not had this trouble with her elder daughter, Julia, who had grown up isolated at Vicovaro and had then gone straight to the far south to marry the Prince of Bisignano. Felice might have been in favour of Clarice's marriage to Guidobaldo, but she could not afford any more discord with family members. Even as Guidobaldo begged Francesco Maria to let him marry her, Felice was arranging another marriage for Clarice with Don Luigi Carafa, the Prince of Stigliano. Carafa, like Julia's husband, the Prince of Bisignano, was a prince with an estate deep into southern Italy, hundreds of miles from the court of Urbino and Guidobaldo.[10] The Carafa were on good terms with the Spanish, and the need to further an Imperial alliance was never far from Felice's mind. Moreover, the Prince's cousin, Giampietro Carafa, was a cardinal of increasing importance, and would become Pope Paul IV in 1555.

Catherine de' Medici, who had resided briefly with Felice when she was a little girl, wrote Felice a charming letter of congratulations, complimenting her on the choice of consort, which the Medici Princess declared could not have pleased her more. She asked that she be recommended to Clarice 'as a sister'.[11] By coincidence, as an infant, Catherine had been betrothed to Guidobaldo and. It was during this engagement that she had spent some months in Felice's house. The intention had been for her to grow up in an environment less hostile to the Urbino della Rovere than the Medici household in Florence. The Medici quickly had Catherine removed from Felice's care once the marriage negotiations broke down. Yet, despite her youth, Catherine had not forgotten Felice, and indeed perhaps remembered her example later in life, when she, in her turn, became a regent with sons too young to rule.

If Clarice was sorry to lose Guidobaldo, she kept it to herself. She wrote from Stigliano to her mother in loving terms and maintained an active interest in her family's affairs from the castle in the south.

Guidobaldo married Julia Varano in 1534. The famous *Venus of Urbino* by the painter Titian, the picture of the nude with the long golden hair, sprawled on her bed, is believed to have been commissioned to celebrate the event. Paintings of beautiful naked women were often hung in Renaissance bedchambers as an incentive to spur on a husband in the dutiful act of sexual intercourse. As Guidobaldo gazed at this fictive goddess, perhaps he thought ruefully that he would have had no need of her were it Clarice beside him. He and Julia Varano had no children. He soon acquired mistresses and had three illegitimate daughters. To name any of them Clarice would have drawn overt attention to his former love, who was by then respectably married. But he did name one of them Felice. He and Felice remained on good terms. In fact, a sign that Felice was aware of how Francesco Maria had insulted her is that she stopped writing to the cousin who had once addressed her as *soror amantissima*, 'most beloved sister'. When she had news to impart, or was in need of help from the Urbino family, she wrote to his son instead.

The Boys

Felice now had to turn her attention to her sons, who were causing her far more in the way of problems. However unjust Francesco Maria had been in his dismissal of Felice as simply a bastard member of the house of della Rovere, he did have a point about the Orsini men. All the indications are that they shared a tendency to suffer from mental problems in varying degrees, as well as laziness and cruelty, rashness and impetuousness. Felice della Rovere was not a bad mother, but as sole parent there was only so much she could do. Renaissance sons did not look to their mothers to learn how to shape their characters; instinctively they looked to their father, and Francesco's and Girolamo's father was dead. That did not mean that Felice's sons dismissed their widowed mother as being of no consequence; even as men they were remarkably dependent on her. Being unable because of their social conditioning to use their mother as a role model, Francesco and Girolamo did not know how to learn from her wisdom, her ability to manipulate situations to her advantage, or the necessity of looking after those who served them. They also did not have her hunger, her need to succeed. They had been born into privilege, and accepted all it had to offer them without question.

In 1530, Felice's eldest son, Francesco, who was now eighteen, received the abbothood of Farfa. Farfa had belonged to Napoleone, but he had

Maarten van Heemskerck, *Young Man Leaning over a Balcony*

relinquished the office in order to marry Claudia Colonna, although he continued to be referred to as 'L'Abate'. The Abbey of Farfa was located to the south of Rome, with its territory bordering that of Vicovaro. It was an enormous holding, and its administration required as steady a hand as that guiding the rest of the Orsini estates. Unfortunately, Francesco, who never married but who did spawn a huge flock of illegitimate children, did not have his mother's commitment to estate management. He left it in the hands of officials with whom he rarely corresponded, and who, left to their own devices, allowed corruption and anarchy to reign.

By 1531, even Pope Clement VII had heard of the mistreatment of the vassals who laboured within the terrain of the Abbey and, given that Farfa was Church property, he was most displeased. Felice was equally unhappy with her son. She had spent almost twenty years working tirelessly to ensure as much contentment as possible on the part of those who served her, and Francesco's inattentive ways were to cause her anxiety for the rest of her life. She was also worried that her son had angered the Pope, as she knew how much she and her children depended on his favour. In one stern letter to Francesco she told him that his vassals at Farfa had good reason to be unhappy. 'Because I am your mother, and a good mother,' she wrote, 'I am obliged not to be remiss in any of the lessons I should provide for you and so you should know it causes me a great deal of bother to learn of your dealings at the Abbey.' She went on to warn him that he should immediately change his representatives in charge at Farfa, as otherwise 'all the water in the sea will not wash away the dirt your officials have brought'.[1]

She was also prepared to cover for his administrative failings. When Francesco was late with the payment of taxes, Felice wrote to the Roman auditor, 'I am sure that this money has been paid to you, to the satisfaction of my son the Abbot. However, we will pay it again in order to satisfy you, so we will send you 5 *scudi* if you will be patient.'[2] It seems more likely that Felice knew very well that Francesco had never sent the money at all and she was attempting to allow her son to save face.

Francesco, for his part, wrote letters to his mother assuring her that everything was under his control and then attempted to distract her with matters more pleasurable. He wrote to her in one letter, 'I am sending you three figs from the trees that grow here and if for love of me they are to your taste, I will continue to send them to you.' Lazy and incompetent as Francesco clearly was, he and Felice were close. She wrote to him often, in affectionate and vivid terms, with none of the rather chilly protocol usually evident in correspondence between a noble woman and her adult son in Renaissance Italy.

Girolamo, however, proved to be more complicated and less controllable. Although he was the younger son, Felice selected him to inherit the title of Lord of Bracciano. The grounds for her choice are not clear. Perhaps she thought him more intelligent than his brother, or more likely to make a good leader. He was certainly his father's son in a way that Francesco was not. Francesco took after any number of his male della Rovere cousins, men such as the Riario cousins or Girolamo Basso della Rovere, who were content to receive innumerable benefices from their uncle Pope Sixtus IV and let them be run by others, as Felice's stepfather Bernardino de Cupis had served Girolamo della Rovere. Felice's Girolamo, on the other hand, although named for his della Rovere cousin, was very much Gian Giordano's son. He was seized, from an early age, with the desire to be a *condottiere* and lead troops of his own. Eventually he would sever the traditional Orsini tie to France and serve the Holy Roman Emperor on expeditions against the Turks. Francesco Sansovino, however, in his 1565 biography of the family, in an attempt to whitewash the Orsini's most recent history, was obliged to write somewhat obliquely that the extent of Girolamo's international military deeds was limited by his 'domestic commitment'. Such 'commitment' nearly cost Girolamo his life, not to mention the livelihood of the Bracciano Orsini.

Felice was aware of her son's hot-headedness and, for as long as she was able, she attempted to keep him away from Rome and out of the reach of Napoleone. But this became more difficult as Girolamo grew to manhood. In 1530, Felice had sent him to stay with his sister Julia deep in the south at Bisignano. Girolamo soon grew restless and Julia's husband, the Prince of Bisignano, had to write to Felice, 'Girolamo wants to return to Rome, and all the entreaties that I and the Princess have placed upon him will not dissuade him.'[4]

As Girolamo grew to adulthood, so did his hatred and anger towards Napoleone. Felice had first viewed Napoleone as an impediment to the prosperity of her own sons and later as an unstable force she needed to neutralize. She might not have actively cultivated animosity towards Napoleone in her own children, but her decision to keep him away from them at all costs undoubtedly sharpened their perception of him as a monster, constantly plotting their downfall. While for Felice Napoleone was a dangerous nuisance, for Girolamo he was an adversary. Girolamo had no interest in his mother's traditional methods of confronting and deflecting his half-brother, constantly seeking papal arbitration and support. Girolamo was a typical young noble of the Italian Renaissance, quick to anger where an insult was perceived. The male adolescent saw insults in the smallest of actions, which resulted all too readily in a willingness to fight and kill in order to restore his sense of honour and self-esteem. Napoleone and Girolamo were fighting over more than just the concept of honour. Their real battle was over the dearest thing to any man's heart, his patrimony. Napoleone viewed Girolamo as the cuckoo in the nest, the one who had denied him his rightful place as his father's successor. Napoleone also saw the dishonour of effectively being disinherited by the son of a pope's bastard daughter. By his own logic, he was absolutely convinced of his own infinite superiority as the son of the bastard daughter of the King of Spain. Girolamo, in his turn, viewed his half-brother as an interloper who was refusing to accept his own father's wishes, who had dedicated his life to disturbing his family's peace, and who was a constant threat to his own seamless accession to the title of Lord of Bracciano.

In previous centuries, the great division in Rome had been between the Orsini and the Colonna families. Now the split was within the Orsini family. The vitriol between Francesco and Girolamo on one side and Napoleone on the other far outstripped their hatred for any other family. Tales of the brothers' enmity travelled beyond Italy. It was not in France's interests to see division between members of the one Roman noble family on which France had always been able to count for support. The French ambassador wrote to Felice on behalf of King Francis I, informing her,

> I have no need to mention the affection and servitude that your husband and yourself have shown towards the French crown, and to His Majesty. However, His Majesty is greatly displeased to learn of the contention between your sons and the Abbot their brother, as he has let me know. He feels certain that where there is such a close tie of blood matters

should end lovingly, and he does not believe this should be a difficult matter with so many honourable personages as there are in your house. And I exhort your ladyship to willingly adopt and effectuate such matters.[5]

Francis I laid the responsibility of restoring peace at Felice's door. As the French King had given Napoleone Gian Giordano's 12,000 ducat pension, which Felice had asked him to confer on Francesco, she hardly regarded him as an ally. Yet even had Felice wished to accommodate Francis, events were soon to reach beyond her, or indeed anyone else's, control. Girolamo's aggressive challenges to Napoleone sent his half-brother into ever-increasing spirals of rage and belligerence. At the beginning of 1532, Napoleone, who was no friend to the Pope, had received from Clement VII a safe conduct valid for one year, providing he reached an accord with his brothers. But by now such a treaty had become psychologically impossible for both parties.

CHAPTER 13

The War of Vicovaro

Since relinquishing the abbothood of Farfa, Napoleone had been able to concentrate on his skills as a warrior, which he had been exercising since invading Palo and in the aftermath of the Sack of Rome. He was now a *condottiere*, a soldier for hire like so many of his relatives, including his father, and he had been employed by Florence in action against the Medici. Napoleone's military service had made him wealthy enough to afford troops of his own, men recruited in part from the sprawling Orsini estates. He was now a force in his own right, and he was intent on flexing this military might.

Felice had decided that Girolamo's own bellicose instincts might be better channelled by organized soldierly activity. In September 1532, despite some aversion to the Gonzaga family, she had given her nineteen-year-old son leave to serve under Ferrante Gonzaga to fight against the Turks in Hungary. Girolamo had men of his own, and had sent two hundred of them ahead to Mantua, leaving himself all but unprotected, with a company of only ten men. Somehow, Napoleone received word of his half-brother's vulnerability just as Girolamo was preparing to leave Vicovaro, the Orsini castle to the south of Rome. Losing no time, Napoleone marched on his family's home, at the head of a force of three hundred men. At Vicovaro, as a report of 11 September to Venice had it, Girolamo

Vicovaro, sixteenth century

was 'taken prisoner by his brother, named Signor Napoleone, the former Abbot of Farfa . . . as there are differences between the brothers'.[1] These differences were, of course, the fortresses and fiefs that Napoleone ardently believed were his fair share of his patrimony. And that was the ransom he demanded for the release of Girolamo.

September and October 1532 brought a great deal of anguish and inner conflict for Felice. Her younger son was now being held hostage by his mentally unstable half-brother, who had been nursing a deep hatred of him since the day Girolamo became Orsini heir, at the age of five. Felice wrote, with some poignancy, to her son Francesco that Napoleone was holding Girolamo prisoner 'in the rooms where you were brought up as children'.[2] Felice was forced to reconcile an image of Girolamo as a little boy playing in those rooms with one of him as a nineteen-year-old held there under the watch of an armed guard, in mortal danger.

Many in her position might have compromised and given in to Napoleone's demands. While Felice wanted Girolamo released as soon as possible, she had not spent the last fifteen years of her life holding on tight to the Orsini patrimony for her children only to have Napoleone wrench it from them. She had no reason to believe that Napoleone would keep to the terms of any agreement. As she wrote to Francesco, although Napoleone claimed all he wanted, in exchange for Girolamo's freedom, were the towns of Castelvecchio and San Gregorio, estates to the south of Rome, she did not trust him. 'I am very much afraid', she concluded, 'that Girolamo is in danger of death.'[3] Cardinal del Monte, her father's former secretary and the future Pope Julius III, remembered her kindness to him as a young man, and wrote to her to give her encouragement: 'My most illustrious mother. I have seen what it is to be the son of such a mother, and so I have every hope for Signor Girolamo.'[4]

Felice set to work on her son's behalf. It would not be easy to take back Vicovaro. The castle was set in far more hostile terrain than Bracciano. It was much more mountainous and rocky, and was a favourite hideout for fugitives from Rome. A corps of cardinal negotiators, including Gian Domenico de Cupis, Cardinal Franciotto Orsini and Cardinal Giovanni Salviati set off for Vicovaro. Also *en route* was a body of a thousand men led by the papal commander Luigi Rodomonte (also known as Alysior or Alvise) Gonzaga marching south to Vicovaro. Clement VII authorized the movements of Luigi and his troops. He had no love for Napoleone, who had once plotted to assassinate him. He considered Vicovaro, and Felice's children, as under his protection, and he wished to 'remove Napoleone from that place and restore it to his brothers'.[5]

Military action was, however, the last resort. As the Urbino ambassador reported to Francesco Maria, it was known 'how little reason governs Signor Napoleone'.[6] He commented that accounts of Napoleone's 'bestialities' would take too long to tell, but did remark that to judge Napoleone from his actions no one could ever know that Girolamo was his own brother.

Felice wrote to Luigi Gonzaga, 'I am most certainly grateful to God for your virtue and wisdom, and I am troubled, knowing as I do, of what little prudence Napoleone shows, and I despair of him not harming my son. I beg you to act in accordance with your usual prudence to save the life of my son, for in doing so you will be saving a creature of His Holiness, as well as a servant of yourself. Forgive me if I am too fretful but you must remember that I am a mother.'[7] However, the fretful mother also understood the realities of military activity, and the same pen issued the following practical instructions to her servant Pietro Vicario of Sancto Polo: 'This part of the estate must contribute to the expense of the soldiers. So you must go immediately to Campagno and obtain four *rubbio* of grain, two from Scrofano, one from Formello and two from Isola.'[8] The soldiers camped at the base of the castle needed feeding, one of the primary considerations of a long campaign. Without adequate supplies, an army could become mutinous, and the events of the Sack of Rome were fresh in everyone's mind.

The Urbino ambassador's description of the activities at Vicovaro changed from the 'affair at Vicovaro' to the 'war of Vicovaro', with the realization that what was occurring was a full-bloodied siege. The tediousness of siege warfare, for either side, can only be imagined, the long days of doing absolutely nothing in all weathers, in excessive heat or in pouring rain. Siege strategy was in large part a war of attrition, the besieged normally being the losing side because their supplies would eventually run out. In this instance, Napoleone had the advantage of a hostage. Consequently, considerable time was devoted to attempts to negotiate an agreement between the two sides of this embattled family, to find, as the Urbino ambassador put it, 'concord from the discord'. But proceedings stalled, and at the end of

September Clement sent Luigi north for a period to quell an insurrection in the Adriatic port of Ancona, before recalling him back to Vicovaro. This time, word was sent to Venice: 'The Pope has supplied six pieces of artillery', cannons and mortars.[9]

As Felice continued to refuse to accept Napoleone's price for Girolamo, Napoleone sought ways to put more pressure on her. She received a letter sent in Girolamo's name designed to appeal to her maternal sensibilities. However, the language of the letter is such that it is doubtful Girolamo himself was its author: 'Illustrious mother,' went the letter,

> Up until today I had every faith in you as a mother, but now I am doubt-ful of the care you have for my life, and I should tell you that this will be the last letter that you receive from me. I have found more mercy from our capital enemy Signor Napoleone than I have from you. He is content to let me write to you to tell you, should you wish to do something for my health, which is so bad I more greatly desire death than life . . . If you were to comply with Napoleone's wishes, and meet with his satisfaction, I shall see myself free from Vicovaro.[10]

Given that the author of the letter wrote in a clear hand, while Girolamo's usual style was a near-indecipherable scrawl, Felice might well have seen this letter as a fake, a fraudulent attempt to wrench sympathy from her. She did not respond.

The stand-off between stepmother and stepson continued, and the papal troops waited, camping outside the walls of Vicovaro in the damp autumnal weather. Luigi Gonzaga sent word to Felice on 18 October that he thought they would be ready to storm the fortress within three days. The problem was that it had begun to rain, which greatly hindered their progress in scaling Vicovaro's walls. The weather did indeed deter the papal troops. Reports sent to Urbino on 25 October said that the attempt to penetrate the castle had brought little success. There were greater casualties among the papal troops than among those inside, among them Luigi Gonzaga himself, who received a shoulder wound from an arrow. It turned gangrenous, and he died a long and slow death, lingering until December of that year.

Still Felice did not cede ground. She persuaded the Pope to send in more men from the garrisons at Ostia and Civitavecchia. Her strategic sense did not desert her. Realizing that she might well need military support from Urbino, but being reluctant to ask for it until it was absolutely necessary, she wrote a melancholy letter to Francesco Maria's son, Guidobaldo. Lamenting the lack of progress made by the troops under Luigi Gonzaga, she told Guidobaldo, 'I am sure Your Highness can understand how, among all the other afflictions and pains that I have had, my maternal love moves me to even greater lamentation, and you know what an affectionate servant Your Highness possesses in my son. I hope that God in his mercy will cause this affliction to cease . . .'[11] But Felice did more than rely on the assistance of others. She herself paid for soldiers led by the mercenary Francesco da Cinguli, which were sent to Vicovaro on 28 October. Despite her deep involvement in the Vicovaro siege, Felice did not neglect her duties as Orsini governor. During the siege, among other actions, she authorized the release of a horse and other belongings of the late Guido Corso, 'our good and faithful servant' to his widow, Madonna Angela; the release of the son of another servant, Basilio de Montepoli, from prison, and attended to the selling of Bracciano's hay.

Napoleone continued to be a tenacious adversary. On 4 November, impatient that his enemy had not yet met his demands, and seeing that the number of troops attempting to storm Vicovaro had not diminished, he attempted to escape, taking Girolamo with him. However, soldiers impeded his way and Napoleone retreated back into the castle. A few days later he contrived to escape by himself, but not without taking, as one of Felice's servants informed her, 'all the silver from the church and crosses and altar cloths, and everything. All he has left is one cloth for the saying of the Mass.'[12]

Napoleone's departure precipitated the capitulation of the castle, and Girolamo was finally released. When the soldiers stormed Vicovaro, only three of Napoleone's men were left guarding Girolamo. At the sight of his rescuers Girolamo declared that he thought he would never be released. Napoleone was gone for the moment, but all knew he would return before too long. For the time being, at least, the business was concluded, as a summary was sent to Venice: 'Signor Alvise Gonzaga has retaken Vicovaro, Signor Napoleone had fled, Signor Alvise was thus able to take the land, and Signor Girolamo brother of the said Napoleone who was imprisoned is now liberated.'[13]

The war of Vicovaro had been costly, not only to Felice personally, but also to the papacy. Not only had Clement spent a great deal of money, he had also lost a papal commander far more reliable than Renzo da Ceri or Francesco Maria della Rovere. He made it clear to Felice that in order to avoid a repetition, the situation between the Orsini brothers must be resolved. France put pressure on Clement too. In 1533, 'through the intercession of King Francis I', Clement passed an act absolving Napoleone for his actions, along with his band of sixty-six men.[14] A division of Orsini property had also to take place, known simply as *la divisione*. However, Napoleone was not to be found, and was thought to have escaped to France. Girolamo too disappeared for much of that year, so little progress was made with the partitioning of the estate.

CHAPTER 14

A Brother's Revenge

Appearance was still a critical matter for Felice. It did not matter that the previous year had seen the most public demonstration yet of the rift between the brothers, or that Napoleone might get his way and receive a significant portion of the estate. She had to ensure that her family appeared stronger than ever. The structural restorations to the fabric of Monte Giordano were complete, and she had acquired sumptuous new furniture carved from oak and walnut. Felice began to entertain at the palace in a way she had not done before. For the Shrove Tuesday carnival festivities, she hosted what was to be described as one of the grandest events ever at Monte Giordano. It was traditional for widowed noblewomen to host a carnival celebration to which only women were invited. Felice's guests included the mother and illegitimate daughters of Cardinal Franciotto Orsini, with whom Felice had come to be on better terms since he had attempted to help her in the negotiations with Napoleone at Vicovaro. Also invited were her cousin Maria della Rovere and her daughter, and the wife of Gregorio Casale, a Vatican financier from Bologna. The guest of honour was Portia Colonna, a widowed matriarch like Felice herself, thus her counterpart in the other great Roman family. Portia was accommodated in one of the most magnificent new rooms, described as containing two beds and sumptuous wall hangings. Francesco Orsini's servant wrote

C. Boel, after Antonio Tempesta 'Bourbon sends Troops to Attack' to inform him that 'the party was one of the greatest ever, and a beautiful comedy was performed by servants of the Reverend Trani'.[1]

For Christmas 1533, the whole of Felice's family gathered at Monte Giordano, the first time they had been together since the Jubilee of 1525. Julia came with her husband, the Prince of Bisignano, and their two little girls, as did Clarice, accompanied by the Prince of Stigliano. Francesco and Girolamo were both present and the festivities extended into January. But the relative peace of 1533 proved to be a lull before the storm. As the party ended, word reached the family that Napoleone was riding to Rome, and everything changed.

If Girolamo Orsini had survived the siege of Vicovaro without sustaining much physical harm, the same could not necessarily be said of his mental state. Being taken prisoner and held captive by his half-brother was a deeply humiliating experience for a young man who prided himself on his warrior-like abilities, even if they had never been put to the test. The ways Napoleone baited Girolamo inside Vicovaro can only be imagined. Certainly he would have hurled insults at him, at his brother and especially at his mother, taunting him, declaring that his family must care little for him if they were not prepared to give up land to secure his release. Possibly Girolamo had come to believe this himself, which would account for his absences from his family during 1533. Girolamo might have sworn loyalty to the Pope, but had undoubtedly sworn a personal oath that he would have his revenge on Napoleone.

Napoleone's motivation for coming to Monte Giordano is unclear but appeared to centre around Clarice, and his desire to see her. Supporters of Napoleone claimed all he wished to do was to 'kiss the hand of his sister [Clarice]' prior to her departure south.[2] Such a desire on Napoleone's part was met with trepidation by Felice and her family. It was unlikely that all Napoleone wished to do was to give a formal greeting to Clarice. Napoleone had always recognized her particular value. He had once before tried to force Felice's hand by insisting that he be the one to determine her younger daughter's future. Clarice, for her part, knew how dangerous he was. In his madness had he hatched some new plan to kidnap her and have her violated so that she would no longer be fit to be the Princess of Stigliano? Clarice, the Prince of Stigliano, and the Bisignano left as soon as they could. As the Prince of Bisignano would later report,

'On our departure from Rome we were accompanied part of the way by the Signora Felice, her mother, the Abbot of Farfa [Francesco], and Signor Girolamo. Her mother and the Abbot turned back, and Signor Girolamo stayed to accompany us for some of the way.' Napoleone caught up with them. Girolamo, enraged, turned to his hated half-brother, drew his sword and killed him. 'Some', remarked Bisignano, with perhaps a hint of understatement, 'are of the opinion that the reason for this act is due to the enmity he has from the time that Napoleone captured him.'[3]

Bisignano's account of Girolamo's killing of Napoleone is actually the most detailed in existence. To flesh out the scene any further requires a certain degree of imagination. Girolamo's act of violence was an impetuous one, undoubtedly triggered by his memory of those terrible months as a hostage at Vicovaro. He now found himself facing, for the first time since then, the brother who had never been a brother to him. Girolamo now had the opportunity to take his revenge for his imprisonment, to protect his younger sister, to restore his honour and most importantly, to restore his honour in front of his brothers-in-law, southern princes both, for whom honour was the stuff of life. Few sword thrusts can have been delivered with as much hatred and satisfaction as Girolamo's that day. And few can have been met with as much surprise. It was Napoleone who was the merciless professional soldier with the reputation for cunning, the one driven by an ever blazing rage. Girolamo was over a decade his junior, a mere boy who had never fought in a war, who had spent his life protected by his mother. Yet it was the boy who killed the man.

The scene is of the type that would later appeal to nineteenth-century painters eager to capture the drama and gore of the Italian past. The first work the Pre-Raphaelite painter William Holman Hunt publicly presented was a scene from fourteenth-century Rome, where the Roman hero Cola di Rienzo mourns his brother, killed in a skirmish between the Orsini and Colonna families. The painter vividly captures a road in the Roman *campagna*, the city visible in the distance. The attackers are now riding away, leaving a man to lament over the body of his dead brother. But while Napoleone had followers who mourned his loss, there was no mourning from his brothers, only rejoicing, and a profound sense of satisfaction at honour regained.

CHAPTER 15

Restitution

Girolamo's action shocked the Italian nobility. Fratricide was not uncommon, but it was more normal practice to hire an assassin or a poisoner to do the deed. That Girolamo killed Napoleone with his own hands reflects his deeply entrenched desire to redeem his own honour. That, at least, was something his peers could understand, and was probably what eventually saved him. Although initially Girolamo was condemned to death by the city of Rome, in May of 1534 his death sentence was commuted to a brief term of imprisonment and the payment of a large fine described as *il debito di sangre*, the debt of blood. The prison sentence was purely theoretical. After the murder, Girolamo had continued to ride on with his brothers-in-law and was hiding at Cassano, the Prince of Bisignano's estates deep in the south of Italy.

There is a surprising lack of documentation relating to the murder in the Orsini family's archive. No letter survives referring directly to what had occurred. Clarice wrote to her mother on 22 March 1534, telling her how sorry she was 'to be absent from your ladyship's side at this time'.[1] From April 1534 there is a letter to Felice from Girolamo written in his near illegible scrawl, in which little more than the word 'disgratia' can be deciphered.[2] There is another from this period to Girolamo from Portia Colonna, Felice's guest at Monte Giordano the previous year for the carnival celebrations, in

Maarten van Heemskerck, *People in Front of the Vatican*

which she assures Girolamo, over and over again, of her love for him 'as a sister'.[3] Yet it is as if every other reference to this event has been systematically removed from Orsini records, thus concealing an event that would stain the family's reputation indelibly.

There is, however, a great deal of surviving documentation relating to the business end of the matter, the payment of the 'debt of blood'. From Clement VII's perspective, Girolamo's removal of Napoleone was by no means to the Pope's disadvantage. Napoleone, who had plotted to assassinate Clement and had assisted in a revolt in Tuscany against the Medici, had long been a thorn in the Pope's side. Although Clement had often been exasperated by the behaviour of both Girolamo and Francesco Orsini, he had followed in his cousin Leo's footsteps and always shown favour to their mother, but Napoleone's assassination was not without potential political consequences and Clement could not now put his personal relationship with Felice above all else. Francis I of France had always been sympathetic to Napoleone and his claims, and Clement's niece, Catherine de' Medici, had been married the previous year to Francis's son, Henry. Clement had no desire to provoke any kind of international incident by appearing to ignore Girolamo's action, allowing it to go unpunished. In fact, what Girolamo had done presented Clement with a desperately needed opportunity to swell the papal coffers which were still drastically depleted following the Sack. The Pope confiscated Vicovaro and Bracciano.

The removal of Vicovaro was bad enough, but Bracciano was the hub, the nerve centre, of the Orsini economy. Without the Bracciano estate, the Orsini of Bracciano could no longer function. The removal of their patrinomic lands rendered them nameless and homeless. It was thus Felice della Rovere's task to ensure that this option was not put into effect. To that end, 1534 was to see her perform the greatest acts of diplomacy and financial strategy of her entire life. She knew that if she were to succeed the greatest impediment to her son's smooth succession as Bracciano lord had been removed. She could never have urged Girolamo to kill Napoleone; the consequences were too great. But now that Napoleone was out of the picture, the prospect of a trouble-free horizon spurred her on to retrieve her sons' estate.

The Pope had confiscated the territory but no fixed terms had been set out by which Felice could procure its return. Such ambiguity on Clement's part was deliberate. It was designed to allow his disgruntled papal *nipote*, Cardinal Ippolito de' Medici, who felt he had been denied a role in papal politics, the opportunity to broker the terms of its return to Felice's sons. The first step in the protocol for *la restitutione*, as it was called, was for Felice to go to the Vatican Palace. There, as Lorenzo Bencivenni, Felice's aide in this affair, wrote to Girolamo, she 'kissed the feet of his Holiness and the hand of the Illustrious Cardinal de' Medici and thanked his Holiness and His Illustriousness for the favour they have shown'.[4] All meetings to petition for the restitution had then to take place with Ippolito, who was to serve as Clement's only representative in the matter. Thus, when Clement eventually agreed to restore the estates to Felice's sons, it could appear to the larger world as if this was due to Ippolito's skilful handling of the situation. All concerned were aware of this masquerade, but appearances had to be maintained at all times to appeal to Ippolito's vanity. This event is not without irony: Ippolito de' Medici was no stranger to familial enmity and the following year, 1535, was to become a victim himself when he was poisoned by an emissary of his own hated cousin, Duke Alessandro de' Medici.

It was not simply a question of Clement waiting for the right moment to hand back the territory. A considerable sum of money would have to change hands for this to happen, and the raising of such a sum posed a major problem for Felice. The Orsini coffers were practically empty and Felice's personal resources depleted. The last few years had seen the expense of repairing three large palaces in Rome, the payment of Clarice's dowry and the cost of her wedding. Added to that were payments to the mercenary soldiers sent to rescue Girolamo from Vicovaro, and the fine paid to spare Girolamo's life. There was little grain to sell that could be exchanged for money as heavy floods the previous year had all but destroyed the new crops. To make matters worse, all these negotiations, both diplomatic and financial, were taking place as the sands of time were running out. By the summer of 1534, Clement's health was in rapid decline. Felice knew that if the agreement to return the Orsini lands was not concluded before he died, a new pope could declare the current negotiations null and void.

Both Felice and the papal party recognized that any petition on her part would be pointless unless she had the funds to support her request. Her first priority was the raising of cash. The papacy indicated to Felice that the sum of 10,000 ducats would be one sufficient for her to bring to the bargaining table. This was a large sum of money – Baldassare Peruzzi's yearly salary as architect of St Peter's, for instance, had been 250 ducats. The proposed restitution was perhaps the equivalent of about 2 million pounds in today's money. However, it was not unrealizable. The challenge, though, was to find those willing to lend to Felice. Other members of the Orsini family were unlikely to help. Many were equally cash poor, their wealth tied up in land. Or, if they could have helped her, they had no desire to, either because of personal animosity or because they anticipated that if Felice could not buy back the estates the land might eventually be ceded to another branch of the family.

However, there were members of Felice's extended family who did come to her aid. On 10 July 1534, Felice wrote to Francesco to tell him that 'for the affair of Bracciano I have found 8000 ducats, which the Archbishop of Benevento will give us. With this agreement we will pay 10 per cent interest, and as security he will take Vicovaro and Castelvecchio, but he will take possession in your name.'[5] The rest of the principal was provided by Felice's new son-in-law, the Prince of Stigliano, Don Luigi Carafa. He supplied her with 4000 ducats. Felice retreated for a few days to her palace at Trinità dei Monti, close enough for her to be informed of anything that might occur and private enough to give her some respite.

Felice could now enter into the negotiating process with Cardinal Ippolito de' Medici. Late at night she would send Francesco reports of the day's events, which had usually exhausted her. On 23 July she wrote, 'At this moment I am suffering from great mental fatigue in finding a way to recover our things. May it please God to grant me inspiration when I talk tomorrow with the Reverend de' Medici.' Each day, Felice would arrive at Ippolito de' Medici's Vatican apartments. Much of the time would be spent in rhetorical, largely meaningless, exchanges. She had to assure him over and over again that her sons would be unswervingly loyal subjects to the Pope, that the Orsini would never again cause strife in the city of Rome but would be faithful papal servants.

On 25 July, news of the Pope's poor health reached Felice: 'I have the good fortune to understand the way the wind blows hour by hour, by means of Cardinal Ridolfi and Lucrezia and Lorenzo Salviati [Medici relatives]. Last night His Holiness passed a fairly peaceful night, he did not have a fever, although he did vomit.'[6] But on 30 July, Felice was panic-stricken: 'I told you that the Pope has taken a turn for the worse, and so this morning I went on horseback to go to speak with Cardinal de' Medici about Bracciano. Out on the street leaving Monte Giordano I heard a great noise and saw a great crowd rushing towards Banchi [the banking district within the bend of the Tiber]. I believed the Pope must be dead, so I turned back, and returned home.'[7] Later that day she learned the commotion had been a false alarm: the Pope was still alive. So she set out again.

The next day, when Felice went again to meet with Ippolito, he gave her good news. The Pope's condition had improved somewhat, and he had devoted himself to thinking about the affairs of the Orsini. As yet, there was no official papal ordinance but, as she reported to Francesco, the Pope had promised, 'as a gentleman, that Bracciano would be rendered unto no others than my sons, and this promise I can hold firm'. 'I did not want to lose any time in notifying you,' Felice continued, 'and I want you to let Girolamo know that there will be no more accusations, and everyone will know the virtues of the men I have made.'[8]

It was, even so, a slow process. Vicovaro was released at the beginning of August. Felice wrote to Girolamo to tell him the good news, and that she hoped that they would also have Bracciano back. She instructed him to 'write warmly and often to Cardinal de' Medici, offering him infinite praise, and tell him everything you have you owe to him'.[9] Word came that Clement's main interest was that the Orsini boys should show their appreciation to Ippolito. Letters were duly sent to Ippolito de' Medici in Girolamo's name, even if they were not actually composed by him. One told the Cardinal, 'I have heard from my mother and brother of all the benefits that our house receives every day from your Reverence and lately the restitution of Vicovaro, which we recognize came only from you, and I, along with all the others, remain in perpetual obligation to you.'[10]

Fearful that her son might get over-excited and attempt to return too soon from exile, Felice instructed Girolamo that he should 'not move for anything' and that he should 'show the Prince of Bisignano all your usual obedience'.[11] She continued her practice of visiting Cardinal Ippolito every day until finally the news came that Bracciano was also to be returned. 'Today,' Felice wrote to Girolamo, 'I went to kiss the feet of His Holiness.

You can now rest with a quiet soul for His Holiness was more loving than I can say. God be praised for everything.'[12] From Stigliano, Clarice wrote joyfully 'that there is no way in which I can properly express my happiness at the wonderful and longed-for news of the recovery of Bracciano'.[13] On 25 September, two months after agreeing to return Bracciano, Clement VII died.

Felice della Rovere's work was almost done. She had, single-handedly, raised the restitution money and negotiated tirelessly at the Vatican to save her sons' patrimony. Yet she took no credit for what she had done. Felice knew that she now belonged to the past. For the Orsini family to have a future, she needed her sons to be respected. Ever mindful that appearance was more important than reality, she created the illusion that the rescue of Bracciano had been the work of Francesco, when in fact, the idle Abbot of Farfa had done nothing. Felice wrote to Francesco's brother-in-law, the Prince of Bisignano, that 'if it was not for the prudence and care of the Abbot your brother, our affairs would be completely in ruin'.[14] Whether or not the Prince of Bisignano, who had witnessed his mother-in-law negotiate with a pope to buy his uncle a cardinal's hat, believed her is open to debate.

There was also some subtext to this message. After two decades as Orsini *gubernatrix*, Felice della Rovere knew the time was approaching when, reluctantly or willingly, she had to hand over the reins of power to her sons. She was almost ready to step down. But not quite. Before she could relinquish her role, she needed the outside world to perceive 'the men she had made', who had the blood of Julius the Warrior Pope running through their veins, as worthy and virtuous heirs to the Orsini family. She knew she still had a lot of work to do to establish her sons' positions within the Italian political and social arena. Reliable and trustworthy agents had to be found to work on behalf of Girolamo and Francesco, who could be feckless, reckless and unpredictable. She had to secure a bride for Girolamo, whose reputation was now somewhat tarnished, in order for the dynasty she had created to live on. So Felice della Rovere's final goal was to seal her maternal legacy. It was to this cause that she was now to devote her life.

PART VI

The Most Loving Mother in the World

Final Reckoning

On 10 February 1535, Felice della Rovere wrote to her son Girolamo, who had now taken possession of his titular castle at Bracciano. She told him, 'Being the most loving mother in the world that it is possible to be, I have experienced many things that have been for your benefit and honour, to inflate your greatness, without which my life would be estimated at nothing. So now this loving mother is writing to ask you to send her the profits from the sale of the hay, as there are a lot of debts to pay.'[1]

Felice's words summarize her life as the Orsini regent, keeping the estate in trust for her sons. From the moment her position within the family was established she had battled through an extraordinary variety of encounters and challenges. Everything she had done was with the goal of securing her sons' inheritance. She had pursued that above all else. Felice's life had had many epic moments, and she knew it, but she was also aware of some of its ironies. Everything she had done, she had done for the ultimate benefit of others – her children. And despite the grandiose language associated with such achievement, campaigning for the 'honour' and 'greatness' of Girolamo, finally she was still occupied with mundane practical considerations. She needed money from the sale of Orsini produce in order to pay the family debts that had accrued during those last turbulent years. Now, more than ever, she needed to keep her business in profit, especially in a

'Old Age', from Christofano Bertelli, *The Ages of Woman*, 1580s

difficult Roman economy, which was still suffering the aftershocks of the Sack. A servant in Rome wrote to Girolamo in March of 1535, lamenting the depressed price of grain in the city due to an influx of cheap grain from the north, which was 'less than 2 *scudi* a *rubbio*'. However, 'in the last few days', wrote the servant admiringly, 'Signora Felice has managed to secure a higher price than that'.[2] Orsini finances depended heavily on the sale of grain; low prices were not good news. In such circumstances, Felice was more than prepared to haggle, something deemed unseemly for well-to-do women in the marketplace.

The restitution of the Orsini titular castles had put Felice in a somewhat ambiguous position. The guarantee that the property now belonged to her sons alone allowed Girolamo and Francesco to embark officially on their adult lives. Girolamo would reign as Orsini Lord, while Francesco would continue as Abbot of Farfa and also play his part in the affairs of the Orsini. Their mother's role was due to change from *gubernatrix* to dowager. Sidelined from family affairs, the widowed dowager was expected to be a quiet creature, giving herself over to contemplation and spiritual matters. It was not to be that simple a transition for Felice. Girolamo had interests quite separate from governing his inheritance. He was anxious to establish a career for himself as a *condottiere*, to claim his Orsini birthright, and to prove he was as much a man, if not more so, than his half-brother Napoleone, whose soldierly skills had been beyond question. With the sanguine passivity of privileged youth, Girolamo did not seem fully aware of just how close he had come to losing his birthright, and how much had had to be done to restore it. Not the least of this was the need to pay back the loans his mother had raised. A great deal of responsibility still fell to Felice. That such a position should still be hers did not necessarily displease her. For twenty years she had been at the centre of the house of Orsini and she had never much cared for a marginalized status.

Felice also had to make some personal sacrifices in order to bolster her sons' position and the family economy. In 1535, she found herself obliged to sell her castle of Palo to raise money to pay back the loans she had taken out to retrieve Vicovaro and Bracciano. She wrote to her sons' cousin, Gentile Virginio Orsini, whose estate at Cerveteri bordered the terrain of Palo, 'I have sold Palo to Maestro Phylippo dal Bene in order to pay the 4000 *scudi* that I owe to the Prince of Stigliano, and the aforementioned

Maestro Phylippo desires to have a letter from you that informs him that it pleases you that he takes the holding of Palo and that you will be a good neighbour. So I ask that you are content to write a letter in the appropriate form to his satisfaction, and it would give me singular pleasure, and so I ask that you send this letter to me.'[3]

Over previous decades, Felice had fought hard to maintain Palo, her prized possession, the dazzling purchase of her youth. The waterfront castle had been her trophy. Its location reminded her of her adventures as a child sailing from Rome to Savona, and the property had given her great power in Renaissance Rome. On more than one occasion the castle had aroused Napoleone's jealously and ire and he had tried, unsuccessfully, to take it from her. Now, in death, he had succeeded in doing what he could not in life: he had removed the castle from Felice's ownership. Yet if she felt the sting of parting with the estate that had, in its time, given her both revenue and prestige, securing her the affection of Leo X, her letters do not reveal it. As the most loving mother in the world, she made what sacrifices she had to safeguard Girolamo's and Francesco's inheritance.

Even if Girolamo was not as active a ruler as he should have been, he was still the Orsini Lord. While Felice was still performing administrative tasks, she was now obliged to write to Girolamo to confirm arrangements, ask for his authorization, or remind him to release cash from the Orsini coffers, which only he could sanction. Although she was not loath to play her matriarchal card, as the 'most loving mother', at moments when her son's inattention strained her patience, Felice's diligent observation of estate protocol suggests that she thought it would be good training for her twenty-one-year-old son to assume his responsibilities, to make sure that he understood that he was now Orsini Lord. The tone in which she addresses him is often formal. Before her son had come of age, whenever she had needed wine sent out from Bracciano, Felice would write directly to the keeper of the castle's cellars at Bracciano. Now she would send Girolamo such requests as: 'I ask that you are willing to let Antonio da Menico take a bottle of wine from Bracciano that he can take to Francesco my tailor and old servant and that it pleases you not to go against me.'[4] Felice had been sending wine to Francesco Sarto for well over ten years, and did not want to break tradition with a faithful servant.

In another letter to Girolamo she explained, 'Because Palo [prior to its sale] lacks wine, please could you send a bottle to the castellan from the Bracciano vineyard.'[5] This letter is dated 29 October 1534, only a few days after Bracciano had been officially restored to the family, and is indicative of Felice's decision to make her son aware of what was now his, down to every last bottle of wine. The same letter also informs her son that 'it would also give me great pleasure if you could send forty pounds of gunpowder, a bit of lead, and lend two arquebusiers'. Clearly the events of recent years had made Felice sensitive to security issues at the seaside castle.

The same need for Girolamo's sanction applied to other foodstuffs, and Felice was anxious the complicated system of exchange and favours she had carefully instituted over the years went undisturbed: 'Cardinal Cibo is insistent about receiving the barley that we owe him, so I need you now to authorize sending him the little that we have stored at Trevignano.'[6] On another occasion, she needed him to 'send me your mules on Monday evening, as I wish to send my ladies to Galera, and from Galera they will go to Bracciano'.[7]

The process of Felice's stepping down as official head of the Orsini family reveals just how seriously she had taken the duty of pastoral care. She was now very anxious that Girolamo should also attend assiduously to those on the Orsini estate who could not help themselves: 'Illustrious and beloved son. Among the many cases I put to you before leaving Bracciano, I did not make any recommendation for poor little Fra Francesco. But I do beg of you for the love of God that it will please you to immediately give an order for him to receive a quarter of grain and a pound of meat, and if you do this it will be a good work and give me singular pleasure.'[8] A similar request: 'The son of the late Troiano di Dovaro is now deprived of a father and mother, and if you do not give him a bit of charity he is going to die of hunger, so I beg you to order that he shall be given half a *rubbio* of grain and to order that every year he shall be given a *rubbio* and a half of grain.' In case Girolamo felt he might like independent corroboration of the orphaned boy's pitiful state, Felice added, 'I learned about him from Giovanni Valdecchio, who has been virtuous and faithful servant.'[9]

Girolamo now had to arbitrate in judicial matters just as Felice had once done, and she encouraged him to side with a protégé of her own during a dispute: 'I wanted to write to you to let you know that Menico is an affectionate and loving vassal and servant, and for love of me I would like you to support this young man.'[10]

Another letter served to remind Girolamo of Felice's vision of his obligations to his familial past: 'The bearer of this letter will be Captain Romazzato, who was an affectionate servant of my lord Papa Julio, and at the same time a great friend of your father. He has come to continue his friendship, and to let you know that his two nephews extend their friendship to you, so I ask that you treat him with great affection and honour.'[11] In a similar letter she told her son, 'Maestro Acantio is coming, the son of Francesco de Fiano, to visit you and do you reverence, so for the love of his father be affectionate towards him.'[12]

For many years, Felice had received letters of introduction from associates who hoped she could find positions for or otherwise assist their own cohorts. She, who had been *patrona et benefatrix*, now found herself calling on Girolamo to assume that position. One such letter she wrote concerned a friend of hers and of her daughter Julia: 'You must know that Signor Carlo Mirobaldo has always been an affectionate friend because of the demonstrations he has made towards me and the Princess your sister, so we are very obliged to him. Because of this I would like you to accept the son of Signor Carlo which would give me a great and most singular pleasure, so tell me, and I will send him to you, so do not write to me and disappoint me.'[13] On a similiar note, she also wrote in January of 1535, 'A few months ago, I promised Carlo Brancha, my dear friend, the office of Campagna, and I would now like to offer him a similar position.'[14]

There can be little doubt that Girolamo did not find his new obligations very interesting. He was much more concerned about commencing a military career than attending to the distribution of grain and wine or hearing hard-luck stories. Although his father, Gian Giordano, had served the French crown, this allegiance was not one Girolamo intended to pursue. Francis I had transferred Gian Giordano's French pension to Napoleone and had supported his right to the Orsini inheritance. Girolamo thus had his own grievances against France, and consequently wanted to ally himself with and work for France's most powerful enemy, Charles V, the Holy Roman Emperor. Shortly after he had received his inheritance, Girolamo began to make plans to serve as a soldier in the Emperor's army. On 22 January 1535, Antonio Romero, an agent of the Emperor, who was planning a campaign against France, wrote to Girolamo at Bracciano. He told him that the Emperor's ambassadors would be passing through Rome, *en route* for Genoa to meet with the naval captain Andrea Doria, of whom Felice was fond, 'in order to give the necessary orders for this expedition'. He went on to tell Girolamo, 'It would be well if you could come secretly to Rome to meet with the ambassador.'[15]

Felice, however, was unenthusiastic about her son's current career plans. A few years earlier, she had been prepared to send him off to war because it would stop him fighting Napoleone. She had never been particularly interested in military matters and was rather unimpressed by *condottieri*. On sending a priest to Bracciano she told her son to 'make sure that he is housed in a room separate from your soldiers, in such a place where he can be quiet and study at his leisure'.[16] She felt Girolamo would be better off attending to his new duties as Lord of Bracciano. It was only eight years earlier that her city had been so viciously sacked by the soldiers of the Holy Roman Emperor, forcing her into exile, and then into a massive and costly restoration programme on her return. Her feelings, now that Girolamo would effectively be one of those soldiers, were mixed, at the least. On 1 February, Antonio Romero wrote to Girolamo to tell him, 'The negotiation for you to serve has not yet been expedited because it has not been possible to open the hand of the Lady Felice, although the solicitude of myself and the ambassador will not cease in asking her over and over again, and we have yet to reach a final conclusion, so I am still hopeful.'[17] That Felice still had the power to stand in the way of her son's ambitions says a great deal about the amount of control and influence that she still wielded. He might now be Lord of Bracciano, but Girolamo still did not want to cross his mother.

Felice's correspondence with Girolamo on that same day was to tell him, 'Today Maestro Giovanni di Nepi came to see me, as he has found one of his cows at Bracciano.' The implication was the cow had been stolen by an Orsini servant. Her brief note, which contained no mention of Girolamo's soldierly ambitions, was clearly intended to emphasize certain points: that a lack of vigilance on his part would see Bracciano's servants engaging in criminal activity, which would cause bad relations with Girolamo's neighbours, and do Girolamo's seigneurial reputation no good, and that Giovanni di Nepi apparently thought that he would get more effective help from Felice than from the new Lord of Bracciano, which did not bode well for girolamo's ability to command respect.

Girolamo, did, however, get his way in the end, and succeeded in pursuing his soldierly ambitions. The following year, 1536, he met Charles V in Rome, and by May he was fighting for the Emperor in Provence against France. Felice might always have intended to relent, but the promise of money from Girolamo's commission to help defray Orsini debts was undoubtedly a deciding factor. She did, however, worry about her son when he was away on the military campaign. She wrote to Francesco on 10 July 1536, 'I am sending you some letters which Signor Girolamo, your brother, sent to me, and God knows that they have given me the greatest consolation.'[18] Girolamo, it seems, was proving better at keeping in touch than he had in the year before he killed Napoleone, when he had disappeared without trace for a period of time.

When not occupied with trying to train Girolamo to become a responsible lord of the manor, Felice spent time concerning herself with her other son, Francesco. Despite their proximity in age, the two brothers were not especially close; one of very few surviving letters Francesco ever sent his brother was simply to inform him that 'Madonna Francesca [de Cupis] has sent you a pair of slippers, which I am sure will please you.'[19] Francesco was particularly in thrall to his mother, so did not voice publicly any resentment that it was his brother who had become Lord of Bracciano. However, Felice went to some lengths to ensure he did not feel left out when it was time to secure a bride for Girolamo.

In July 1535, Felice wrote to Francesco, 'Today the Bishop of Sutri came to solicit me about making a match between the daughter of Count Bosio and Signor Girolamo. He would like to know if you would be happy with a good church, bishopric or archbishopric worth around 4000 *scudi* up until the time that you would get *il capello* [the cardinal's hat]. I replied that I knew nothing, but that I would write to you.'[20]

Felice preferred to arrange marriages for her children where her family could gain extra benefits, such as the deal she and Leo struck to sell a cardinal's hat to the uncle of Julia's husband, the Prince of Bisignano. That she should be seeking extra benefits for Francesco was part of a similar strategy. She had also waited a little while for things to settle down after the restitution before she instituted a search for a wife for

Girolamo. But when she did, she went seeking a bride who met her requirements for the protection and promotion of her children. The daughter of Count Bosio was such a bride. Bosio was the Count of Santa Fiora, in the province of Emilia Romagna, not far from Parma. The Count of Santa Fiora was not of major importance himself but his wife Costanza was the daughter of Alessandro Farnese, who in October 1534 had been elected Pope Paul III. This meant that Girolamo and his potential betrothed, Bosio's and Constanza's daughter Francesca, were both the grandchildren of popes.

Felice had long sought an alliance with the Farnese family, a desire they had reciprocated. She had hoped to marry her daughter Clarice to Paul's son Ranuccio, before he was killed in the Sack of Rome, and had commenced negotiations accordingly. As Cardinal Alessandro Farnese, Pope Paul III had accrued substantial wealth. Initially, he had received papal favours because he was the brother of Alexander VI's lover Giulia Farnese, a situation that had earned him the nickname 'the petticoat cardinal'. But Alessandro was highly able and had been greatly respected by subsequent popes, Felice's father among them. Felice's eagerness for the Farnese alliance undoubtedly emerged from a supposition that Alessandro would eventually be elected pope. After her bad experiences with Hadrian of Utrecht in the early 1520s, she wanted to ensure that she and her children always maintained a favoured position at the papal court. From the perspective of Alessandro Farnese, an alliance with the Orsini was as useful for him as it had been for Julius, with the added benefit that at the family's helm was a woman who truly understood the workings of the papacy.

Thanks to Gian Domenico de Cupis, Felice had inside knowledge of the outcome of the 1534 papal election As she wrote to Francesco at the start of conclave, 'The common opinion is that Farnese will be elected.'[21] Paul's election made Felice all the more anxious to secure a Farnese bride. She courted the good will of other influential members of the Farnese family, including Paul's son Pier Luigi. She was very pleased in April 1535 to be able to thank Francesco for sending her a 'stag, by way of the Reverend Trani [Gian Domenico] which I have kept to make lots of pies to give to his lordship Pier Luigi who Tuesday will lodge with your brother Girolamo at Isola [a small island with good hunting on a small lake near Bracciano] and Signor

Girolamo wants to make convenient provisions. So it is best I rush these pies off to them, which I think will be just the thing.'[22] It is rare to find Felice in such a mood of culinary agitation, but it was important to her that Pier Luigi should feel that his niece would enter a loving and caring family.

It was also important to Felice that Francesco should profit from the match as well. It seems unlikely that the Bishop of Sutri came unbidden to offer Francesco benefices. Felice wanted to ensure he was an important part of the process.

The ultimate prize for Francesco, was, of course, a cardinal's hat, but even Felice, anxious as she was to gain promotion for her sons, might have realized that such a goal was beyond Francesco's capabilities. She loved him a great deal, but she also worried about his character and his ability to run his estates effectively. Only a few years earlier she had warned him to take care of his lands and who minded them. In 1535, she had to write to him regarding two vats of oil he had sent her: 'One of the vats you sent is missing a third of its content. I think your ministers are stealing and you do not know anything about it.'[23] On another occasion she wrote to him, 'With a great deal of anger, annoyance and sorrow I have heard about the cruellest of cruelty that has been used in Galera.'[24] Although she did not specify the actual nature of this act, Felice was upset Francesco had clearly done nothing in response. Francesco acknowledged his shortcomings, at least to his mother, telling her, 'I have received everything you have written to me, and I understand very well what you write. I beg of you that you do not accuse me of arrogance. I will not be lacking in the affairs of the castle, and I will not spend any more money than I have to.'[25]

But while Francesco was afraid of his mother holding a poor opinion of him, he compensated for his incompetence with cruelty. This did not escape Felice's attention, as she was constantly called on to intervene: 'Ioacchino di Magnalardo of your Abbey of San Salvatore has been to see me, to explain the situation regarding his father Giovanni d'Antonetto. He tells me that you wish to impose penalties upon him on account of his having built a house. Although he is an old man and his mistake is not grave, I hear you are unhappy about the house, and want to tear it down to the ground. So I am asking you cordially not to do so in order to reassure the said Giovanni.'[26] In a similar fashion, Felice wrote to tell Francesco, 'Today

Madonna Paulina Carrezia di Fara came to see me together with Madonna Angela who strongly begged me to pray to you that you would restore their property to them.'[27]

It was not just the laity Francesco tormented. Felice had to write on yet another occasion, when, 'The Vicar General of the Third Order of St Francis came to see me and told me that you have made accusations against two friars of that order, questioned them in Castel Sant' Angelo, and taken one of them prisoner, so I beg of you to release him as quickly as possible, and in doing so you would be doing me a great and singular pleasure.'[28]

To counteract Francesco's reputation for malevolence, Felice also tried to encourage him to perform small acts of kindness: 'I received a visit from Signora Panthasilea d'Alviano on account of a will made by a poor little man, which he will explain to you more fully, for he wishes to ask of you that his will is kept in a safe place, and that you will ensure its execution. In helping him you would be doing a pious act.'[29]

Although Felice had hardly retired, now her sons were playing – for better or worse – active roles in the governing of the estate, she could find time for recreation and personal projects. One request she sent Francesco was to ask if he would 'send me my books, which would be granting me the most singular pleasure'.[30] As a young woman, Felice had avidly acquired books from the Venetian printer Manutius. The demands on her time in the past few decades had given her precious little opportunity to read for enjoyment. Now she hoped she might be able do so.

Although she had had to sell Palo, Felice compensated for its loss by turning her attention to her palace on the Pincian Hill, at Trinità dei Monti. Imagining that she would now spend more time there, in August 1536 she embarked on a project that would bring more light to the palace. She concentrated on the part of the building that bore her name, the tower that was the old *campanile* of the church of San Felice. She wanted to put solar windows in the room made from the tower, using materials from the Orsini estates. She had asked Francesco to facilitate matters. Predictably, he was less than helpful. On 31 August 1536, she wrote, 'For the love you bear me, send me the fifty planks of wood about which I have written to you in the past. I have the greatest need of them to make the tower's thermal windows, and in doing so you would be giving me the greatest pleasure.'[31]

On 5 September, Felice wrote, 'Maestro Ascanio of Canemorto sent me twenty plates of bricks which are too soft, and no good, so I need you to send a letter to him on my behalf. I also need to get wood for making a big door, and then I can finish the tower's solar windows. I have written to you many times, so send me forty planks of chestnut wood.'[32] The planks still had not arrived by 11 September, when another letter to Francesco began, 'As I have written to you many times, I really need to make those solar windows in the tower . . . '[33]

Felice's anxiety to see her solar windows in place might have been exacerbated by her feeling that she was running out of time. In the early summer of 1535, her health had begun to fail her, although she refused to let it interrupt her activities. Her condition is unspecified, but it had rendered her frail and unable to get about very easily. She proposed to get round this by using a litter bed, a long curtained sedan chair. Her friend Leo X had used one when his gout made it impossible for him to walk. On 3 May 1536, she wrote to Francesco, 'Because for the last two days I have not been in a very good way I decided to get a litter bed made for me. For this, I have given some money to Maestro Paolo Cacciguerra to make it for me. All it needs are nails, everything else is finished. I have begged him to get nails as quickly as possible, as I want to leave Rome, and I am certain that if I were to stay here to await the end of my [unspecified] business, I will be here in perpetuity, so it is best that I have decided to leave as soon as my litter bed is made for me.'[34] Two days later, the combination of unfinished litter and unfinished business were making her testy: 'I still have not left Rome, as I wrote to you before, as my litter is unfinished and these blessed affairs seem to be eternal . . . '[35] She also asked Francesco to go to the Brothers of Santo Cosimato at Vicovaro, as they were keeping for her 'a luxurious sedan chair which belonged to Papa Julio'.[36] Julius as an ageing pope had been carried around the Vatican Palace in such a contraption, and a portrait had even been painted of him on it by Raphael, with the artist depicted as one of the litter-bearers.

Felice's weakened condition did not diminish her desire to respond to the needs of others. In the same letter concerning her litter bed, she also wanted to make sure that Francesco would make provision for the daughters of her long-serving maid, Madonna Daniela, 'who is old . . . and I want you to give her daughters a *rubbio* of grain and twelve bottles of oil'.[37]

In June 1536, she told Francesco that he ought to come to Rome because she had made progress on behalf of various Orsini servants in their lawsuit against the Cenci, a neighbouring Roman family. And in late August, she wrote again to him, having heard about 'a drunkard, who when he is drunk goes mad and beats his wife. I want him to be fetched immediately and imprisoned, until he gives security that he will no longer beat her, otherwise the poor girl is lost for sure.'[38]

Felice's duties and convictions, not to mention the events of the previous years, took their toll on her. A letter of 6 September to Francesco concludes, 'Do not admire the signature at the bottom of the letter as it is not in my hand. As you know, I am feeling a little indisposed today.'[39] The last letter in the Orsini archive written by Felice is dated 15 September 1536. She tells Francesco, 'An associate of the Cardinal of Naples came to see me Sunday evening, asking me to write to you to see if you would grant him a place at the Abbey of Farfa.'[40] Up until her last days, Felice was still doing favours for cardinals, in the expectation that they would be reciprocated in some way, for the benefit of her family.

Less than two weeks later, on 27 September, Felice wrote her last will and testament. The document has a very different tone from that of the one she had composed back in April 1518, almost twenty years earlier. That first will reflects the exhilaration she was finding in her new position as Orsini *gubernatrix*. Then, a thirty-five-year-old Felice imagined a glorious life after death. Masses were to be sung for her in every corner of Rome, her body entombed in a splendid sepulchre in her chapel at Trinità dei Monti. The memory of Felice della Rovere would endure in the public realm. But times were different now. Money was short, and a tired Felice was perhaps hoping for a quiet afterlife, with rest her major ambition. So instead, 'Felix de Ruver de Ursini, of a weak body but a sound mind, lying in bed in her palace at Monte Giordano' composed a very simple will in the presence of her testators.[41] Present at her bedside were Francesca de Cupis, a friar of San Agostino and the vicar of Santa Maria del Popolo, who were there to give her comfort. The will was witnessed by Galeotto Ferreolo, her consistorial lawyer for many years now; Francesco Vanuzzi, a Roman cleric, and Felice di Massimo, a nobleman, who lived in a neighbouring palace.

Felice asked for her body to be buried in the church of Santa Maria del

Popolo, the della Rovere family church, where among other family members her cousin Girolamo Basso della Rovere was also buried. Mass at the church was to be sung in perpetuity every year. Without specifying the amount, she left Girolamo and Francesco as her *eredes universalis*. Relatively little was left. Not long after her death her sons sold the Trinità dei Monti palace in order to realize its cash value. Their dowries were all that was left to her daughters Julia and Clarice; back in 1518 they had been supplemented by a legacy of 3000 ducats apiece. But Felice did think of beneficiaries other than her children: the Ssters of Angelica at the church of San Agostino near the de Cupis palace received 100 ducats, her maidservant Camilla 200. Felice's doctor, Angelo di Nepi, received 100 ducats 'for his services'. Her half-sister Francesca received 2000, money that, after the death of her philandering husband, Angelo del Bufalo, Francesca would use to institute a small convent. Gian Domenico de Cupis, she did not mention, undoubtedly because the Cardinal was already fantastically wealthy in his own right, largely thanks to the efforts of his half-sister. Felice also asked that 'every single year, on the anniversary of her death, alms will be given to the poor and the sick, in the form of bread and wine of portions sufficient for everyone'.

Felice's final request was that 'the servants and maidservants in the house at present, at the time of her death will be retained'. This last appeal ensured that the servants who had been so great a part of her life for several decades would be assured of employment following her demise. It also ensured that Felice placed her seal on the house she had shaped; changes were not to be made to the household structure that had not been authorized by her. At the end of her days, lying in what she described as 'her palace' at Monte Giordano, Felice, who had evolved from cardinal's daughter to pope's daughter, exited this world as Orsini matriarch. Her legacy would not be found in an elaborate tomb or eternal hosannas; it was as the loving mother who had dedicated herself to creating a strong and stable environment for the sons she herself had created.

Not long after she made her will, Felice died. For an elite, well-nourished woman, who had survived her childbearing years and who had taken pains to take care of herself, fifty-three was no great age. The stresses and the strains of the previous decade, from the Sack of Rome to the siege of Vicovaro, the murder of Napoleone and the negotiations to recover the estates, can only have taken their toll on Felice's mind and body. No specific date can be determined for the day of her death but she was dead by 9 October. On that day, the Archbishop of Benevento, who had loaned Felice money for the return of the Orsini estate, sent a letter of condolence to Francesco. He wrote, 'God knows how much I mourn the death of the Illustrious Lady Felice, your mother, to the extent that truly there could be no other thing that could make me more unhappy. I am certain that all of the other great men at court are also deeply sad, for, for many decades, the goodness and wisdom of her ladyship has been such that there have been none like her at this court. The great reputation that she leaves behind her must provide us with some consolation in our sorrow.'[42] Implicit in the Archbishop's words is the sense that at Felice's passing, another time and place, the Rome of Julius and Leo, both long gone, passed with her.

Others who mourned her death were also anxious about the changes it would mean for them now her sons were completely in charge. Cardinal Contarini wrote to tell Francesco that his mother had always sent him 'a quantity of Bracciano wine, which I found suited my taste and stomach' and hoped that Francesco would continue to do the same.[43] A similar note, signed 'Agnellis' informed Francesco that every year Felice had sent three bottles of Bracciano red and three of Spanish white to his house and servants.[44] In November, a servant at Vicovaro, Hieronimo di Pompeo, asked Francesco if he could have a little grain, in memory of 'our illustrious lady . . . words cannot express how sorry I am, her grace was such that every time she saw me, she would give me more affection than I deserved, and I and her other servants are still weeping and sorrowing at her death'.[45]

Felice might not have missed attending constantly to endless requests, which did not cease even after her death. That she did not live to see Girolamo marry was undoubtedly another matter. Absent for much of 1536, including the time of his mother's death, on his military secondment, he did not wed Francesca Sforza until October 1537. By then, Felice had been dead a full year. The delay was partly a mark of respect to her, and partly because negotiations had been so completely in her hands that it took time to recommence them. The wedding was a sumptuous affair; Pope Paul III's granddaughter was adorned with gold ornaments designed by the papal goldsmith Benvenuto Cellini. Girolamo himself did not live for more than a few years after his marriage. He did, however, produce an heir, Paolo Giordano, whose turbulent life was to make the exploits of his father pale in comparison, and he had a son and heir in his turn. And so it was the blood of the pope's daughter that coursed through the veins of the subsequent generations of Orsini.

Epilogue: Felice's Legacy

As sad as it is that Felice did not live to witness Girolamo's wedding or the birth of her first grandson, it was as well that she did not live to see the fates of her other children. Julia met a tragic end, strangled in 1539 by the Prince of Bisignano, frustrated at his wife's inability to give him a son.[1] Following his mother's death, Francesco made a perhaps inevitable descent into a dissolute and corrupt way of life. Despite their family ties, Pope Paul III condemned him to death in 1543, although Francesco saved himself by fleeing into exile; he lived until 1567. It is not known when Clarice died, but she did not outlive her husband, as the Prince of Stigliano was to take a second wife, Lucrezia del Tufa. Had Felice herself still been living, her presence might have prevented Julia's murder and Francesco's decline. But she could only do so much, and death comes to us all. During her tumultuous life, Felice della Rovere certainly did all she could for her family. Yet she could not control a future in which she could play no part.

Until now, Felice della Rovere's life after death has been a quiet one, generating little commentary. Her children, however, did hope that she would live on in their own daughters, in whom her strength, intelligence, will, duty and sense of commitment would be replicated. Julia and Girolamo had girls they christened Felice; Guidobaldo della Rovere named one

Jean Thomas Thibault, *View of Bracciano*, c.1810

of his illegitimate daughters after her as well. None of them had as remark-able a life as that of their intrepid namesake. However, were she to have had a favourite, Felice might have selected Girolamo's daughter, whose combination of charm and intelligence seem very much like that of her aunt, Clarice. Among all the daughters of the Orsini family it is this Felice who is extolled in Francesco Sansovino's *History of the House of Orsini* of 1565. He praises her with these words, which indicate what he believed to be the source of her good qualities: 'This lady shares the name of Felice with her grandmother, who was the daughter of Pope Julius II. And she shares not just her name, but also the nobility of her thoughts, the great-ness of her soul and the excellence of her regal manner, for which she numbers among the most illustrious personages of the Orsini family.'[2]

In the 1560s, the memory of Felice della Rovere was still vivid to those who had known her. Catherine de' Medici had become Regent of France, after several decades of shame and humiliation at the hands of her husband Henri II and his mistress Diane de Poitiers. As a three-year-old, Catherine had spent a few months in Felice's care and retained sufficiently fond mem-ories to write a decade later to congratulate Felice on the marriage of her 'sister' Clarice. As Catherine finally attained power, her recollections of Felice could have served only to inspire her, and it is interesting how much they have in common. Both knew what it was like to be an outsider; both largely disliked their husbands' relatives, and dealt ruthlessly with those they felt were a threat to their rule. Both were unquestionably committed to their children, and both had sons who were far less capable than their mothers. Felice would have perfectly understood everything that Catherine felt she was required to do, all the deeds that have made her monstrous in the eyes of history. Both, to a greater or lesser degree, were Machiavellian *Principesse*. Whether Elizabeth I was familiar with the life of Felice della Rovere is open to question, but again there are parallels between the Italian and the English-woman. Both had complex relationships with their fathers, one a king, the other a pope, and both spent time as young women on the periphery, uncertain of their future. Both had experiences that served only to further their resolve and ambition.

Felice, however, unlike a Catherine or an Elizabeth, has been almost for-gotten by history. Her stage, of course, was so much smaller; she ruled a family and not a country. And she did something else that contributed to her disappearance; essentially she sacrificed her personal legacy for the good of her children. She sold her personal possessions to claim back the Orsini estate and she made a will of remarkable simplicity and humility. No building bears her name or her coat of arms; there are no altarpieces in which she is depicted in a donor portrait. And yet her story in all its amazing detail was preserved, waiting to be uncovered in an archive in Rome.

It is this detail that allows Felice, a pope's bastard child, to teach us as much as a queen of England or France or an acquisitive Marchesa of Mantua. Felice has many lessons to impart about self-belief, about standing one's ground, knowing when and when not to compromise, and about the value of decorum, *bella figura, sprezzatura.* If she is sometimes intimidating, she is always worthy of admiration and respect. It might have taken almost half a millennium to resurrect her, but Felice is well worth the wait. Her archive of dusty papers is still there in Rome, to be perused by the occasional scholar, and Rome and its environs are replete with memories of her. Travel to Bracciano, and you can look at the *fonte* she commissioned, which is now attached to a nineteenth-century wash-house. The castle still stands there; guided tours never mention Felice, but this is where she gave birth, where she had her tapestries made, and it was Felice who organized its cleaning and repainting. In Rome you might pass by the Palazzo de Cupis on Piazza Navona and imagine a cardinal's young daughter peering from its upper windows or stand below the palace of Monte Giordano and see the Orsini *Signora* standing at the top of the entrance slope handing out Christmas boxes to the servants. And if you were to go and look at Raphael's *Mass of Bolsena* in the Vatican Palace apartments where Julius II once lived, you could seek out, among the frescoed figures, a dark-haired young woman fixing her gaze on her father, the Pope.

Bibliography

ARCHIVAL SOURCES

Rome

Archivio di Stato Capitolino (ASC): *Archivio Orsini*
Archivio di Stato di Roma (ASR): *Archivio del Collegio dei Notai; Archivio Santa Croce*
Biblioteca Angelica: MS 1349

Florence

Archivio di Stato di Firenze (ASF): *Mediceo Avanti il Principato; Ducato di Urbino, Classe Prima*

Mantua

Archivio di Stato di Mantova (ASM): *Archivio Gonzaga*

Los Angeles

University of California, Los Angeles (UCLA) Special Collections: 902, *Orsini Archive*

PRINTED WORKS

Achillini, Giovanni Filiteo, *Viridario*, Bologna, 1513
Ait, Ivana, and Manuel Vaquero Piñciro, *Dai casali alla fabbrica di San Pietro, i Leni: uomini d'affari del Rinascimento*, Rome, 2000
Albertini, Francesco, *Opusculum de mirabilibus novae et veteris urbis Romae*, Rome, 1515
Allegrezza, Franca, *Organizzazione del potere e dinamiche familiari; gli Orsini dal duecento agli inizi del Quattrocento*, Rome, 1998
Assereto, G. (ed.), *Cronache savonesi*, Savona, 1887
Bandello, Matteo, *Novelle*, Alessandria, 1992
Bari, Hubert et al., *Diamanti; Arte, Storia, Scienza*, Rome, 2002
Barocchi, P., and R. Ristori (eds.), *Il carteggio di Michelangelo*, 5 vols.:, Florence, 1965–83
Beaune, Colette, 'François de Paule et les roix de France', in Yves Bruley (ed.), *La Trinité-des-Monts redécouverte*, Rome, 2002
Bell, Rudolph M., *How to Do It; Guides to Good Living for Renaissance Italians*, Chicago, 1999
Bellonci, Maria, *Lucrezia Borgia; La sua vita e i suoi tempi*, Milan, 1939
–, *Lucrezia Borgia*, London, 1953
Benzi, Fabio (ed.), *Sisto IV: Le arti a Roma nel primo rinascimento*, Rome, 2000
Bianchi, Lidia, *La villa papale della Magliana*, Rome, 1942
Bini, Daniele (ed.), *Isabella d'Este primadonna del Rinascimento*, Modena, 2001
Bisticci, Vespasiano da, *Lives of Illustrious Men*, London, 1926

Bloodgood, Linda Fleitmann, *The Saddle of Queens; The Story of the Side Saddle*, London, 1959

Bober, Phyllis Pray and Rubenstein, Ruth, *Renaissance Artists and Antique Sculpture; A Handbook of Sources*, Oxford and New York, 1986

Bosticco, Sergio, et al., *Piazza Navona; Isola dei Pamphilij*, Rome, 1978

Brummer, Hans Henrik, *The Statue Court in the Vatican Belvedere*, Stockholm, 1970

Bullard, Melissa Meriam, 'Grain Supply and Urban Unrest in Renaissance Rome: The Crisis of 1533–1534', in P. A. Ramsey (ed.), *Rome in the Renaissance; The City and The Myth*, Binghampton, New York, 279–92

Burckhardt, Jacob, *The Civilization of the Renaissance in Italy*, New York, 2002

Campana, Augusto, 'Dal Calmeta al Colocci', in Trezzini et al. (eds.), *Tra Latino e volgare per Carlo Dionisotti*, Padua, 1974

Campbell, Thomas P., *Tapestry in the Renaissance; Art and Magnificence*, New Haven, 2002

Caprile, Giovanni, *Villa Malta, dall'antica Roma a 'civiltà cattolica'*, Rome, 1999

Cartwright, Julia, *Isabella d'Este*, London, 1903

Castiglione, Baldessar, *The Courtier of Counte Baldessare Castiglione*, London, 1603

–, *The Book of the Courtier*, translated by George Bull, London, 1976

Cavallero, Anna, et al., *Bracciano e gli Orsini nel '400*, Rome, 1981

Ceci, Giuseppe, and Benedetto Croce, *Lode di dame napoletane del decimosesto*, Naples, 1894

Celletti, Vincenzo, *Gli Orsini di Bracciano*, Rome, 1963

Cellini, Benvenuto, *My Life,* translated and edited by Julia Conway Bondanella and Peter Bondanella, Oxford and New York, 2002

Cerisola, Nello, *Storia di Savona*, Savona, 1983

Cerretani, Bartolomeo, *Ricordi,* edited by Giuliana Berti, Florence, 1993

Chamberlin, E. R., *The Sack of Rome*, London, 1979

Chastel, André, *The Sack of Rome, 1527,* Princeton, 1983

Coffin, David, *The Villa in the Life of Renaissance Rome*, Princeton, 1979

Condivi, Ascanio, *The Life of Michelangelo*, translated and edited by Alice Sedgwick Wohl and Hellmut Wohl, University Park, PA, 1999

Cook, Bill, et al., *All the Queen's Horses*, Prospect, KY, 2003

Coppi, A., 'Alsio, Palo e Palidoro', *Dissertazioni della ponitificia academia romana di archeologia*, VII, 1836

Cornini Guido, et al., *Raphael in the Apartments of Julius II and Leo X*, Milan, 1993

Curia, Rosario, *Bisignano nella storia del Mezzogiorno: dalle orgini al xix secolo*, Cosenza, 1985

D'Amico, John F., *Renaissance Humanism in Papal Rome: Humanists and Churchmen on the Eve of the Reformation*, London and Baltimore, 1973

De Cupis, Cesare, *Regesto degli Orsini secondo documenti conservati nell'archivio della famiglia Orsini e nell' Archivio Segreto Vaticano*, Sulmona, 1903

De Vecchi, Pierluigi (ed.), *The Sistine Chapel; A Glorious Restoration*, New York, 1994

Dennis, George, *The Cities and Cemeteries of Etruria*, London, 1848

Dent, Anthony, et al., *The Reign of the Horse: The Horse in Print, 1500–1715*, Washington DC, 1991

Duffy, Eamon, *Saints and Sinners: A History of the Popes*, London, 1997

Dunkerton, Jill, and Michael Hirst, *The Young Michelangelo*, London, 1994

Egger, Herman, *Römische Verduten: Handzeichnungen aus dem XV, bis XVIII Jahrhundert zur Topographie der Stadt Rom*, Vienna, 1931–32

Eiche Sabine, 'Fossombrone, Part 1: Unknown Drawings and Documents for the *Corte* of

BIBLIOGRAPHY

Leonora Gonzaga, Duchess of Urbino and her Son, Giulio della Rovere', in *Studi di Storia dell'Arte*, 2, 1991, 103–28

–, (ed.), *Ordine et officij de casa de lo illustrissimo Signor Duca de Urbino*, Urbino, 1999

Erasmus, Desiderio, *Julius Exclusus*, edited by Paul Pascal and J. Kelley Sowards, Bloomington and London, 1968

Evitascandalo, Cesare, *Il Maestro di Casa, dialogo. Nel quale si contine di quanto il maestro di casa dev'essere istrutto e quanto deve sapere ciascun altro che vogila esecitare offitio in corte*, Viterbo, 1620

Feliciangeli, B., *Notizie e documenti sulla vita di Caterina Cibo-Varano*, Camerino, 1891

Ferino Pagden, Silvia (ed.), *Vittoria Colonna; Dichterin und Muse Michelangelos*, Vienna, 1997

Fernández, Henry Dietrich, 'The Patrimony of Saint Peter: The Papal Court in Rome', John S. Adamson ed., London, *The Princely Courts of Europe*, 2000, 140–163

–, *Bramante's Architectural Legacy in the Vatican Palace; A Study in Papal Routes*, Ph.D. dissertation, University of Cambridge, 2003

Ferrajoli, Alessandro, *Il ruolo della corte di Leon* Rome, 1984

Firenze, Fra Mariano da, *Itinerarium urbis romae*, edited by E. Buletti, Rome, 1931

Firenzuola, Agnelo, *Opere*, Florence, 1958

Frapiccini, David, 'Il Cardinale Girolamo Basso della Rovere e la sua cerchia tra contesti marchigiani e romani', in Marco Gallo (ed.), *I cardinali di santa romana chiesa; collezionisti e mecanati*, Rome, 2001

Frettoni, M., 'Felice della Rovere', in *Dizionario biografico degli italiani*, Rome, 1989; 337–8

Frommel, Christopher Luitpold, *Der Römische Palastbav der Hochrenaissance*, 3 vols, Tübingen, 1973

Gennaro, Clara, 'La "Pax Romana" del 1511', *Archivio della società romana di storia patria*, XC, 1967, 2–60

Giaccone, Carla Michelli, *Bracciano e il suo castello*, Rome, 1990

Giustiniani, Antonio, *Dispacci di Antonio Giustinian*, Florence, 1876

Gnoli, Domenico, *La Roma di Leon X*, Rome, 1938

Gouwens, Kenneth, *Remembering the Renaissance; Humanist Narratives of the Sack of Rome*, Leiden, 1998

Guicciardini, Luigi, *The Sack of Rome*, translated by James H. McGregor, New York, 1983

Guidoni, Enrico, 'Michelangelo: La vita contemplativa (Vittoria Colonna) e la vita attiva (Faustina Manici) nel monumento a Guilio II in S. Pietro in Vincoli', *Strenna dei Romanisti*, MMDCCVL, April 2000, 321–38

Hale, John, et al., *L'età della Rovere; V convegno storico savonese*, Savona, 1985

Haskins, Susan, 'Isabella d'Este', in Jill Berk Jiminez (ed.), *Dictionary of Artists' Models*, London, 2001

Hatfield, R, *The Wealth of Michelangelo*, Rome, 2002

Hirst, Michael, and Jill Dunkerton, *The Young Michelangelo*, London, 1994

Hook, Judith, *The Sack of Rome, 1527*, London, 1972

Ingersoll, Richard, *The Ritual Use of Public Space in Renaissance Rome*, Ann Arbor, 1985

Krautheimer, Richard, *Rome; Profile of a City, 312–1308*, Princeton, 1980

Lanciani, Rodolfo, *Storia Scavi di Roma*, 7 vols, Rome, 1989–2002

Litta, Pompe, *Le famiglie celebri italiane*, Milan, 1868, vols. 7, 9

Luzio, Alessandro, *Isabella d'Este ed Il Sacco di Roma*, 1908

–, *Isabella d'Este di fronte a Giulio II negli ultimi tre anni del suo pontificato*, Milan, 1912

Luzio, Alessandro, and Rodolfo Renier, *Mantova e Urbino; Isabella d'Este ed Elizabetta Gonzaga nelle relazioni famigliari e nelle vicende politiche*, Torino/Rome, 1893

Macdougall, Elizabeth B., 'The Sleeping Nymph: Origins of a Humanist Fountain',
   Art Bulletin, LVII, 1975, 357–65

Machiavelli, Niccolò, *The Prince*, London, 1975

Magnuson, Torgil, *Studies in Roman Quattrocento Architecture*, Stockholm, 1958

Mallett, Michael, *The Borgia; The Rise and Fall of a Renaissance Dynasty*, London, 1969

–, *Mercenaries and their Masters; Warfare in Renaissance Italy*, London, 1974

Marcucci, Roberto, *Francesco Maria della Rovere*, Senigallia, 1903

Marucci, Valerio (ed.), *Pasquinate del cinque e seicento*, Rome, 1988

Mazari, Mario (ed.), *Navi di legno; Evoluzione tecnica e sviluppo della cantieristica nel Mediterraneo dal
   XVI secolo a oggi*, Trieste, 1998

Mena Marqués, Manuela, *Sebastiano del Piombo e l'España*, Madrid, 1995

Milanesi, Carlo (ed.), *Il Sacco di Roman del MDXXVII*, Florence, 1867

Millon, Henry, et al. (eds.), *The Renaissance from Brunelleschi to Michelangelo; The Representation of
   Architecture*, Milan, 1994

Minois, Georges, *Anne de Bretagne*, Paris, 1999

Mode, Robert, 'Masolino, Uccello and the Orsini Uomini Famosi', *Burlington Magazine*, 114,
   1972, 369–78

Moncallero, G. L., *Epistolario di Bernado Dovizi da Bibbiena*, I, Florence, 1935

Muntz, Eugène, *La tiare pontificale du VIIIe au XVI siècle; extrait des mémoires de l'Académies des
   inscriptions et belles-lettres*, Paris, 1897

Musacchio, Jacqueline Marie, *The Art and Ritual of Childbirth in Renaissance Italy*, New Haven/
   London, 1999

Nolhac, Pierre de, 'Les Correspondents d'Alde Manuce', in *Studi e documenti di storia e diritto*, 8,
   1887

Panizza, Letizia (ed.), *Women in Italian Renaissance Culture and Society*, Oxford, 2000

Partner, Peter, *Renaissance Rome, 1500–1555*, Berkeley, 1976

–, *The Pope's Men: The Papal Civil Service in The Renaissance*, Oxford, 1990

Partridge, Loren W, and Randolph R. Starn, *A Renaissance Likeness; Art and Culture in Raphael's
   Julius II*, Berkeley, 1980

Paschini, Pio, *Roma nel Rinascimento*, Bologna, 1940

Pastor, Ludwig, *The History of the Popes*, London, 1894–97:, vols. IV–VIII

Pazzelli, Raffaelle, *St Francis and the Third Order: The Franciscan and pre-Franciscan Penitential Movement*,
   Chicago, 1989, 70–73

Pecchiai, Pio, *Roma nel Cinquecento*, Rome, 1948

–, *Palazzo Taverna a Monte Giordano*, Rome, 1963

Perogalli,C., *Castelli del Lazio,* Milan, 1968

Petrucci, F., 'Gian Domenico de Cupis', in *Dizionario biografico degli italiani*, Rome, 1989, 602–5

Pieri, P., 'Jacopo Appiano', in *Dizionario biografico degli Italiani*, Rome, 1961, 629–31

Pon, Lisa, *Raphael, Dürer and Marcantonio Raimondi; Copying and the Italian Renaissance Print*, London
   and New Haven, 2004

Reiss, Sheryl, 'Cardinal Giulio de' Medici and Mario Maffei: A Renaissance Friendship and the
   Villa Madama', in Lars R. Jones and Louisa C. Matthew (eds.), *Coming About . . . A Festschrift
   for John Shearman*, Cambridge, 2002, 281–8

Rodocanachi, E., *La Première Renaissance; Rome au temps de Julius II et de Leon X*, Paris, 1912

–, *Le pontificat de Julius II*, Paris, 1928

Romano, P., and P. Partini, *Piazza Navona nella storia e nell'arte*, Rome, 1947

Roscoe, William, *The Life and Pontificate of Leo the Tenth*, London, 1888

Rowland, Ingrid D., *The Culture of the High Renaissance; Ancient and Moderns in Sixteenth-Century Rome*, Cambridge, 1998

Sansovino, Francesco, *L'historia di casa Orsini*, Venice, 1565

Sanuto, Marino, *I diarii di Marino Sanuto (1496–1533)*, Venice, 1879–1903

Scaraffia, Lucetta, *Loreto*, Bologna, 1998

Schiavo, Armando, 'I Rovereschi alla "Mesa di Bolzena" di Raffaello', *Lunario Romano*, 1980, 301–64

–, 'Donna Felice della Rovere in ritratti di Raffaello e Michelangelo', *L'Urbe*, 47, 1984

Shaw, Christine, *The Political Role of the Orsini Family in the Papal States, c. 1480–1534*, Ph.D., Oxford, 1983

–, *Julius II: The Warrior Pope*, Oxford, 1993

Shearman, John, 'The Vatican Stanze, Functions and Decorations', in *Proceedings of the British Academy*, 57, 1971

–, *Only Connect; Art and the Spectator in the Italian Renaissance*, Princeton, 1992

–, 'Una nota sul progetto di Papa Giulio', in *Michelangelo; La Capella Sistina documentazione e interpretazioni*, III, Novara, 1994, 29–36

Simpson, W. A., 'Cardinal Giordano Orsini as a Prince of the Church and a Patron of the Arts', *Journal of the Warburg and Courtauld Institutes*, 29, 1966, 136–7

Stinger, Charles, *The Renaissance in Rome*, Bloomington, 1998

Strabo, *Geography*, translated by Horace Leonard Jones, Cambridge, MA, 1948

Testa, Laura, 'Gli affreschi absidali della chiesa di Sant'Onofrio al Gianicolo: committenza, interpretazione et attribuzione', in *Storia dell'arte*, 1990, 171–86

Tolnay, Charles de, *The Tomb of Julius II*, Princeton, 1954

–, *Michelangelo; The Final Period, Last Judgement*, Princeton, 1971

Tomas, Natalie, *The Medici Women; Gender and Power In Renaissance Florence*, Burlington, VT, 2003

Triff, Kristin, *Patronage and Public Image in Renaissance Rome: Three Orsini Palaces*, Ann Arbor, 2000

Uhl, Alois, *Papstkinder; Lebensbilder aus der Zeit der Renaissance*, Düsseldorf, 2003

Urago, Benito, *Stigliano sotto gli Spagnuoli*, Stigliano, 1964

Valone, Carolyn, 'The Art of Hearing: Sermons and Images in the Chapel of Lucrezia della Rovere', in *Sixteenth Century Journal*, XXI, 3, 2000

–, 'Why Women Built in Early Modern Rome', in Sheryl Reiss and David Wilkins (eds.), *Beyond Isabella; Secular Women Patrons of Art in Renaissance Italy*, Kirksville, MO, 2001

Varaldo, Carlo, *Istoria d'arte del centro storico di Savona*, Savona, 1995

Vasari, Giorgio, *Le vite de' più eccelenti pittori, scultori ed architettori*, 1568 edn, Florence, 1878–85

–, *Lives of the Painters, Sculptors and Architects*, translated by Gaston de Vere, edited by David Ekserdjian, New York, 1996, 1

Vattasso, Marco, 'Antonio Flaminio e le principali poesie dell'autografo Vaticano 2870', *Studi e testi*, 1, 1900, 55–6

Venturi, Aldo, 'Gian Cristoforo Romano', *Archivio storico dell'arte*, 1, 1888

Westfall, Carroll William, *In This Most Perfect Paradise: Alberti, Nicolas V, and the Invention of Conscious Urban Planning in Rome, 1447–1455*, University Park, PA, 1974

WEB-BASED INFORMATION

http://digilander.libero.it/adamaney/immaginisavonaedintorni/dellarovere.htm
http://www.martignano.com/casale%20di%20Martignano.htm@end:

Notes

1 Felice's Father

1 The most recent biography of Julius II is by Christine Shaw, *Julius II: The Warrior Pope*, Oxford, 1993.
2 This account of the career of Francesco della Rovere, later Pope Sixtus IV, is adapted from Ludwig Pastor, *The History of the Popes*, London, 1894–97, IV, 197 ono.
3 Ibid., 235.
4 Pio Paschini, *Roma nel Rinascimento*, Bologna, 1940, 245.
5 Letter from Giovanni Pietro Arrivabene, Mantuan emissary, cited in Pastor, IV, 269.
6 Shaw, 9–50.
7 Desiderio Erasmus, *Julius Exclusus*, edited by Paul Pascal and J. Kelley Sowards, Bloomington/London, 1968, 60.
8 Paschini, 313.
9 For a recent compendium of papal children, see Alois Uhl, *Papstkinder; Lebensbilder aus der Zeit der Renaissance*, Düsseldorf, 2003.

2 Felice's Mother

1 See F. Petrucci, 'Gian Domenico de Cupis' and M. Frettoni, 'Felice della Rovere' in *Dizionario biografico degli italiani*, Rome, 1987, 1989; 602–5 and 337–8.
2 Richard Krautheimer, *Rome; Profile of a City, 312–1308*, Princeton, 1980, 51.
3 Raffaelle Pazzelli, *St Francis and the Third Order: The Franciscan and pre-Franciscan Penitential Movement*, Chicago, 1989

3 The Birth of Felice

1 P. Romano and P. Partini, *Piazza Navona nella storia e nell'arte*, Rome, 1947, 79.

4 Felice's Stepfather

1 Laura Testa, 'Gli affreschi absidali della chiesa di Sant'Onofrio al Gianicolo: committenza, interpretazione et attribuzione', in *Storia dell'arte*, 1990, 171–86.
2 Cesare Evitascandalo, *Il Maestro di Casa, dialogo. Nel quale si contine di quanto il maestro di casa dev'essere istrutto e quanto deve sapere ciascun altro che vogila esecitare offitio in corte*, Viterbo, 1620.
3 David Frapiccini, 'Il Cardinale Girolamo Basso della Rovere e la su cerchia tra contesti marchigiani e romani', in Marco Gallo (ed.), *I Cardinali di santa romana chiesa; collezionisti e mecanati*, Rome, 2001, 8–23.
4 For the history of the Piazza Navona see P. Romano and P. Partini, *Piazza Navona nella storia e nell'arte*, Rome, 1947, and Sergio Bosticco et al., *Piazza Navona; Isola dei Pamphilij*, Rome, 1978.
5 Francesco Albertini, *Oposculum de mirabilibus novae et veteris urbis Romae*, Rome, 1515, 88v.
6 Ascanio Condivi, *The Life of Michelangelo*, translated and edited by Alice Sedgwick Wohl and Hellmut Wohl, University Park, PA, 1999, 6–7.

5 Felice's Rome

1 For a history of Rome in the fourteenth and fifteenth centuries, see Richard Krautheimer, *Rome; Profile of a City, 312–1308*, Princeton, 1980, as well as, among others, Pio Paschini, *Roma nel Rinascimento*, Bologna, 1940, and Torgil Magnuson, *Studies in Roman Quattrocento Architecture*, Stockholm, 1958.

2 Eugène Muntz, *La tiare pontificale du VIIIe au XVI siècle; extrait des mémoires de l'Académies des inscriptions et belles-lettres*, Paris, 1897.

3 Vespasiano da Bisticci, *Lives of Illustrious Men*, London, 1926, 29–30.

4 Paschini, 162.

5 Magnuson, 47.

6 Ibid., 35–6.

7 Carroll William Westfall, *In This Most Perfect Paradise: Alberti, Nicolas V, and the Invention of Conscious Urban Planning in Rome, 1447–1455*, University Park, PA, 1974.

8 Giorgio Vasari, *Lives of the Painters, Sculptors and Architects*, translated by Gaston de Vere, edited by David Ekserdjian, New York, 1996, I, 87.

9 Henry Dietrich Fernández (trans.), *Bramante's Architectural Legacy in the Vatican Palace; A Study in Papal Routes*, Ph.D. dissertation, University of Cambridge, 2003, appendix.

10 For the most recent comprehensive account of Sixtus' patronage, see Fabio Benzi (ed.), *Sisto IV: Le arti a Roma nel primo rinascimento*, Rome, 2000.

6 Felice's Childhood

1 See Peter Partner, *The Pope's Men: The Papal Civil Service in The Renaissance*, Oxford, 1990.

2 Christine Shaw, *Julius II: The Warrior Pope*, Oxford, 1993, 51–79.

3 Ludwig Pastor, *The History of the Popes*, London, 1894, V, 242.

7 Enter the Borgia

1 See Michael Mallett, *The Borgia; The Rise and Fall of a Renaissance Dynasty*, London, 1969.

2 Maria Bellonci, *Lucrezia Borgia*, London, 1953, 110.

8 Felice's Departure

1 Pio Paschini, *Roma nel Rinascimento*, Bologna, 1940, 318.

2 Ludwig Pastor, *The History of the Popes*, London, 1894, V, 424.

3 For Giuliano's years of exile see Christine Shaw, *Julius II: The Warrior Pope*, Oxford, 1993, 81–115.

4 Mario Mazari (ed.), *Navi di legno; Evoluzione tecnica e sviluppo della cantieristica nel Mediterraneo dal XVI secolo a oggi*, Trieste, 1998.

9 The Adolescent Felice

1 Nello Cerisola, *Storia di Savona*, Savona, 1983.

2 Carlo Varaldo, *Istoria d'arte del centro storico di Savona*, Savona, 1995.

3 http://digilander.libero.it/adamaney/immaginisavonaedintorni/dellarovere.htm.

10 Felice's First Marriage

1 Antonio Giustiniani, Dispacci di Antonio Giustinian, Florence, 1876, III, 393 ono, discussed in greater detail in Part II, Chapter 4.

PART II: THE POPE'S DAUGHTER

1 The New Pope

1 Ludwig Pastor, *The History of the Popes*, London, 1894, VI, 131–4.
2 Ibid., 192.
3 Ibid., 208.
4 David Frapiccini, 'Il Cardinale Girolamo Basso della Rovere e la sua cerchia tra contesti marchigiani e romani', in Marco Gallo (ed.), *I cardinali di santa romana chiesa; collezionisti e mecanati*, Rome, 2001, 17.
5 Pastor, VI, 212.
6 Desiderio Erasmus, *Julius Exclusus*, edited by Paul Pascal and J. Kelley Sowards, Bloomington/London, 1968, 83.
7 Giorgio Vasari, *Le vite de' più eccelenti pittori, scultori ed architettori*, 1568 edn, Florence, 1878–85, IV, 338.

2 The Reluctant Bride

1 Ludwig Pastor, *The History of the Popes*, London, 1894, VI, 223.
2 Ibid., 104–7.
3 Marino Sanuto, *I diarii di Marino Sanuto (1496–1533)*, Venice, 1879–1903, V, 784.
4 Ibid., 844.
5 For other examples of this, see Sheryl Reiss, 'Cardinal Giulio de' Medici and Mario Maffei: A Renaissance Friendship and the Villa Madama', in Lars R. Jones and Louisa C. Matthew (eds.), *Coming About . . . A Festschrift for John Shearman*, Cambridge, 2002, 281–8.
6 David Frapiccini, 'Il Cardinale Girolamo Basso della Rovere e la sua cerchia tra contesti marchigiani e romani', in Marco Gallo (ed.), *I cardinali di santa romana chiesa; collezionisti e mecanati*, Rome, 2001, 17.
7 See P. Pieri, 'Jacopo Appiano' in *Dizionario biografico degli Italiani*, Rome, 1961, 629–31.
8 Sanuto, V, 798.
9 Ibid., 935.
10 G. Assereto (ed.), *Cronache savonesi*, Savona, 1887, 347.
11 Pastor, VI, 230.

3 The della Rovere Women in Rome

1 Antonio Giustiniani, *Dispacci di Antonio Giustinian*, Florence, 1876, III, 129.
2 Ibid., 138.
3 Ibid., 143.
4 Henry Dietrich Fernández (trans.), *Bramante's Architectural Legacy in the Vatican Palace; A Study in Papal Routes*, Ph.D. dissertation, University of Cambridge, 2003, appendix.

5 See, among other sources, correspondence of the Mantua ambassadors, ASM.
6 Hans Henrik Brummer, *The Statue Court in the Vatican Belvedere*, Stockholm, 1970.
7 Alessandro Luzio and Rodolfo Renier, *Mantova e Urbino; Isabella d'Este ed Elizabetta Gonzaga nelle relazioni famigliari e nelle vicende politiche*, Torino/Rome, 1893, 159.
8 Giustiniani, 175.
9 Maria Bellonci, *Lucrezia Borgia; La sua vita e i suoi tempi*, Milan, 1939, 439-40.

4 The Prince of Salerno

1 Christine Shaw, *Julius II: The Warrior Pope*, Oxford, 1993, 63-4.
2 Antonio Giustiniani, *Dispacci di Antonio Giustinian*, Florence, 1876, III, 393-4.
3 Ibid., 418.
4 Ibid.

5 Self-Promotion

1 Agnolo Firenzuola, 'Epistola a Claudio Tolomei', in *Opere*, Florence, 1958, 183.
2 This version, *The Courtier of Counte Baldessare Castiglione*, London, 1603, is the one I have used for translated passages. More easily accessible versions include *The Book of the Courtier*, translated by George Bull, London, 1976.
3 Castiglione, Book I.
4 Ibid.
5 Ibid., Book II.
6 Ibid.
7 Ibid.
8 Ibid., Book I.
9 Ibid. See also A. R. Humphreys, introduction to *Much Ado About Nothing*, London, 1981, 16.
10 Like Lucrezia Borgia, Isabella d'Este has generated a great deal of literature. The most comprehensive biography of her, however, still remains Julia Cartwright, *Isabella d'Este*, London, 1903.
11 For Isabella as patron, see Daniele Bini (ed.), *Isabella d'Este primadonna del Rinascimento*, Modena, 2001.
12 Aldo Venturi, 'Gian Cristoforo Romano', *Archivio storico dell'arte*, I, 1888, 149-50.
13 Susan Haskins, 'Isabella d'Este' in Jill Berk Jiminez (ed.), *Dictionary of Artists' Models*, London, 2001, 186.

6 The Education of Felice della Rovere

1 Giovanni Filiteo Achillini, *Viridario*, Bologna, 1513, 195 r.
2 Augusto Campana, 'Dal Calmeta al Colocci', in Trezzini et al. (eds.), *Tra Latino e volgare per Carlo Dionisotti*, Padua, 1974
3 Ibid.
4 The letters are published in Pierre de Nolhac, 'Les Correspondents d'Alde Manuce', in *Studi e documenti di storia e diritto*, 8, 1887, 284-6.
5 Ibid.

7 Enter the Orsini

1 See Michael Hirst and Jill Dunkerton, *The Young Michelangelo*, London, 1994.
2 Christoph L. Frommel in Henry Millon et al. (eds.), *The Renaissance from Brunelleschi to Michelangelo; The Representation of Architecture*, Milan, 1994, 400–401.
3 Ludwig Pastor, *The History of the Popes*, London, 1894, VI, 465.
4 Francesco Sansovino, *L'historia di casa Orsini*, Venice, 1565.
5 For the origins of the Orsini family see Franca Allegrezza, *Organizzazione del potere e dinamiche familiari; gli Orsini dal duecento agli inizi del Quattrocento*, Rome, 1998.
6 Pio Pecchiai, *Palazzo Taverna a Monte Giordano*, Rome, 1963.
7 For an overview of the Orsini Roman palaces see Kristin Triff, *Patronage and Public Image in Renaissance Rome: Three Orsini Palaces*, Ann Arbor, 2000.
8 Robert Mode, 'Masolino, Uccello and the Orsini Uomini Famosi', *Burlington Magazine*, 114, 1972, 369–78.
9 W. A. Simpson, 'Cardinal Giordano Orsini as a Prince of the Church and a Patron of the Arts', *Journal of the Warburg and Courtauld Institutes*, 29, 1966, 136–7.

8 Gian Giordano

1 Francesco Sansovino, *L'historia di casa Orsini*, Venice, 1565, 77.
2 See Michael Mallett, *Mercenaries and their Masters; Warfare in Renaissance Italy*, London, 1974.
3 B. Feliciangeli, *Notizie e documenti sulla vita di Caterina Cibo-Varano*, Camerino, 1891, 129.
4 Sansovino, 77.
5 Feliciangeli, 132.
6 ASC, *Archivio Orsini*, IIA, XX, 38.
7 Ibid., 41.

9 The Orsini Wedding

1 Marino Sanuto, *I diarii di Marino Sanuto (1496–1533)*, Venice, 1879–1903, VI, 348.
2 Paris de Grassis's account of the wedding is transcribed in Armando Schiavo, 'Donna Felice della Rovere in ritratti di Raffaello e Michelangelo', *L'Urbe*, 47, 1984, 98, note 11.
3 Alessandro Luzio and Rodolfo Renier, *Mantova e Urbino; Isabella d'Este ed Elizabetta Gonzaga nelle relazioni famigliari e nelle vicende politiche*, Torino/Rome, 1893, 179.
4 Ibid., 179–80.
5 Schiavo, 99, note 11.

PART III: FELIX OF THE OAK AND THE BEAR

1 A Bride at Bracciano

1 See, among other works, Anthony Dent et al., *The Reign of the Horse: The Horse in Print, 1500–1715*, Washington DC, 1991, and Bill Cook et al., *All the Queen's Horses*, Prospect, KY, 2003.
2 For a history of the side-saddle, see Lida Fleitmann Bloodgood, *The Saddle of Queens; The Story of the Side Saddle*, London, 1959.

3 For the history of Bracciano, see Anna Cavallero et al., *Bracciano e gli Orsini nel '400*, Rome, 1981, and Carla Michelli Giaccone, *Bracciano e il suo castello*, Rome, 1990.

4 See Franca Allegrezza, *Organizzazione del potere e dinamiche familiari; gli Orsini dal duecento agli inizi del Quattrocento*, Rome, 1998, and Christine Shaw, *The Political Role of the Orsini Family in the Papal States, c. 1480–1534*, Ph.D., Oxford, 1983.

5 Ludwig Pastor, *The History of the Popes*, London, 1894, IV, 518–19.

6 Marino Sanuto, *I diarii di Marino Sanuto (1496–1533)*, Venice, 1879–1903, VI, 359.

2 Felice and the Orsini

1 ASC, *Archivio Orsini*, I, 400, 46.

2 ASF, Acquisiti e Doni, 142, 8, No. 3.

3 ASC, *Archivio Orsini*, I, 400, 271.

4 Ibid, 272.

3 Felice and Gian Giordano

1 ASC, *Archivio Orsini*, I, 93, 1.

2 E. Rodocanachi, *La Première Renaissance; Rome au temps de Julius II et de Leon X*, Paris, 1912, 398.

3 ASC, *Archivio Orsini*, I, 400, 46.

4 ASM, *Archivio Gonzaga*, 2996, Libro 30, 860, 87.

5 ASC, *Archivio Orsini*, IIA, XX, 51.

6 Ibid., 54.

7 Marino Sanuto, *I diarii di Marino Sanuto (1496–1533)*, Venice, 1879–1903, VI, 616.

8 The only way we know this child was called Julio is from a letter written in 1528, referring to him as *quondam* (once or former). He was not alive when Felice's other children were born, as no mention is made of him in the provisions for the expenses for the children.

4 Father and Daughter Reunion

1 E. Rodocanachi, *La Première Renaissance; Rome au temps de Julius II et de Leon X*, Paris, 1912, 84.

2 Ibid., 398–9.

3 Richard Ingersoll, *The Ritual Use of Public Space in Renaissance Rome*, Ann Arbor, 1985, 136, note 62.

5 The Castello of Palo

1 See David Coffin, *The Villa in the Life of Renaissance Rome*, Princeton, 1979; A. Coppi, 'Alsio, Palo e Palidoro', *Dissertazioni della pontificia academia romana di archeologia*, VII, 1836, 377–86, and C. Perogalli, *Castelli del Lazio,* Milan, 1968, 129–30.

2 ASC, *Archivio Orsini*, IIA, XX, 56.

3 UCLA Special Collections, 902, *Orsini Archive*, Box 154.

4 George Dennis, *The Cities and Cemeteries of Etruria*, London, 1848.

5 http://www.martignano.com/casale%20di%20Martignano.htm

6 The Entrepreneur

1 Ivana Ait and Manuel Vaquero Piñeiro, *Dai casali alla fabbrica di San Pietro, i Leni: uomini d'affari del Rinascimento*, Rome, 2000.

2 UCLA, Special Collections, 902, *Orsini Archive*, Box 154.

7 Vatican Ambassadress

1 See John Shearman, 'The Vatican Stanze, Functions and Decorations', in *Proceedings of the British Academy*, 57, 1971.

2 Clara Gennaro, 'La "Pax Romana" del 1511', *Archivio della società romana di storia patria*, XC, 1967, 2–60.

3 E. Rodocanachi, *La Première Renaissance; Rome au temps de Julius II et de Leon X*, Paris, 1912, 84.

4 Christine Shaw, *Julius II: The Warrior Pope*, Oxford, 1993, 209–43.

5 Marino Sanuto, *I diarii di Marino Sanuto (1496–1533)*, Venice, 1879–1903, VIII, 139.

6 Ibid., 135.

7 Ludwig Pastor, *The History of the Popes*, London, 1894, VI, 651.

8 Felice and the Queen of France

1 Marino Sanuto, *I diarii di Marino Sanuto (1496–1533)*, Venice, 1879–1903, IX, 496–7.

2 Ibid., XII, 301.

3 Baldessar Castiglione, *The Courtier of Counte Baldessare Castiglione*, London, 1603, II, 22.

4 Alessandro Luzio, *Isabella d'Este di fronte a Giulio II negli ultimi tre anni del suo pontificato*, Milan, 1912, 60.

5 Ibid., 83.

6 Ibid., 204.

9 Madonna Felice is Everything

1 G. L. Moncallero, *Epistolario di Bernado Dovizi da Bibbiena*, I, Florence, 1935, 338.

2 Ibid., 366.

3 Alessandro Luzio, *Isabella d'Este di fronte a Giulio II negli ultimi tre anni del suo pontificato*, Milan, 1912, 165.

4 Moncallero, 466.

5 ASM, *Archivio Gonzaga*, 2996, 30, 858, 552.

6 Marino Sanuto, *I diarii di Marino Sanuto (1496–1533)*, Venice, 1879–1903, XII, 441.

10 Code Name Sappho

1 Ludwig Pastor, *The History of the Popes*, London, 1894, VI, 327–8.

2 ASM, *Archivio Gonzaga*, 2996, vol. 30, 150.

3 Alessandro Luzio, *Isabella d'Este di fronte a Giulio II negli ultimi tre anni del suo pontificato*, Milan, 1912, 60.

4 ASM, *Archivio Gonzaga*, 860, 137.

5 Ibid., 129.

6 Ibid., 2996, 30, 42.

7 Ibid., 860, 141.
8 Ibid., 137.

11 The Julian Legacy

1 ASM, Archivio Gonzaga, 860, 468.
2 Ludwig Pastor, *The History of the Popes,* London, 1894, vi, 434.
3 See, among other accounts of Julius's death, Rodoconachi, *Le pontificat de Julius II,* Paris, 1928, 178–80.
4 Ibid., 179.
5 Schiavo proposed that the full-length woman leaning towards Julius was an image of Felice, but the young woman in black is far more likely to be her.
6 Marco Vattasso, 'Antonio Flaminio e le principali poesie dell'autografo Vaticano 2870', *Studi e testi,* 1, 1900, 55–6.
7 Ingrid D. Rowland, *The Culture of the High Renaissance; Ancient and Moderns in Sixteenth-Century Rome,* Cambridge, 1998, 180 ono.
8 Elizabeth B. Macdougall, 'The Sleeping Nymph: Origins of a Humanist Fountain', *Art Bulletin,* LVII, 1975, 357–65.
9 Rowland, 183–4.
10 Ingrid D. Rowland, *The Culture of the High Renaissance; Ancient and Moderns in Sixteenth-Century Rome,* Cambridge, 1998, 184.

12 Felice, Michelangelo and the Pincian Hill

1 See, for example, André Chastel, *The Sack of Rome, 1527,* Princeton, 1983, 200-207.
2 John Shearman, 'Una nota sul progetto di Papa Giulio', in *Michelangelo; La Capella Sistina documentazione e interpretazioni,* III, Novara, 1994, 29–36.
3 Fra Mariano da Firenze, *Itinerarium urbis romae,* edited by E. Buletti, Rome, 1931, 221.
4 Giorgio Vasari, *Lives of the Painters, Sculptors and Architects,* translated by Gaston de Vere, edited by David Ekserdjian, New York, 1996, vii, 174.
5 Charles de Tolnay, Michelangelo; *The Final Period, Last Judgement,* Princeton, 1971.
6 ASR, Archivio del Collegio dei Notai, Sabba Vanucci, 1836, 103r.
7 Colette Beaune, 'François de Paule et les roix de France', in Yves Bruley (ed.), *La Trinité-des-Monts redécouverte,* Rome, 2002.
8 Carolyn Valone, 'The Art of Hearing: Sermons and Images in the Chapel of Lucrezia della Rovere', in *Sixteenth Century Journal,* XXI, 3, 2000, 759–61.
9 Ibid., 761–3.
10 Giovanni Caprile, *Villa Malta, dall'antica Roma a 'civiltà cattolica',* Rome, 1999.

PART IV: PATRONA ET GUBERNATRIX

1 A Trip to Loreto

1 G. L. Moncallero, *Epistolario di Bernado Dovizi da Bibbiena,* I, Florence, 1935, 255.
2 Lucetta Scaraffia, *Loreto,* Bologna, 1998.
3 David Frapiccini, 'Il Cardinale Girolamo Basso della Rovere e la su cerchia tra contesti

marchigiani e romani', in Marco Gallo (ed.), *I Cardinali di santa romana chiesa; collezionisti e mecanati*, Rome, 2001, 16.

4 See Rudolph M. Bell, *How to Do It; Guides to Good Living for Renaissance Italians*, Chicago, 1999, 16 ono.

5 ASC, *Archivio Orsini*, IIA, 1284, 68v.

2 Childbirth and its Aftermath

1 Jacqueline Marie Musacchio, *The Art and Ritual of Childbirth in Renaissance Italy*, New Haven/London, 1999.

2 Rudolph M. Bell, *How to Do It; Guides to Good Living for Renaissance Italians*, Chicago, 1999, 129.

3 The Pope's Daughter Becomes the Pope's Friend

1 ASF, *Mediceo Avanti il Principato*, Filza 117, fol. 153.

2 Bartolomeo Cerretani, *Ricordi*, edited by Giuliana Berti, Florence, 1993, 320.

4 The Pope Goes Hunting

1 E. Rodocanachi, *La Première Renaissance; Rome au temps de Julius II et de Leon X*, Paris, 1912, 61–71.

2 Peter Partner, *Renaissance Rome, 1500–1555*, Berkeley, 1976, 94.

3 Ivana Ait and Manuel Vaquero Piñeiro, *Dai casali alla fabbrica di San Pietro, i Leni: uomini d'affari del Rinascimento*, Rome, 2000, 147.

4 ASC, *Archivio Orsini*, I, 83, 453.

5 Ait and Piñeiro, 167, 174, 191, 208.

6 Biblioteca Angelica, Rome: Paolo Nomentano, *Sylvicolae*, MS 1349, Ode XXIII

5 Papal Payback

1 ASC, *Archivio Orsini*, IIA, XXI, 27.

6 Orsini Signora Revisited

1 ASC, *Archivio Orsini*, II, 1284.

7 Bracciano's *fonte*

1 Carolyn Valone, 'Why Women Built in Early Modern Rome', in Sheryl Reiss and David Wilkins (eds.), *Beyond Isabella; Secular Women Patrons of Art in Renaissance Italy*, Kirksville, MO, 2001, 321, 332, n. 25.

2 UCLA Special Collections, *Orsini Archive*, Box 13, 3.

3 Kristin Triff, *Patronage and Public Image in Renaissance Rome: Three Orsini Palaces*, Ann Arbor, 2000, 328.

8 Weaving

1 UCLA Special Collections, 902, *Orsini Archive*, Box 13, 1.
2 ASC, 902, *Archivio Orsini*, IIA, XX, I, 55.

9 Personal Reckoning

1 UCLA Special Collections, *Orsini Archive*, Box 13, 1.

10 A Slave to the House of Orsini

1 ASR, *Archivio Santa Croce*, 771, 73.
2 ASC, *Archivio Orsini*, I, 93, 43.
3 Ibid., IIA, XXI, 44.
4 Ibid., 41.
5 Ibid, I, 93, 68.

11 More Reckoning

1 ASR, *Archivio del Collegio dei Notai*, Sabba Vanucci, 1836, 103r.
2 Several copies of the inventory exist; the best transcribed is ASR, *Archivio Santa Croce*, 771, 95–107.

12 The Temporal Mother

1 ASC, *Archivio Orsini*, I, 93, 111.
2 Ibid., 95, 314.
3 Ibid., 299.
4 Ibid., 318.
5 Ibid., 93, 151.
6 Ibid., 95, 196.
7 Ibid., 326.
8 Ibid., 95, 293.
9 Ibid., 93, 558.
10 Ibid., 93, 258.
11 Ibid., 477.
12 Ibid., 93, 130.
13 Ibid., 95, 240.
14 Ibid., 93, 211.
15 Ibid., 143.
16 Ibid., 167.
17 Ibid., 93, 357.
18 Ibid., 95, 164–70.
19 Ibid., 556.
20 Ibid., 95, 82.
21 Ibid., 369.
22 Ibid., 91.
23 Ibid., 487.

13 Statio

1 ASC, *Archivio Orsini*, 1, 333.
2 Ibid., 400, 79.
3 Ibid., 76.
4 Ibid., 93, 43.
5 Strabo, *Geography*, translated by Horace Leonard Jones, 11, Cambridge, MA, 1948, 375.
6 ASC, *Archivio Orsini*, 1, 96, 145.
7 Ibid., 95, 280.
8 Ibid., 93, 234.
9 Ibid., 287.
10 Ibid., 437.

14 Family Matters

1 ASC, *Archivio Orsini*, 1, 48.
2 Valerio Marucci (ed.), *Pasquinate del cinque e seicento*, Rome, 1988, 61, 84.
3 ASC, *Archivio Orsini*, 1, 96, 360.
4 Matteo Bandello, *Novelle*, 111, LXII, Alessandria, 1992.
5 ASC, *Archivio Orsini*, 1, 96, 521.
6 Ibid., 95, 76.
7 Ibid., 93, 398.
8 Ibid., 147.
9 Ibid., 232.
10 Ibid., 105.
11 Ibid., 93, 56.
12 Ibid., 428.
13 Ibid., 261.
14 Ibid., 95, 202.
15 Ibid., 210.
16 Ibid., 429.
17 Ibid., 93, 147.
18 Ibid., 11, 1285.

15 Dowries and the Great Queen

1 ASC, *Archivio Orsini*, 11A, XXI, 54.
2 Ibid., 1, 93, 283.
3 For a history of Bisignano, see Rosario Curia, *Bisignano nella storia del Mezzogiorno: dalle orgini al xix secolo*, Cosenza,1985.
4 ASC, *Archivio Orsini*, 1, 93, 332.
5 E. Rodocanachi, *La Première Renaissance; Rome au temps de Julius II et de Leon X*, Paris, 1912, 84.
6 Marino Sanuto, *I diarii di Marino Sanuto (1496–1533)*, Venice, 1879–1903, XXX, 8.
7 ASC, *Archivio Orsini*, 1, 93, 586.
8 Rodocanachi, 84.
9 Sanuto, XXX, 52.

10 ASC, *Archivio Orsini*, I, 93, 685.
11 Ibid., 95, 229.
12 Ibid., 95, 268.
13 Sanuto, XXX, 52.

16 Napoleone

1 ASC, *Archivio Orsini*, I, 400, 69.
2 Ibid., 93, 571.
3 E. Rodocanachi, *La Première Renaissance; Rome au temps de Julius II et de Leon X*, Paris, 1912, 84.

17 The Taking of Palo

1 ASF, *Ducato di Urbino, Classe Prima*, 113v.
2 Ibid., 108, 7, 10, 13,
3 ASC, *Archivio Orsini*, I, 93, 673.
4 ASF, *Ducato di Urbino, Classe Prima*, 7, 28.
5 Ibid., 132, 11, 278.
6 ASC, *Archivio Orsini*, I, 95, 226.
7 Ibid., 98.
8 ASF, *Ducato di Urbino, Classe Prima*, 108, 7, 29.

18 Papal Reprieve

1 ASC, *Archivio Orsini*, I, 95, 16.
2 Ibid., 400, 40.
3 UCLA Special Collections, 902, *Orsini Archive*, Box 25, 26.

PART V: DISPOSSESSED AND REPOSSESSED

1 At Prayer

1 ASC, *Archivio Orsini*, I, 95, 208.
2 Ibid., 115.
3 Ibid., II, 1931.

2 The Fall of Rome

1 Two fundamental histories of the Sack are E. R Chamberlin, *The Sack of Rome*, London, 1979, and Judith Hook, *The Sack of Rome, 1527*, London, 1972.
2 Luigi Guicciardini, *The Sack of Rome*, translated by James H. McGregor, New York, 1983, 98.
3 Ibid., 104.
4 Ibid., 83-4.
5 Ibid., 80.
6 Marino Sanuto, *I diarii di Marino Sanuto (1496–1533)*, Venice, 1879-1903, XXXXV, 45, 187.

3 Hostages

1 Pio Pecchiai, *Palazzo Taverna a Monte Giordano*, Rome, 1963, 20.
2 'Del Sacco di Roma, lettera del Cardinale di Como al suo segretario', in Carlo Milanesi (ed.), *Il Sacco di Roman del MDXXVII*, Florence, 1867, 478–9.
3 Ibid., 483–4.
4 Ibid., 479.
5 Marino Sanuto, *I diarii di Marino Sanuto (1496–1533)*, Venice, 1879–1903, XXXXV, 45, 191.
6 Milanesi, 480–81.

4 Escape from Rome

1 Marino Sanuto, *I diarii di Marino Sanuto (1496–1533)*, Venice, 1879–1903, XXXXV, 45, 208.
2 Ibid., XXXXIV, 277.

5 Fossombrone

1 ASC, *Archivio Orsini*, I, 95, 355.
2 ASF, *Ducato di Urbino, Classe Prima*, 108, 8, 2–4.
3 ASC, *Archivio Orsini*, I, 95, 334.
4 Ibid., 335.
5 Ibid., 342.
6 ASF, *Ducato di Urbino, Classe Prima*, 108, 8, 5.
7 ASC, *Archivio Orsini*, I, 95, 341.
8 Sabine Eiche (ed.), *Ordine et officij de casa de lo illustrissimo Signor Duca de Urbino*, Urbino, 1999, 68–9.
9 Sabine Eiche, 'Fossombrone, Part 1: Unknown Drawings and Documents for the *Corte* of Leonora Gonzaga, Duchess of Urbino and her Son, Giulio della Rovere', in *Studi di Storia dell'Arte*, 2, 1991, 103–28.

6 The Exiled

1 ASC, *Archivio Orsini*, I, 95, 336.
2 Ibid., 377.
3 Ibid., 373.
4 Ibid., 334.
5 Alessandro Luzio, *Isabella d'Este ed Il Sacco di Roma*, 1908, 90.
6 ASC, *Archivio Orsini*, I, 95, 415.
7 ASM, *Archivio Gonzaga*, 2999, 47, 18.
8 Ibid., 19 and 27.
9 Ibid., 31.
10 Ibid., 2996, 876, 540.
11 ASC, *Archivio Orsini*, I, 95, 431.
12 Ibid., 507.

7 The Return to Rome

1 ASC, *Archivio Orsini*, I, 95, 489.
2 Ibid., 96, 35.
3 Ibid., II, 777.
4 Ibid., I, 400, 285.
5 Melissa Meriam Bullard, 'Grain Supply and Urban Unrest in Renaissance Rome: The Crisis of 1533–1534', in P. A. Ramsey (ed.), *Rome in the Renaissance; The City and The Myth*, Binghampton, NY, 279–92.
6 ASC, *Archivio Orsini*, II, 777, 13v.

8 Rebuilding

1 Giorgio Vasari, *Lives of the Painters, Sculptors and Architects*, translated by Gaston de Vere, edited by David Ekserdjian, New York, 1996, IV, 601.
2 ASC, *Archivio Orsini*, II, 777, 13r.
3 Ibid., I, 95, 502.

9 At the Trinity

1 ASC, *Archivio Orsini*, I, 453.
2 Ibid., II, 777, 4–11.
3 Ibid., I, 96, 231.

10 A Memorial to the Past

1 Kenneth Gouwens, *Remembering the Renaissance; Humanist Narratives of the Sack of Rome*, Leiden, 1998, 91.
2 P. Barocchi and R. Ristori (eds.), *Il carteggio di Michelangelo*, Florence, 1965–83, III, 356.
3 First proposed by Armando Schiavo in his essay in *L'Urbe*.
4 Charles de Tolnay, *The Tomb of Julius II*, Princeton, 1954, 72.

11 Clarice

1 ASC, *Archivio Orsini*, I, 95, 93.
2 Ibid., 93, 390.
3 Ibid., 147.
4 Ibid., 499.
5 Ibid., 203.
6 Ibid., 96, 98.
7 Ibid., II, 777, 31r.
8 Ibid., I, 96, 98.
9 See B. Feliciangeli, *Notizie e documenti sulla vita di Caterina Cibo-Varano,* Camerino, 1891, 125 ono, for the correspondence cited between Guidobaldo and his parents, regarding Clarice Orsini.
10 For a history of Stigliano, see Benito Urago, *Stigliano sotto gli Spagnuoli*, Stigliano, 1964.
11 ASC, *Archivio Orsini*, I, 96, 169.

12 The Boys

1 ASC, *Archivio Orsini*, I, 73, 432.
2 Ibid., 96, 190.
3 Ibid., 149.
4 Ibid., 11.
5 Ibid., 95, 254.

13 The War of Vicovaro

1 Marino Sanuto, *I diarii di Marino Sanuto (1496–1533)*, Venice, 1879–1903, LVII, 57, 930.
2 ASC, *Archivio Orsini*, I, 672, 503.
3 Ibid., 74, 72.
4 Ibid., 96, 219.
5 Sanuto, LVIII, 94.
6 ASF, *Ducato di Urbino, Classe Prima*, 132, 71, 3r.
7 ASC, *Archivio Orsini*, I, 96, 206.
8 Ibid., 205.
9 Sanuto, LVIII, 44.
10 Ibid., 73, 330.
11 ASF, *Ducato di Urbino, Classe Prima*, 7, 36.
12 ASC, *Archivio Orsini*, I, 96, 247.
13 Sanuto, LVIII, 258.
14 ASC, *Archivio Orsini*, IIA, XXIII, I.

14 A Brother's Revenge

1 ASC, *Archivio Orsini*, I, 73, 499.
2 Christine Shaw, *The Political Role of the Orsini Family in the Papal States, c. 1480–1534*, Ph.D., Oxford, 1983, 209.
3 ASC, *Archivio Orsini*, I, 391, 143.

15 Restitution

1 ASC, *Archivio Orsini*, I, 96, 355.
2 Ibid., 319.
3 Ibid., 391, 142.
4 Ibid., 56.
5 Ibid., 74, 132.
6 Ibid., 317.
7 Ibid., 479.
8 Ibid., 451.
9 Ibid., 391, 141.
10 Ibid., 45.
11 Ibid., 83.
12 Ibid., 151.
13 Ibid., 74, 473.
14 Ibid., 96, 319.

PART VI THE MOST LOVING MOTHER IN THE WORLD

1 ASC, Archivio Orsini, I, 391, 304.
2 Ibid., 247.
3 Ibid., 400, 289.
4 Ibid., 391, 167.
5 Ibid., 194.
6 Ibid., 147.
7 Ibid., 158.
8 Ibid., 174.
9 Ibid., 207.
10 Ibid., 38.
11 Ibid., 276.
12 Ibid., 293.
13 Ibid., 218.
14 Ibid., 390, 170.
15 Ibid., 391, 216.
16 Ibid., 390, 137.
17 Ibid., 391, 169.
18 Ibid., 75, 404.
19 Ibid., 391, 160.
20 Ibid., 75, 91.
21 Ibid., 74, 404.
22 Ibid., 540.
23 Ibid., 76, 140.
24 Ibid., 75, 425.
25 Ibid., 96, 383.
26 Ibid., 76, 213.
27 Ibid., 75, 407.
28 Ibid., 78, 87.
29 Ibid., 246.
30 Ibid., 75, 404.
31 Ibid., 76, 517.
32 Ibid., 63.
33 Ibid., 520.
34 Ibid., 107.
35 Ibid., 250.
36 Ibid., 78, 35.
37 Ibid., 107.
38 Ibid., 147.
39 Ibid., 77, 63.
40 Ibid., 77, 389.
41 UCLA Special Collections, 902, *Orsini Archive*, 240, 21.
42 ASC, *Archivio Orsini*, 78, 117.
43 Ibid., 104.

44 Ibid., 371.
45 Ibid., 312.

Epilogue: Felice's Legacy

1 Recounted in Giuseppe Ceci and Benedetto Croce, *Lode di dame napoletane del decimosesto*, Naples, 1894.
2 Francesco Sansovino, *L'historia di casa Orsini*, Venice, 1565, Book II, 14v.

List of Illustrations

341

LIST OF ILLUSTRATIONS

PLATE SECTION ONE

Photographs and illustrations in the plate sections are reproduced by kind permission of the following: Vatican Museums and Galleries / www.bridgeman.co.uk (1, 2, 3); Photo Scala, Florence (5, 16, 18); National Gallery, London / www.bridgeman.co.uk (8); Louvre, Paris / www.bridgeman.co.uk (9); Palazzo Vecchio (Palazzo della Signoria) Florence / www.bridgeman.co.uk (10); Galleria degli Uffizi, Florence / www.bridge-man.co.uk (11, 12, 23, 29, 30, 31); Ali Meyer / www.bridgeman.co.uk (13); Kunsthistorisches Museum, Vienna / www.bridgeman.co.uk (14); Museu Nacional d'Art de Catalunya, Barcelona (22); Palazzo Pitti, Flo-rence / Alinari / www.bridgeman.co.uk (24, 26); Galleria Nazionale de Capodimonte, Naples / Giraudon / www.bridgeman.co.uk (25); Private Collection / www.bridgeman.co.uk (32). Henry Dietrich Fernández (6, 17, 19, 20, 21, 28, 33). Plurigraf (27). Archivio di Stato di Firenze (34). The illustration on page 136 is reproduced by kind permission of Fine Arts Library, Harvard University, and those on pages 166 and 313 by permis-sion of Charles Plante Fine Arts / www.bridgeman.co.uk.

Index

Illustrations are entered in bold type